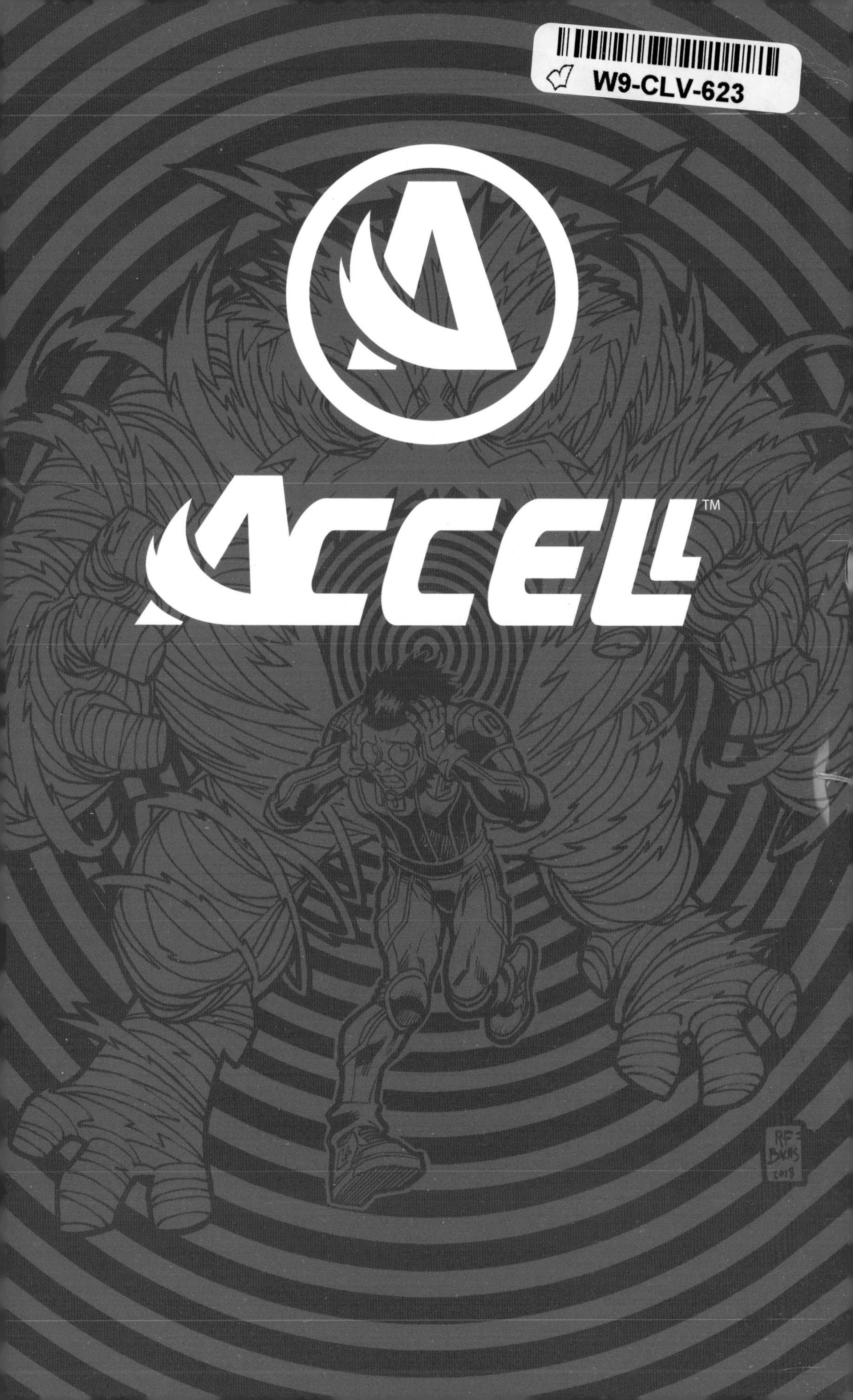
ACCEL™

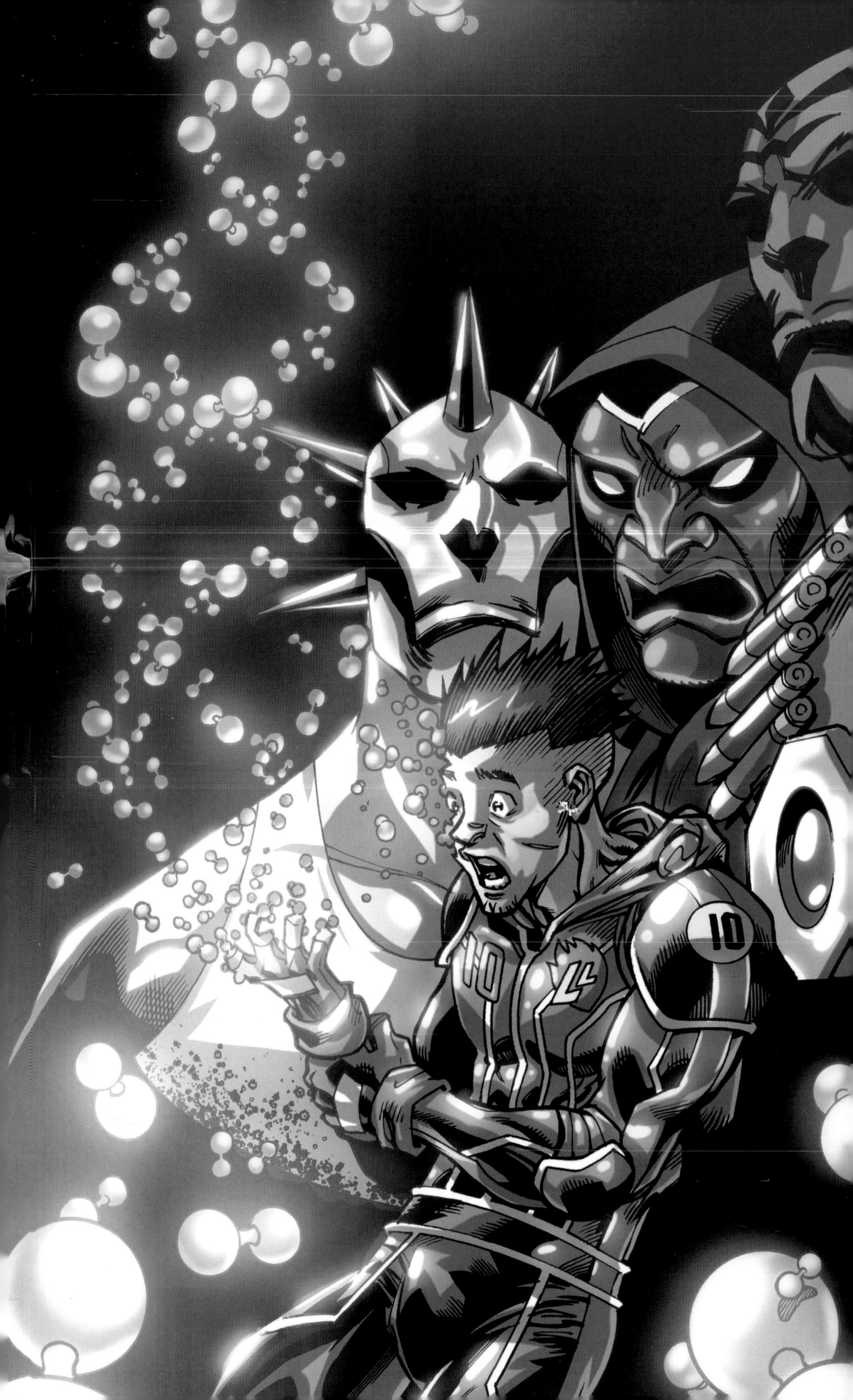

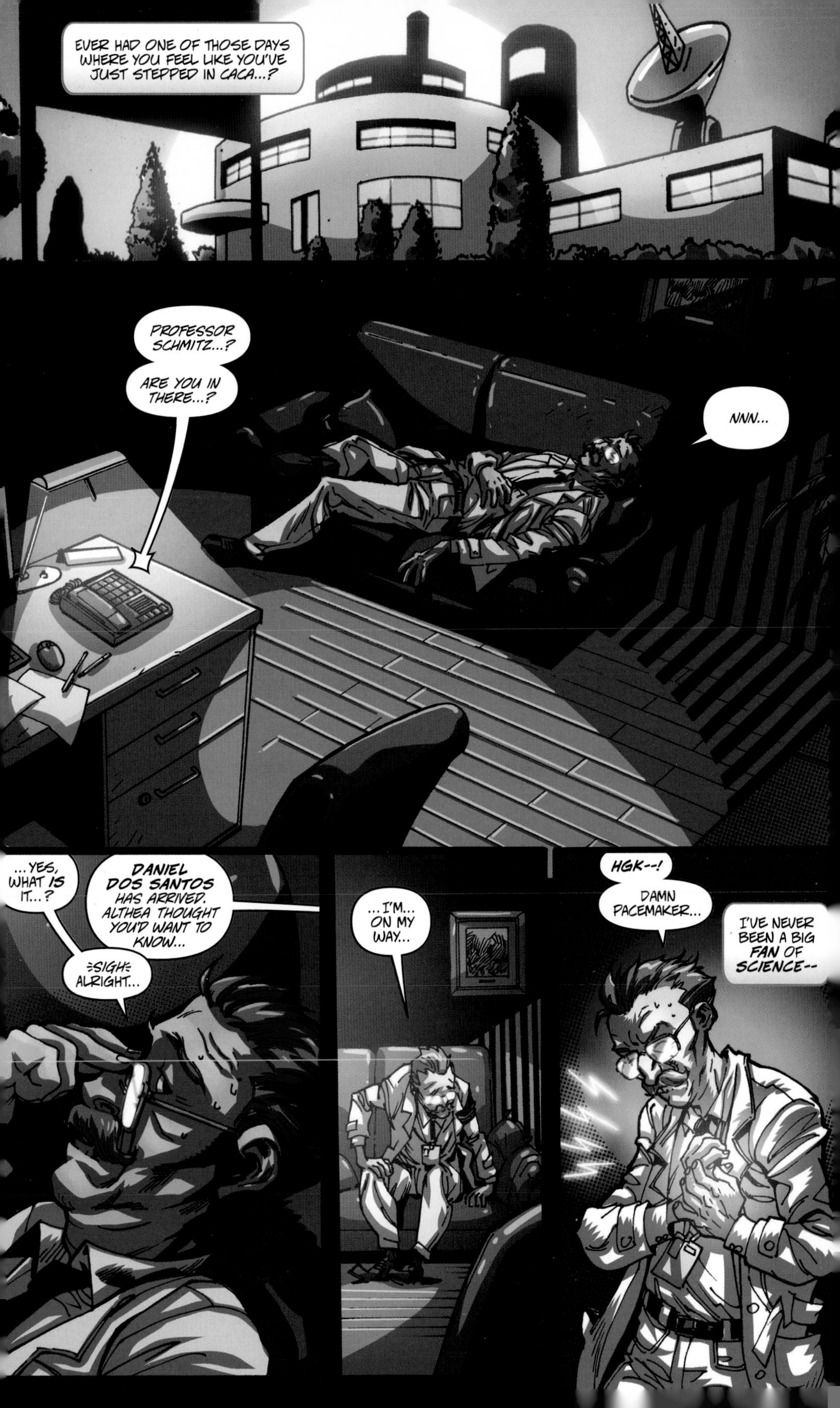
EVER HAD ONE OF THOSE DAYS WHERE YOU FEEL LIKE YOU'VE JUST STEPPED IN CACA...?
PROFESSOR SCHMITZ...?
ARE YOU IN THERE...?
NNN...
...YES, WHAT IS IT...?
DANIEL DOS SANTOS HAS ARRIVED. ALTHEA THOUGHT YOU'D WANT TO KNOW...
=SIGH= ALRIGHT...
...I'M... ON MY WAY...
HGK--!
DAMN PACEMAKER...
I'VE NEVER BEEN A BIG FAN OF SCIENCE--

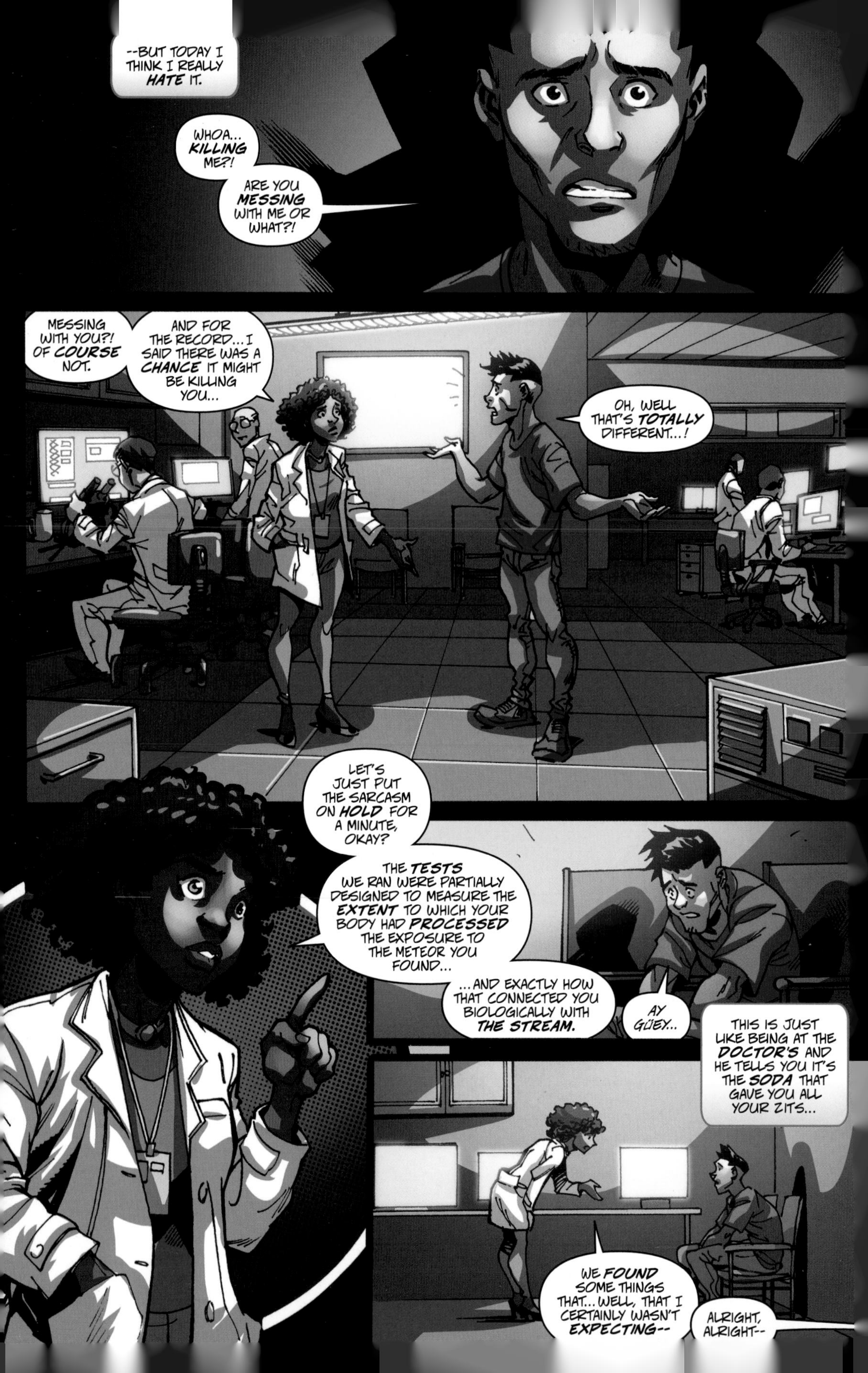
--BUT TODAY I THINK I REALLY HATE IT.
WHOA... KILLING ME?!
ARE YOU MESSING WITH ME OR WHAT?!
MESSING WITH YOU?! OF COURSE NOT.
AND FOR THE RECORD... I SAID THERE WAS A CHANCE IT MIGHT BE KILLING YOU...
OH, WELL THAT'S TOTALLY DIFFERENT...!
LET'S JUST PUT THE SARCASM ON HOLD FOR A MINUTE, OKAY?
THE TESTS WE RAN WERE PARTIALLY DESIGNED TO MEASURE THE EXTENT TO WHICH YOUR BODY HAD PROCESSED THE EXPOSURE TO THE METEOR YOU FOUND...
...AND EXACTLY HOW THAT CONNECTED YOU BIOLOGICALLY WITH THE STREAM.
AY GÜEY...
THIS IS JUST LIKE BEING AT THE DOCTOR'S AND HE TELLS YOU IT'S THE SODA THAT GAVE YOU ALL YOUR ZITS...
WE FOUND SOME THINGS THAT... WELL, THAT I CERTAINLY WASN'T EXPECTING--
ALRIGHT, ALRIGHT--

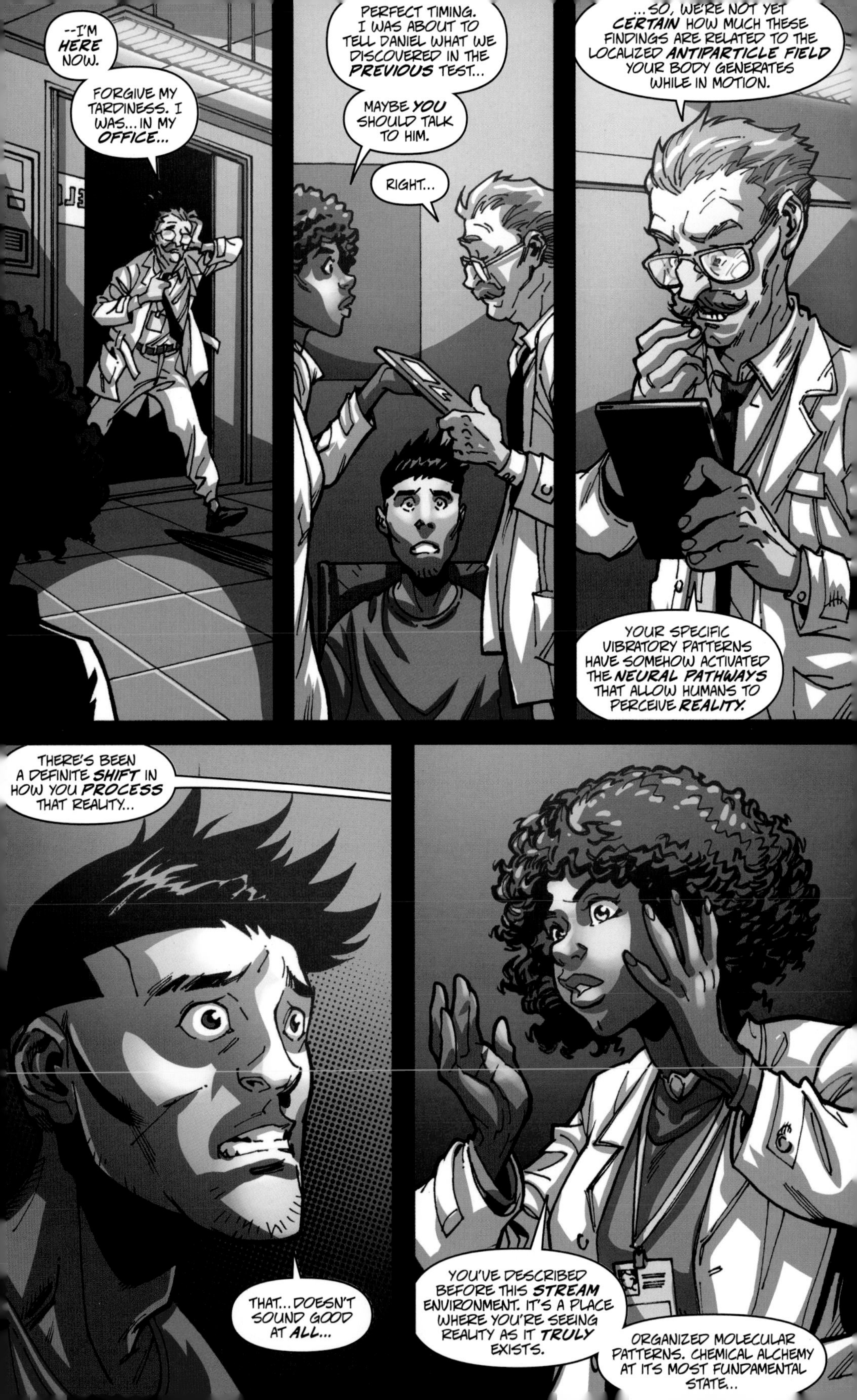
--I'M HERE NOW.
FORGIVE MY TARDINESS. I WAS... IN MY OFFICE...
PERFECT TIMING. I WAS ABOUT TO TELL DANIEL WHAT WE DISCOVERED IN THE PREVIOUS TEST...
MAYBE YOU SHOULD TALK TO HIM.
RIGHT...
...SO, WE'RE NOT YET CERTAIN HOW MUCH THESE FINDINGS ARE RELATED TO THE LOCALIZED ANTIPARTICLE FIELD YOUR BODY GENERATES WHILE IN MOTION.
YOUR SPECIFIC VIBRATORY PATTERNS HAVE SOMEHOW ACTIVATED THE NEURAL PATHWAYS THAT ALLOW HUMANS TO PERCEIVE REALITY.
THERE'S BEEN A DEFINITE SHIFT IN HOW YOU PROCESS THAT REALITY...
THAT... DOESN'T SOUND GOOD AT ALL...
YOU'VE DESCRIBED BEFORE THIS STREAM ENVIRONMENT. IT'S A PLACE WHERE YOU'RE SEEING REALITY AS IT TRULY EXISTS.
ORGANIZED MOLECULAR PATTERNS. CHEMICAL ALCHEMY AT ITS MOST FUNDAMENTAL STATE...

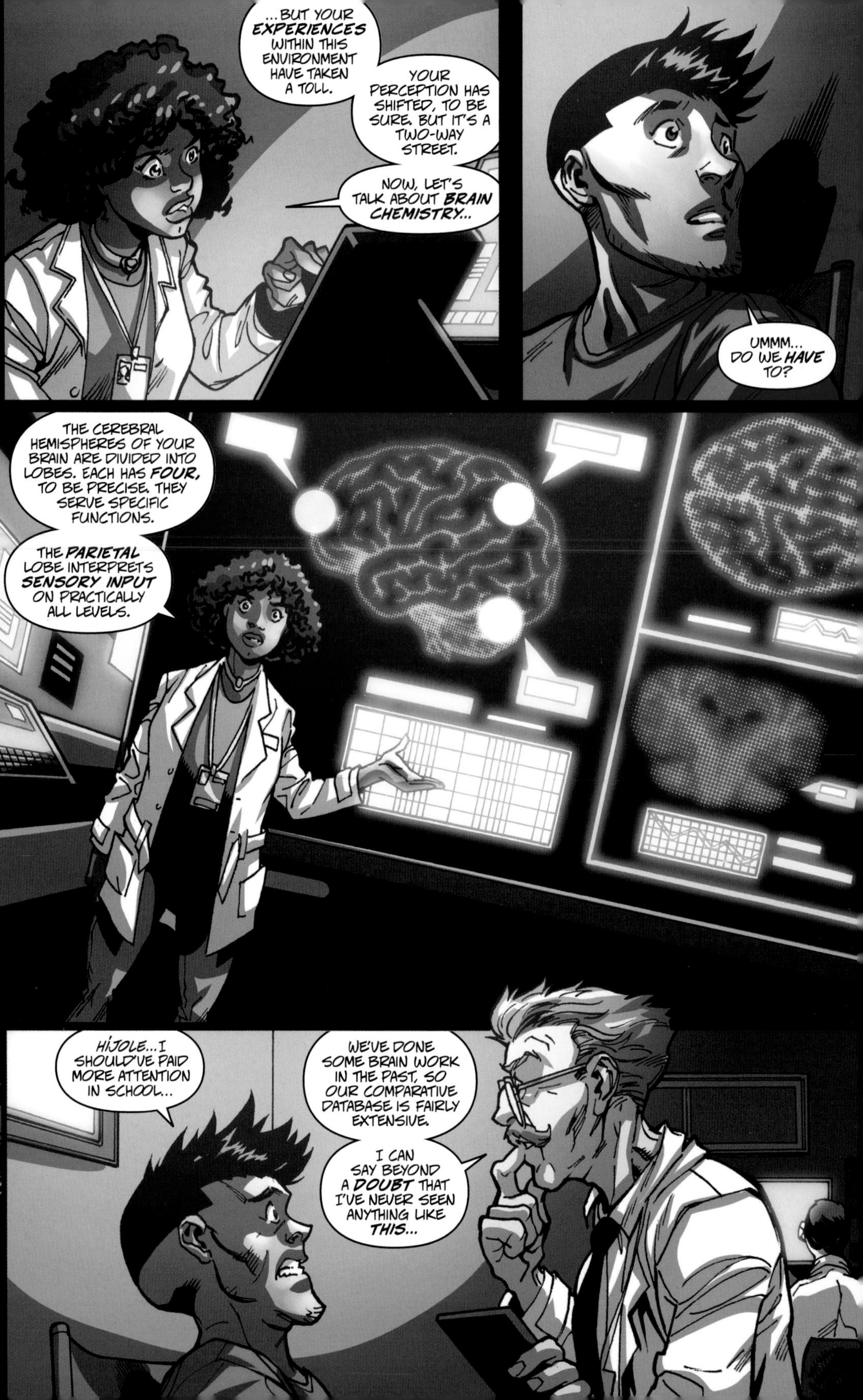

...BUT YOUR EXPERIENCES WITHIN THIS ENVIRONMENT HAVE TAKEN A TOLL.
YOUR PERCEPTION HAS SHIFTED, TO BE SURE. BUT IT'S A TWO-WAY STREET.
NOW, LET'S TALK ABOUT BRAIN CHEMISTRY...
UMMM... DO WE HAVE TO?
THE CEREBRAL HEMISPHERES OF YOUR BRAIN ARE DIVIDED INTO LOBES. EACH HAS FOUR, TO BE PRECISE. THEY SERVE SPECIFIC FUNCTIONS.
THE PARIETAL LOBE INTERPRETS SENSORY INPUT ON PRACTICALLY ALL LEVELS.
HÍJOLE...I SHOULD'VE PAID MORE ATTENTION IN SCHOOL...
WE'VE DONE SOME BRAIN WORK IN THE PAST, SO OUR COMPARATIVE DATABASE IS FAIRLY EXTENSIVE.
I CAN SAY BEYOND A DOUBT THAT I'VE NEVER SEEN ANYTHING LIKE THIS...

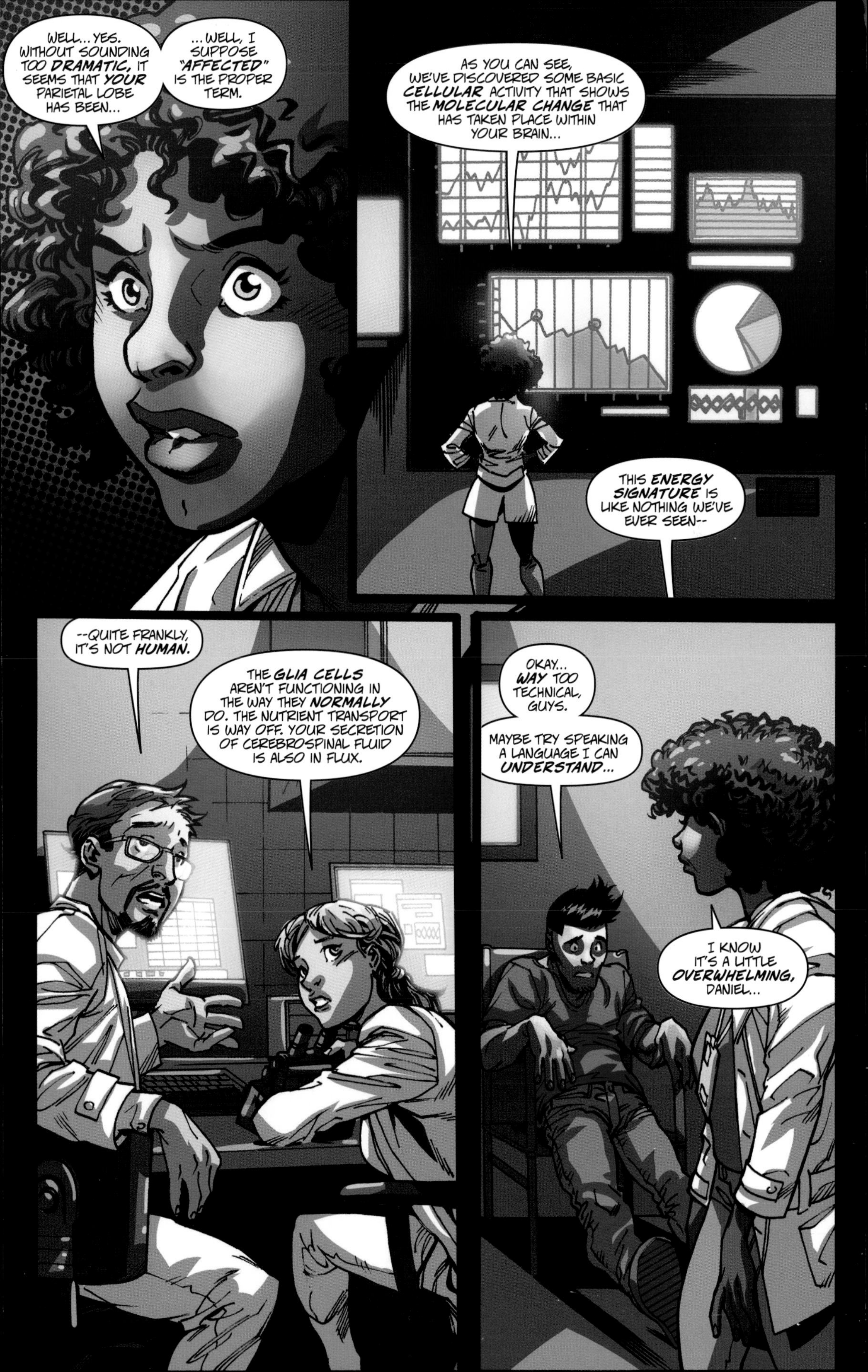
WELL... YES. WITHOUT SOUNDING TOO DRAMATIC, IT SEEMS THAT YOUR PARIETAL LOBE HAS BEEN...
...WELL, I SUPPOSE "AFFECTED" IS THE PROPER TERM.
AS YOU CAN SEE, WE'VE DISCOVERED SOME BASIC CELLULAR ACTIVITY THAT SHOWS THE MOLECULAR CHANGE THAT HAS TAKEN PLACE WITHIN YOUR BRAIN...
THIS ENERGY SIGNATURE IS LIKE NOTHING WE'VE EVER SEEN--
--QUITE FRANKLY, IT'S NOT HUMAN.
THE GLIA CELLS AREN'T FUNCTIONING IN THE WAY THEY NORMALLY DO. THE NUTRIENT TRANSPORT IS WAY OFF. YOUR SECRETION OF CEREBROSPINAL FLUID IS ALSO IN FLUX.
OKAY... WAY TOO TECHNICAL, GUYS.
MAYBE TRY SPEAKING A LANGUAGE I CAN UNDERSTAND...
I KNOW IT'S A LITTLE OVERWHELMING, DANIEL...

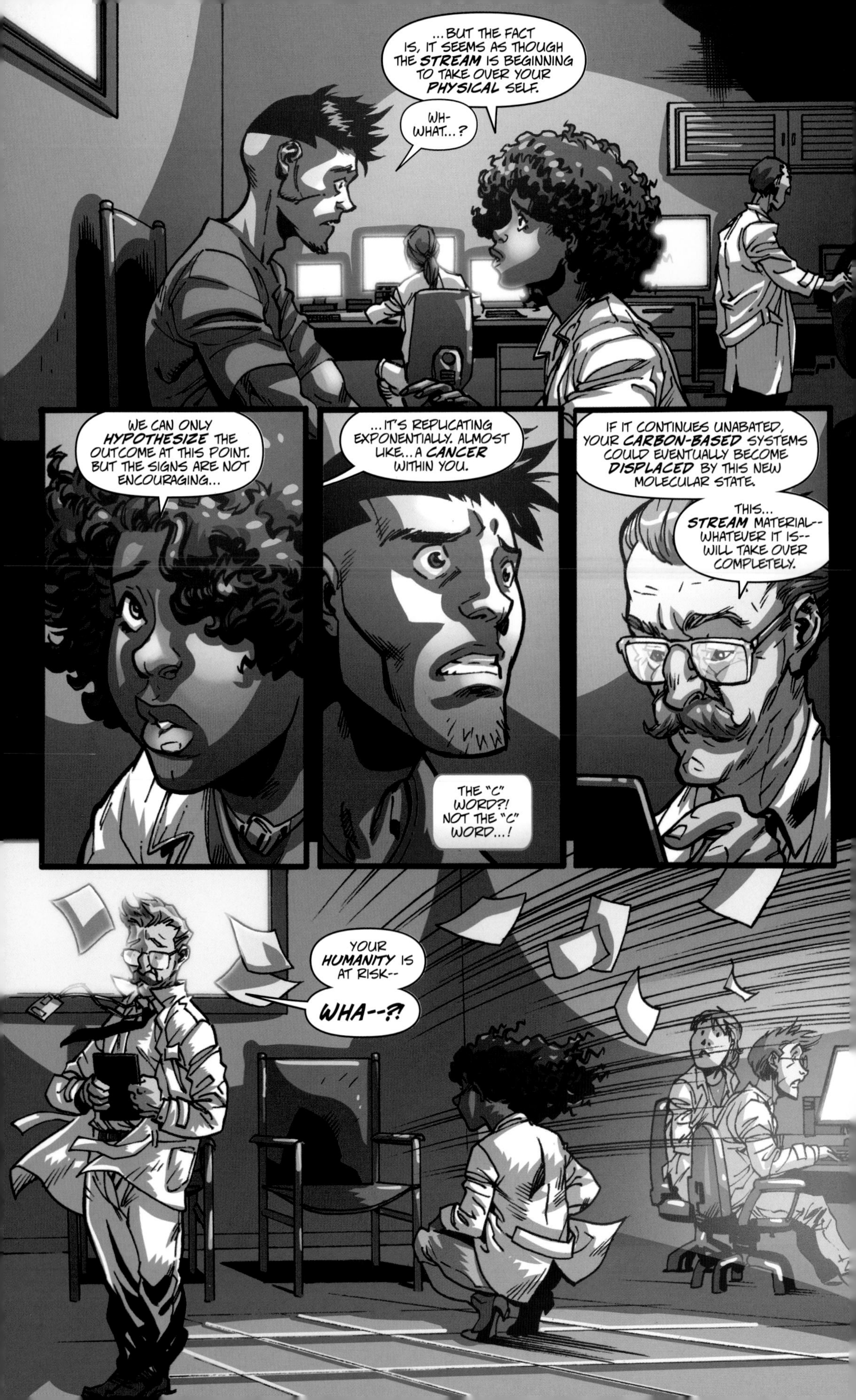
...BUT THE FACT IS, IT SEEMS AS THOUGH THE STREAM IS BEGINNING TO TAKE OVER YOUR PHYSICAL SELF.
WH- WHAT...?
WE CAN ONLY HYPOTHESIZE THE OUTCOME AT THIS POINT. BUT THE SIGNS ARE NOT ENCOURAGING...
...IT'S REPLICATING EXPONENTIALLY. ALMOST LIKE...A CANCER WITHIN YOU.
THE "C" WORD?! NOT THE "C" WORD...!
IF IT CONTINUES UNABATED, YOUR CARBON-BASED SYSTEMS COULD EVENTUALLY BECOME DISPLACED BY THIS NEW MOLECULAR STATE.
THIS... STREAM MATERIAL-- WHATEVER IT IS-- WILL TAKE OVER COMPLETELY.
YOUR HUMANITY IS AT RISK--
WHA--?!

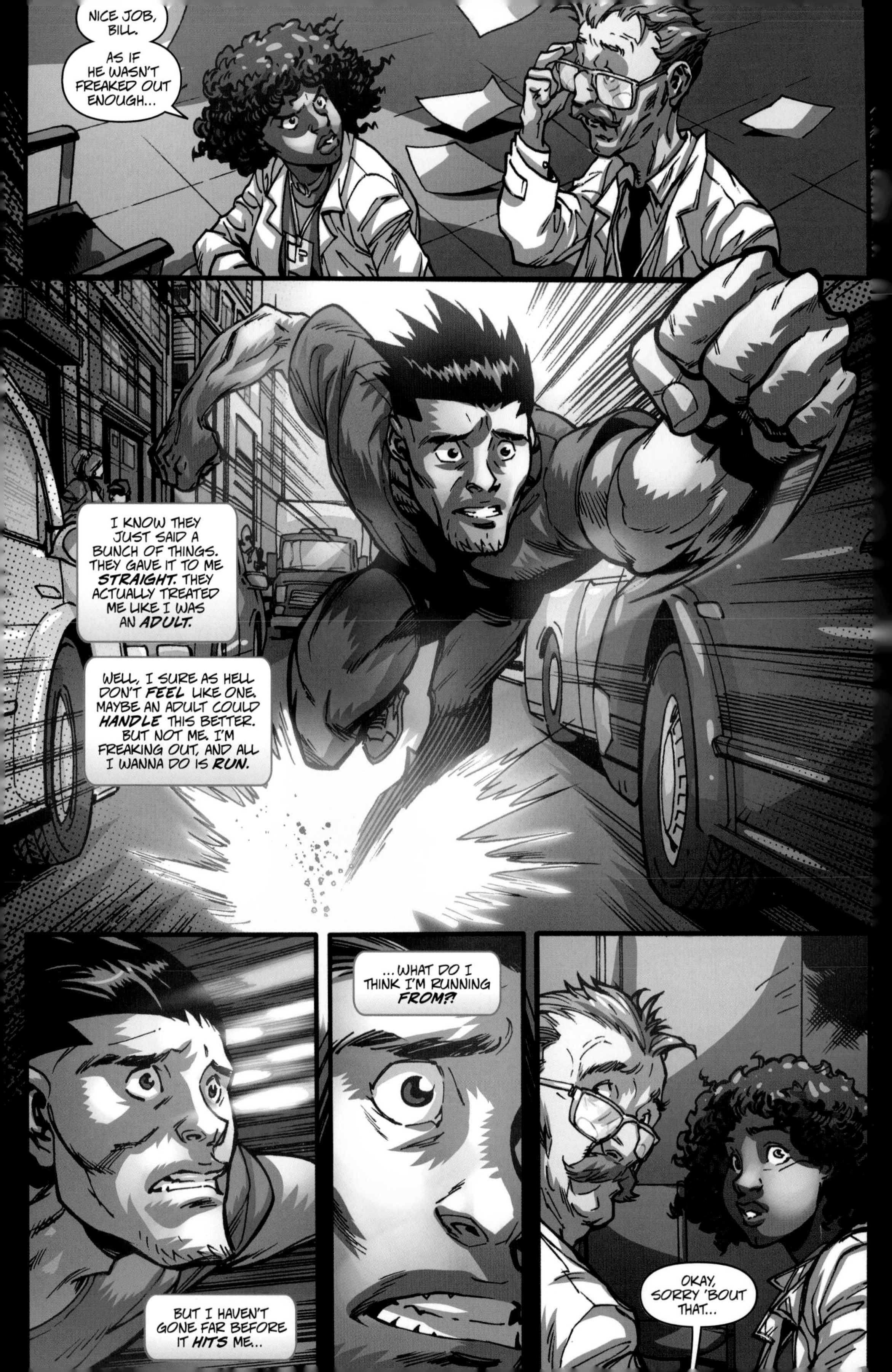
NICE JOB, BILL.
AS IF HE WASN'T FREAKED OUT ENOUGH...
I KNOW THEY JUST SAID A BUNCH OF THINGS. THEY GAVE IT TO ME STRAIGHT. THEY ACTUALLY TREATED ME LIKE I WAS AN ADULT.
WELL, I SURE AS HELL DON'T FEEL LIKE ONE. MAYBE AN ADULT COULD HANDLE THIS BETTER. BUT NOT ME. I'M FREAKING OUT, AND ALL I WANNA DO IS RUN.
BUT I HAVEN'T GONE FAR BEFORE IT HITS ME...
...WHAT DO I THINK I'M RUNNING FROM?!
OKAY, SORRY 'BOUT THAT...

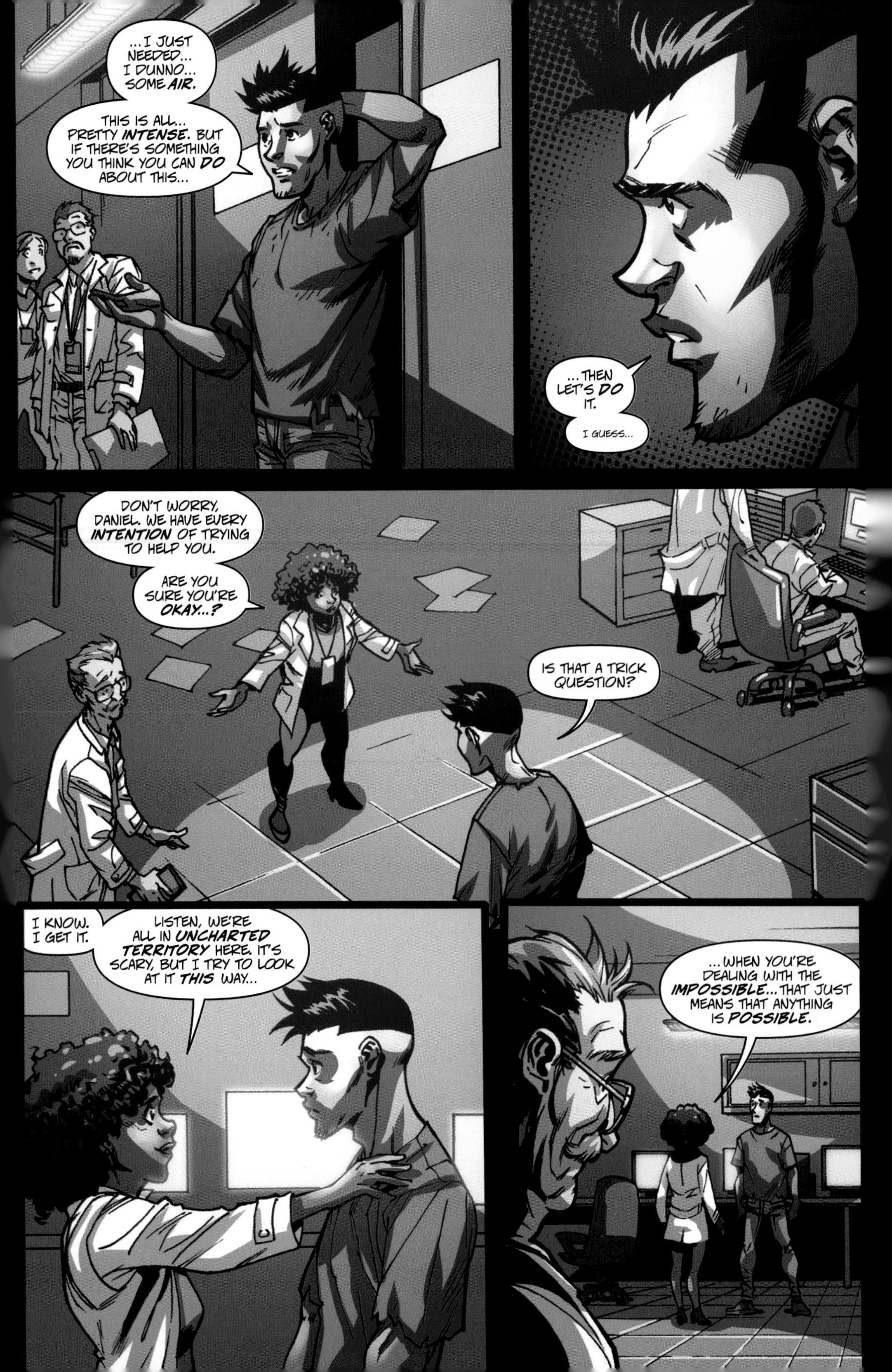
...I JUST NEEDED... I DUNNO... SOME AIR.
THIS IS ALL... PRETTY INTENSE. BUT IF THERE'S SOMETHING YOU THINK YOU CAN DO ABOUT THIS...
...THEN LET'S DO IT.
I GUESS...
DON'T WORRY, DANIEL. WE HAVE EVERY INTENTION OF TRYING TO HELP YOU.
ARE YOU SURE YOU'RE OKAY...?
IS THAT A TRICK QUESTION?
I KNOW. I GET IT.
LISTEN, WE'RE ALL IN UNCHARTED TERRITORY HERE. IT'S SCARY, BUT I TRY TO LOOK AT IT THIS WAY...
...WHEN YOU'RE DEALING WITH THE IMPOSSIBLE... THAT JUST MEANS THAT ANYTHING IS POSSIBLE.

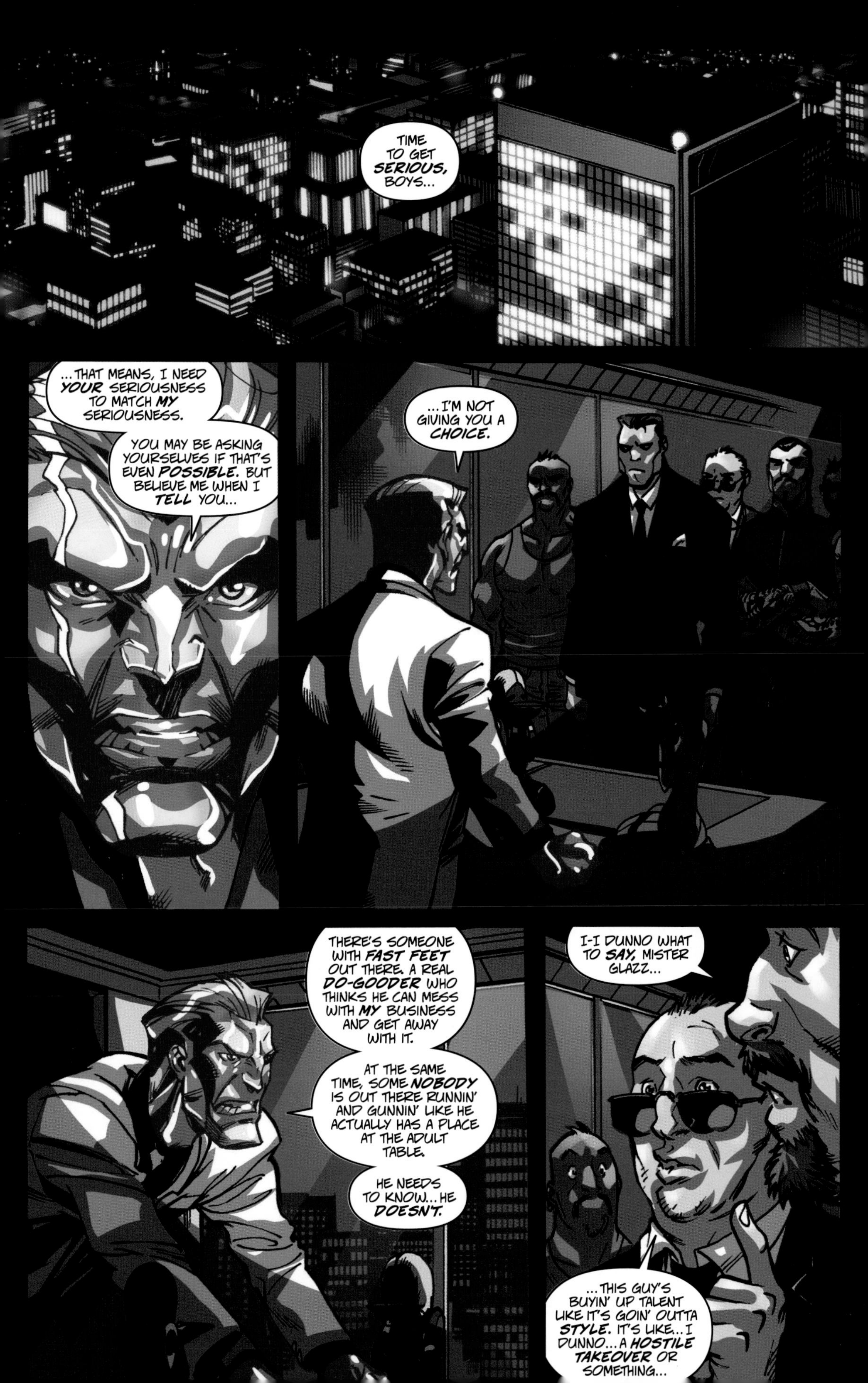
TIME TO GET SERIOUS, BOYS...
...THAT MEANS, I NEED YOUR SERIOUSNESS TO MATCH MY SERIOUSNESS.
YOU MAY BE ASKING YOURSELVES IF THAT'S EVEN POSSIBLE. BUT BELIEVE ME WHEN I TELL YOU...
...I'M NOT GIVING YOU A CHOICE.
THERE'S SOMEONE WITH FAST FEET OUT THERE. A REAL DO-GOODER WHO THINKS HE CAN MESS WITH MY BUSINESS AND GET AWAY WITH IT.
AT THE SAME TIME, SOME NOBODY IS OUT THERE RUNNIN' AND GUNNIN' LIKE HE ACTUALLY HAS A PLACE AT THE ADULT TABLE.
HE NEEDS TO KNOW... HE DOESN'T.
I-I DUNNO WHAT TO SAY, MISTER GLAZZ...
...THIS GUY'S BUYIN' UP TALENT LIKE IT'S GOIN' OUTTA STYLE. IT'S LIKE... I DUNNO... A HOSTILE TAKEOVER OR SOMETHING...

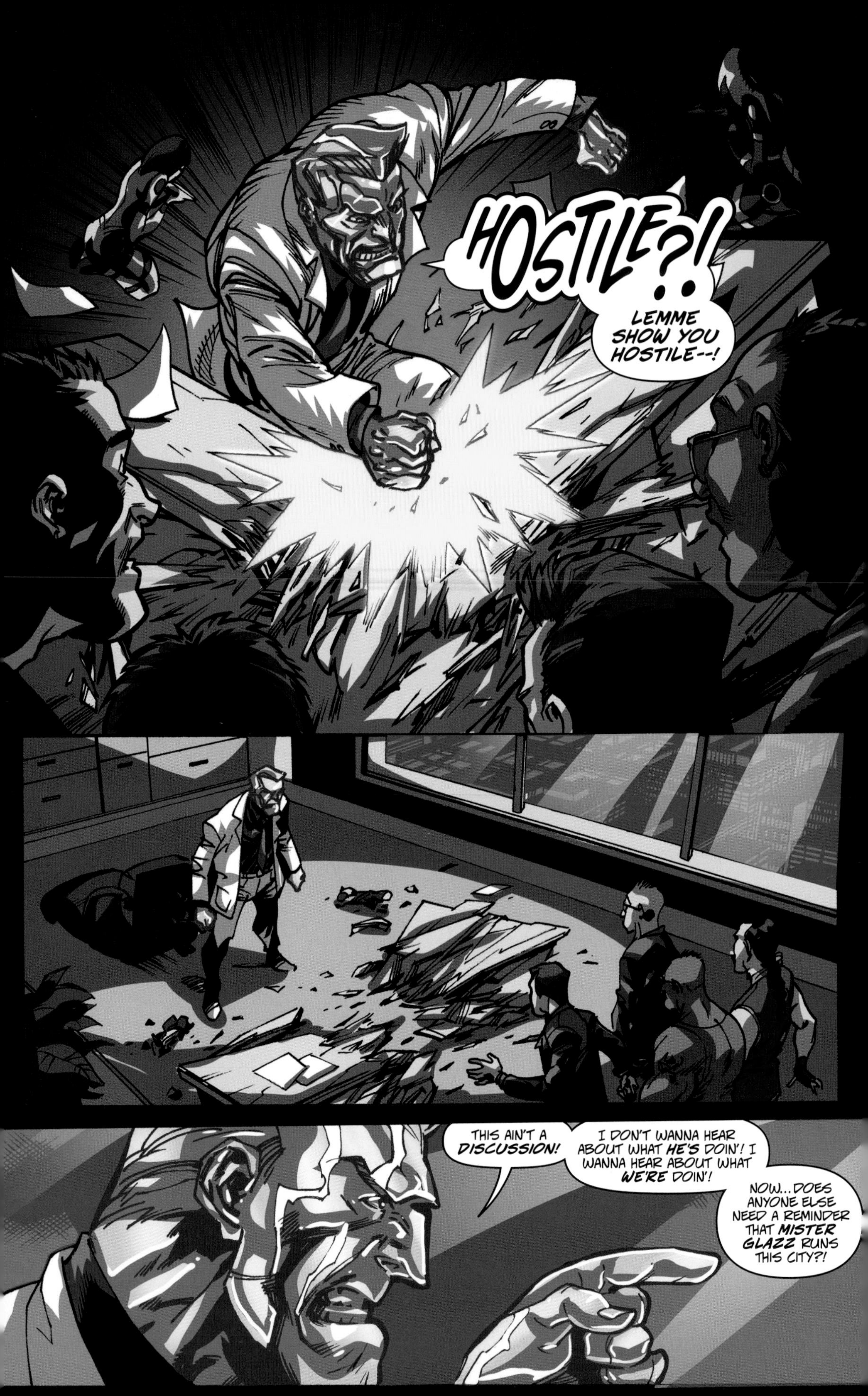
HOSTILE?!
LEMME SHOW YOU HOSTILE--!
THIS AIN'T A DISCUSSION!
I DON'T WANNA HEAR ABOUT WHAT HE'S DOIN'! I WANNA HEAR ABOUT WHAT WE'RE DOIN'!
NOW...DOES ANYONE ELSE NEED A REMINDER THAT MISTER GLAZZ RUNS THIS CITY?!

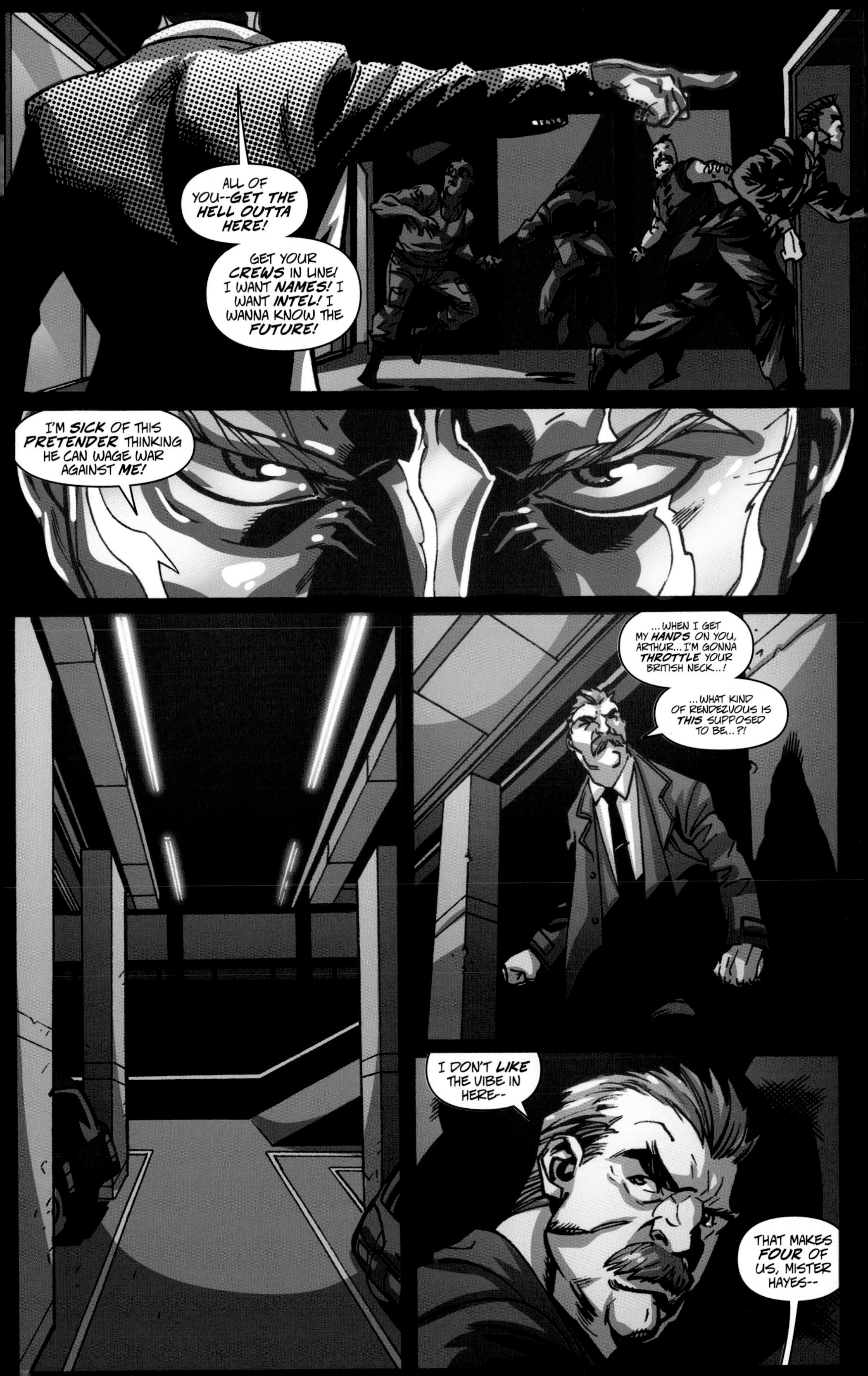
ALL OF YOU--GET THE HELL OUTTA HERE!
GET YOUR CREWS IN LINE! I WANT NAMES! I WANT INTEL! I WANNA KNOW THE FUTURE!
I'M SICK OF THIS PRETENDER THINKING HE CAN WAGE WAR AGAINST ME!
...WHEN I GET MY HANDS ON YOU, ARTHUR... I'M GONNA THROTTLE YOUR BRITISH NECK...!
...WHAT KIND OF RENDEZVOUS IS THIS SUPPOSED TO BE...?!
I DON'T LIKE THE VIBE IN HERE--
THAT MAKES FOUR OF US, MISTER HAYES--

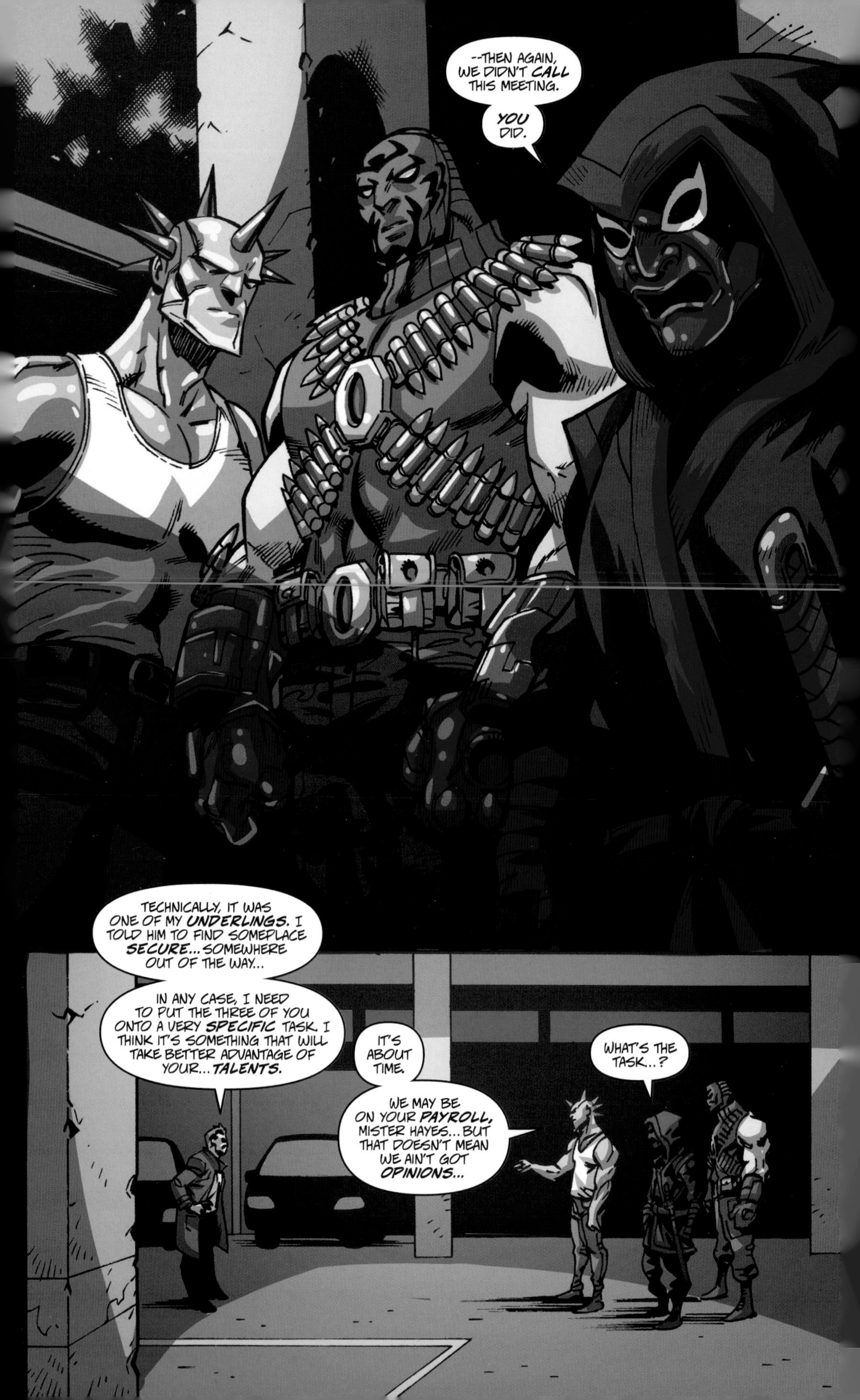
--THEN AGAIN, WE DIDN'T CALL THIS MEETING.
YOU DID.
TECHNICALLY, IT WAS ONE OF MY UNDERLINGS. I TOLD HIM TO FIND SOMEPLACE SECURE... SOMEWHERE OUT OF THE WAY...
IN ANY CASE, I NEED TO PUT THE THREE OF YOU ONTO A VERY SPECIFIC TASK. I THINK IT'S SOMETHING THAT WILL TAKE BETTER ADVANTAGE OF YOUR... TALENTS.
IT'S ABOUT TIME.
WE MAY BE ON YOUR PAYROLL, MISTER HAYES... BUT THAT DOESN'T MEAN WE AIN'T GOT OPINIONS...
WHAT'S THE TASK...?

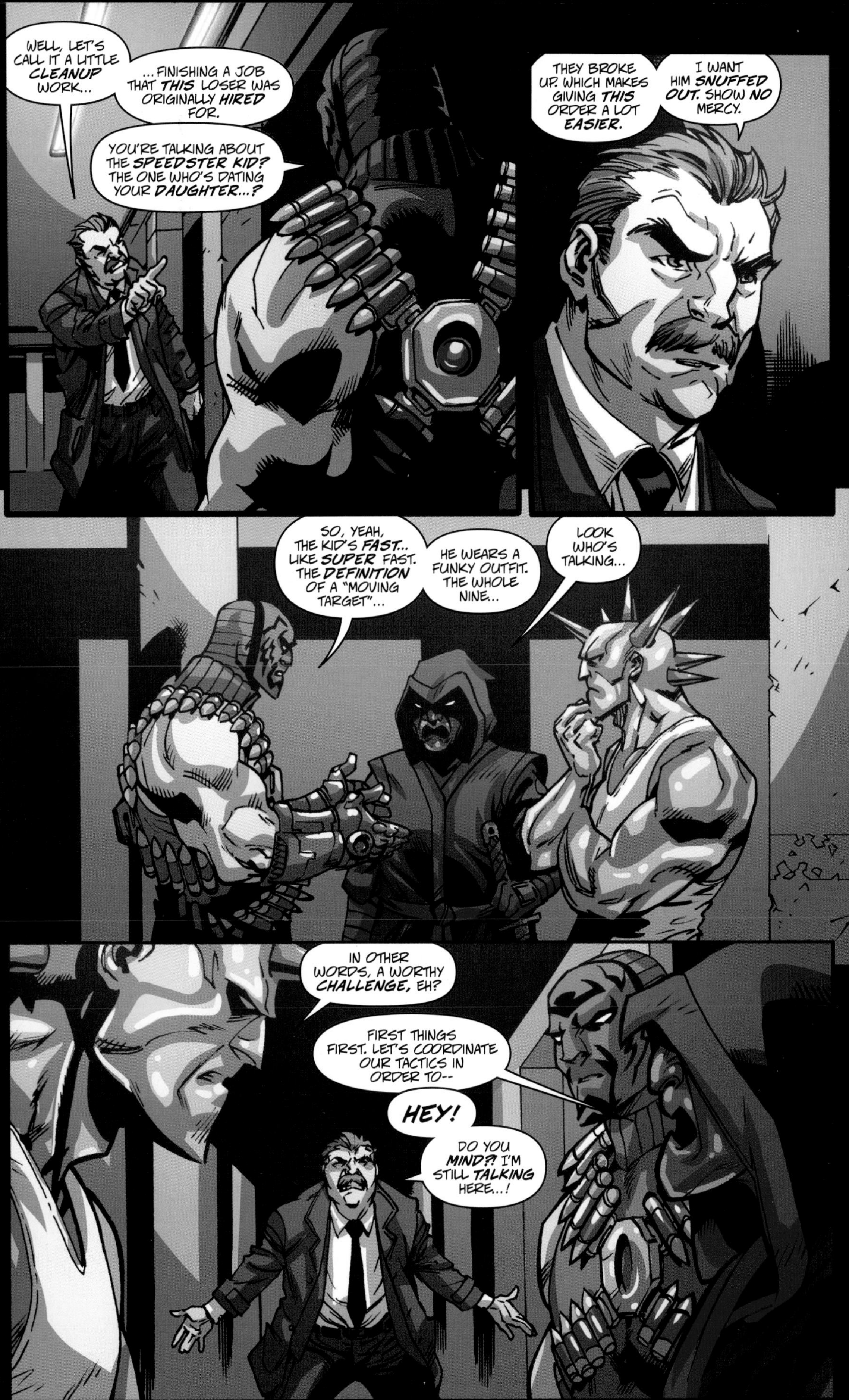

WELL, LET'S CALL IT A LITTLE CLEANUP WORK...
...FINISHING A JOB THAT THIS LOSER WAS ORIGINALLY HIRED FOR.
YOU'RE TALKING ABOUT THE SPEEDSTER KID? THE ONE WHO'S DATING YOUR DAUGHTER...?
THEY BROKE UP. WHICH MAKES GIVING THIS ORDER A LOT EASIER.
I WANT HIM SNUFFED OUT. SHOW NO MERCY.
SO, YEAH, THE KID'S FAST... LIKE SUPER FAST. THE DEFINITION OF A "MOVING TARGET"...
HE WEARS A FUNKY OUTFIT. THE WHOLE NINE...
LOOK WHO'S TALKING...
IN OTHER WORDS, A WORTHY CHALLENGE, EH?
FIRST THINGS FIRST. LET'S COORDINATE OUR TACTICS IN ORDER TO--
HEY!
DO YOU MIND?! I'M STILL TALKING HERE...!

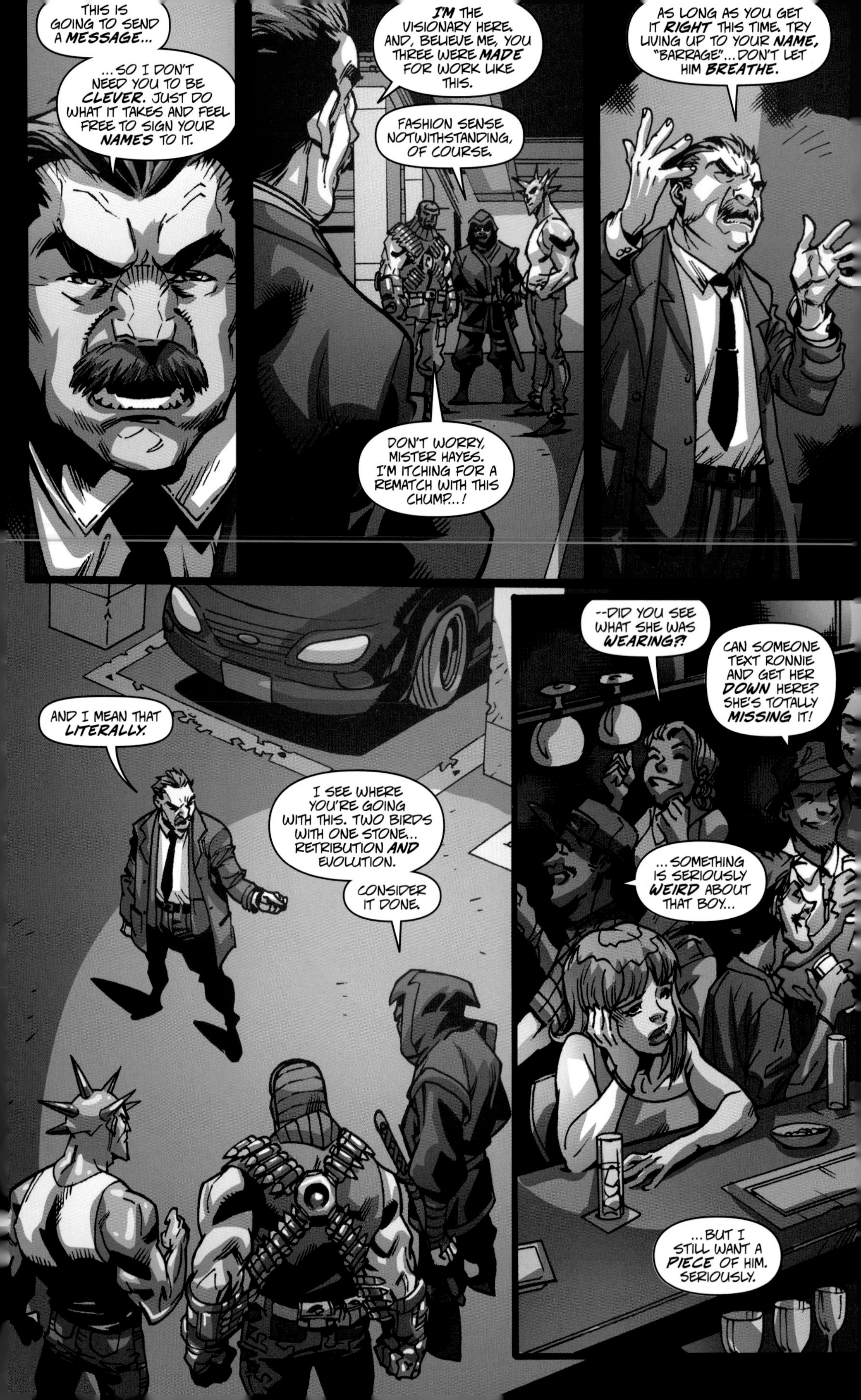
THIS IS GOING TO SEND A MESSAGE...
...SO I DON'T NEED YOU TO BE CLEVER. JUST DO WHAT IT TAKES AND FEEL FREE TO SIGN YOUR NAMES TO IT.
I'M THE VISIONARY HERE. AND, BELIEVE ME, YOU THREE WERE MADE FOR WORK LIKE THIS.
FASHION SENSE NOTWITHSTANDING, OF COURSE.
DON'T WORRY, MISTER HAYES. I'M ITCHING FOR A REMATCH WITH THIS CHUMP...!
AS LONG AS YOU GET IT RIGHT THIS TIME. TRY LIVING UP TO YOUR NAME, "BARRAGE"...DON'T LET HIM BREATHE.
AND I MEAN THAT LITERALLY.
I SEE WHERE YOU'RE GOING WITH THIS. TWO BIRDS WITH ONE STONE... RETRIBUTION AND EVOLUTION.
CONSIDER IT DONE.
--DID YOU SEE WHAT SHE WAS WEARING?!
CAN SOMEONE TEXT RONNIE AND GET HER DOWN HERE? SHE'S TOTALLY MISSING IT!
...SOMETHING IS SERIOUSLY WEIRD ABOUT THAT BOY...
...BUT I STILL WANT A PIECE OF HIM. SERIOUSLY.

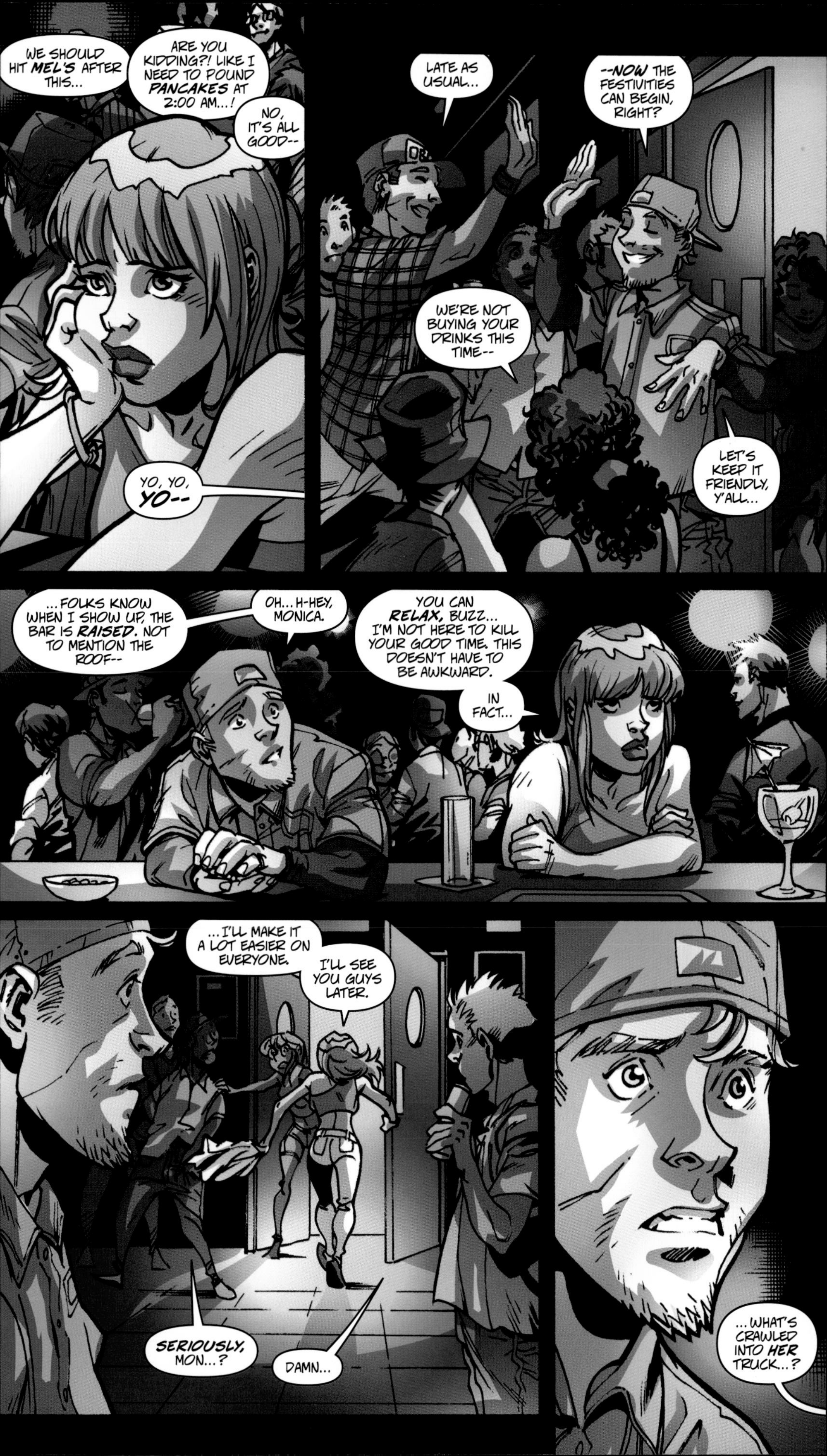
WE SHOULD HIT MEL'S AFTER THIS...
ARE YOU KIDDING?! LIKE I NEED TO POUND PANCAKES AT 2:00 AM...!
NO, IT'S ALL GOOD--
YO, YO, YO--
LATE AS USUAL...
--NOW THE FESTIVITIES CAN BEGIN, RIGHT?
WE'RE NOT BUYING YOUR DRINKS THIS TIME--
LET'S KEEP IT FRIENDLY, Y'ALL...
...FOLKS KNOW WHEN I SHOW UP, THE BAR IS RAISED. NOT TO MENTION THE ROOF--
OH... H-HEY, MONICA.
YOU CAN RELAX, BUZZ... I'M NOT HERE TO KILL YOUR GOOD TIME. THIS DOESN'T HAVE TO BE AWKWARD.
IN FACT...
...I'LL MAKE IT A LOT EASIER ON EVERYONE.
I'LL SEE YOU GUYS LATER.
SERIOUSLY, MON...?
DAMN...
...WHAT'S CRAWLED INTO HER TRUCK...?

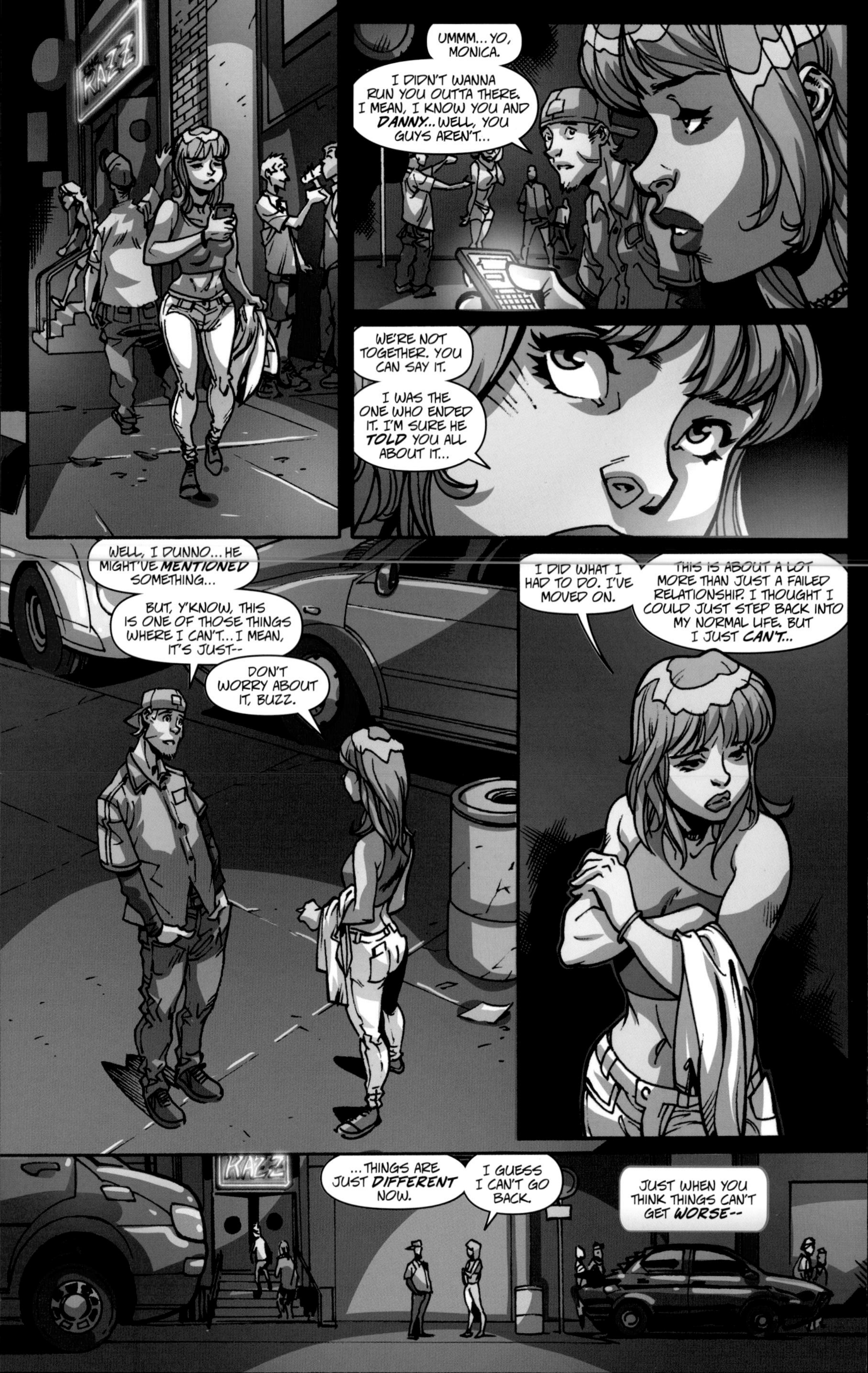
UMMM... YO, MONICA.
I DIDN'T WANNA RUN YOU OUTTA THERE. I MEAN, I KNOW YOU AND **DANNY**... WELL, YOU GUYS AREN'T...
WE'RE NOT TOGETHER. YOU CAN SAY IT.
I WAS THE ONE WHO ENDED IT. I'M SURE HE **TOLD** YOU ALL ABOUT IT...
WELL, I DUNNO... HE MIGHT'VE **MENTIONED** SOMETHING...
BUT, Y'KNOW, THIS IS ONE OF THOSE THINGS WHERE I CAN'T... I MEAN, IT'S JUST--
DON'T WORRY ABOUT IT, BUZZ.
I DID WHAT I HAD TO DO. I'VE MOVED ON.
THIS IS ABOUT A LOT MORE THAN JUST A FAILED RELATIONSHIP. I THOUGHT I COULD JUST STEP BACK INTO MY NORMAL LIFE. BUT I JUST **CAN'T**...
...THINGS ARE JUST **DIFFERENT** NOW.
I GUESS I CAN'T GO BACK.
JUST WHEN YOU THINK THINGS CAN'T GET **WORSE**--

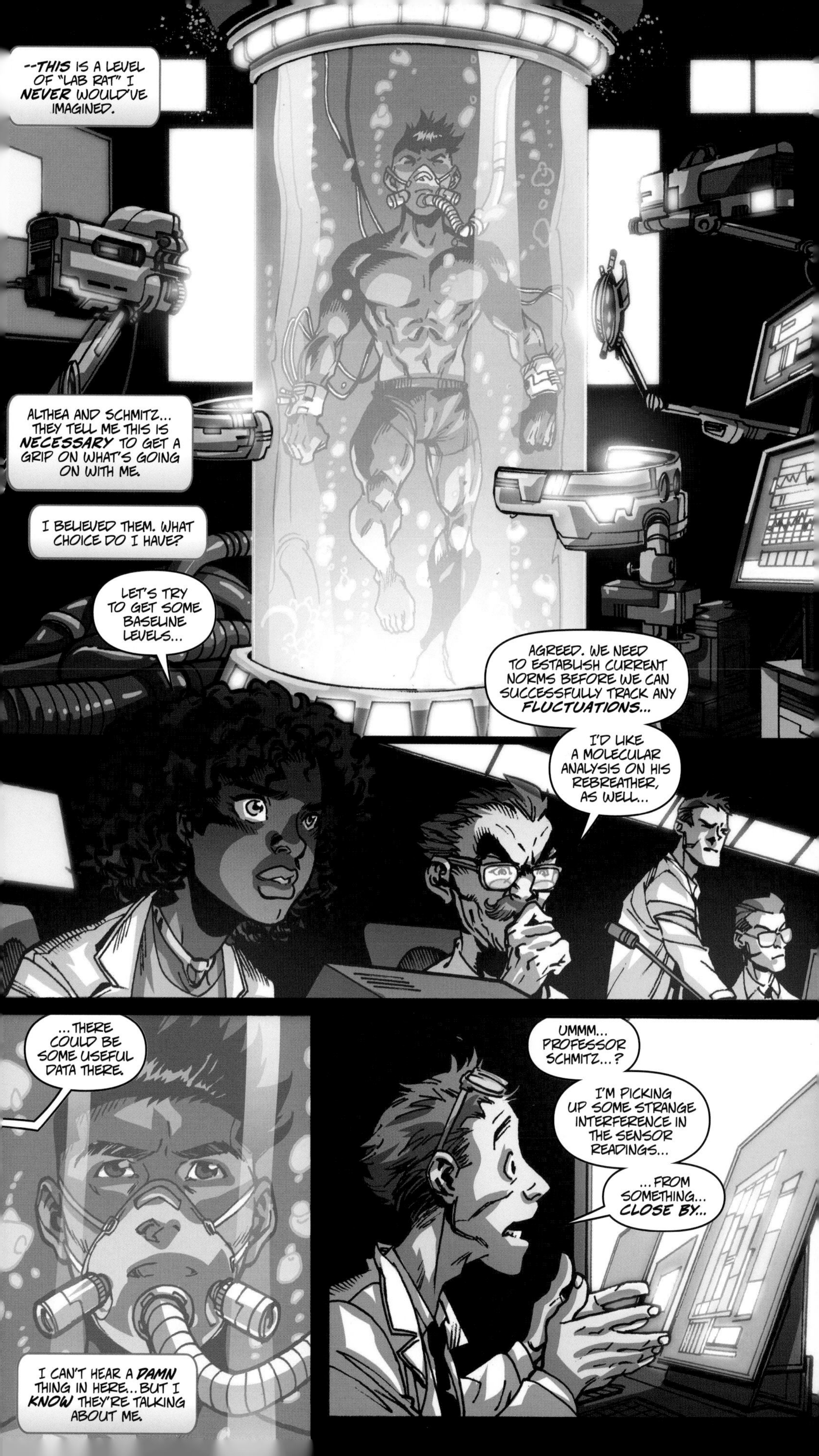

--THIS IS A LEVEL OF "LAB RAT" I NEVER WOULD'VE IMAGINED.
ALTHEA AND SCHMITZ... THEY TELL ME THIS IS NECESSARY TO GET A GRIP ON WHAT'S GOING ON WITH ME.
I BELIEVED THEM. WHAT CHOICE DO I HAVE?
LET'S TRY TO GET SOME BASELINE LEVELS...
AGREED. WE NEED TO ESTABLISH CURRENT NORMS BEFORE WE CAN SUCCESSFULLY TRACK ANY FLUCTUATIONS...
I'D LIKE A MOLECULAR ANALYSIS ON HIS REBREATHER, AS WELL...
...THERE COULD BE SOME USEFUL DATA THERE.
I CAN'T HEAR A DAMN THING IN HERE...BUT I KNOW THEY'RE TALKING ABOUT ME.
UMMM... PROFESSOR SCHMITZ...?
I'M PICKING UP SOME STRANGE INTERFERENCE IN THE SENSOR READINGS...
...FROM SOMETHING... CLOSE BY...

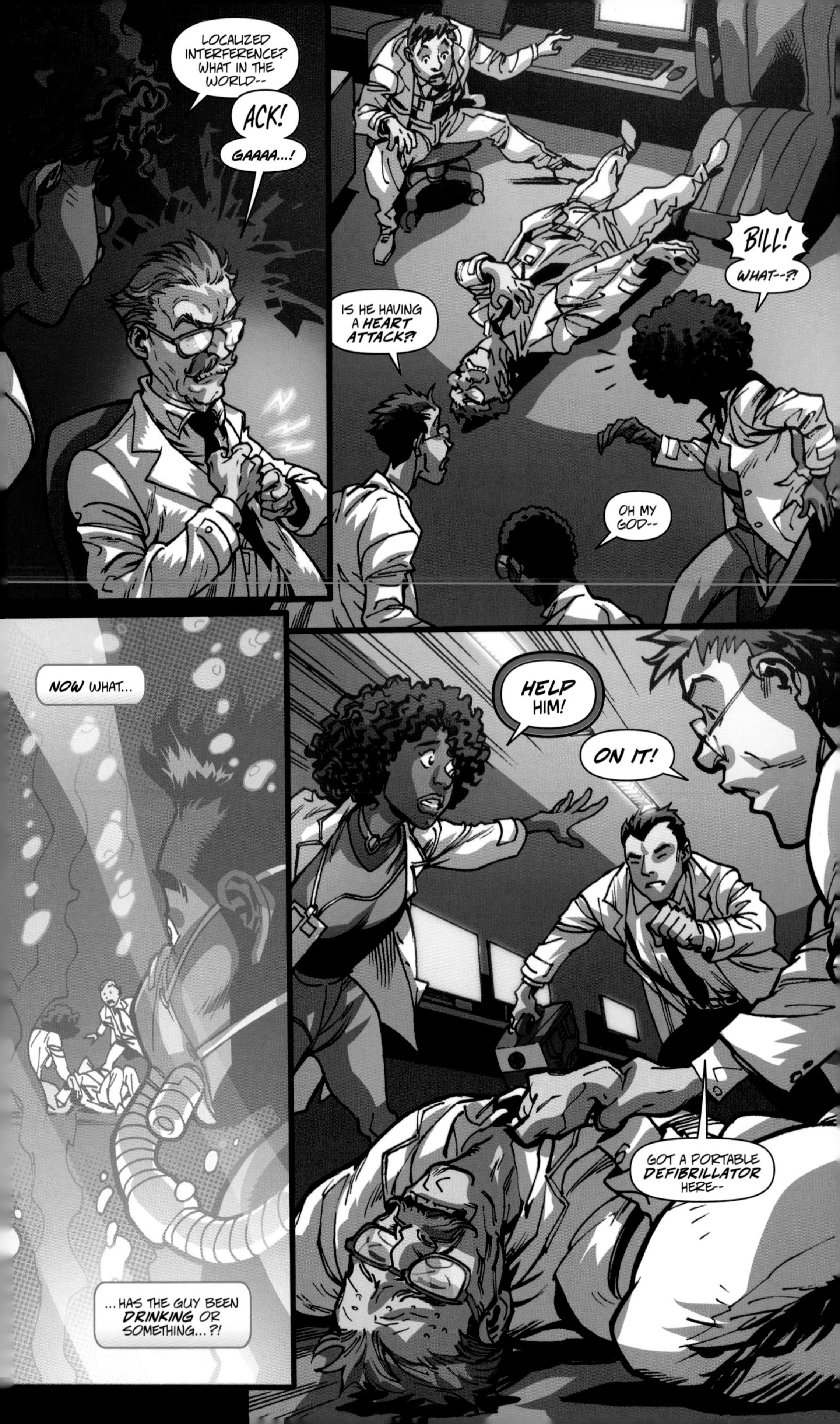
LOCALIZED INTERFERENCE? WHAT IN THE WORLD--
ACK!
GAAAA...!
BILL!
WHAT--?!
IS HE HAVING A HEART ATTACK?!
OH MY GOD--
NOW WHAT...
...HAS THE GUY BEEN DRINKING OR SOMETHING...?!
HELP HIM!
ON IT!
GOT A PORTABLE DEFIBRILLATOR HERE--

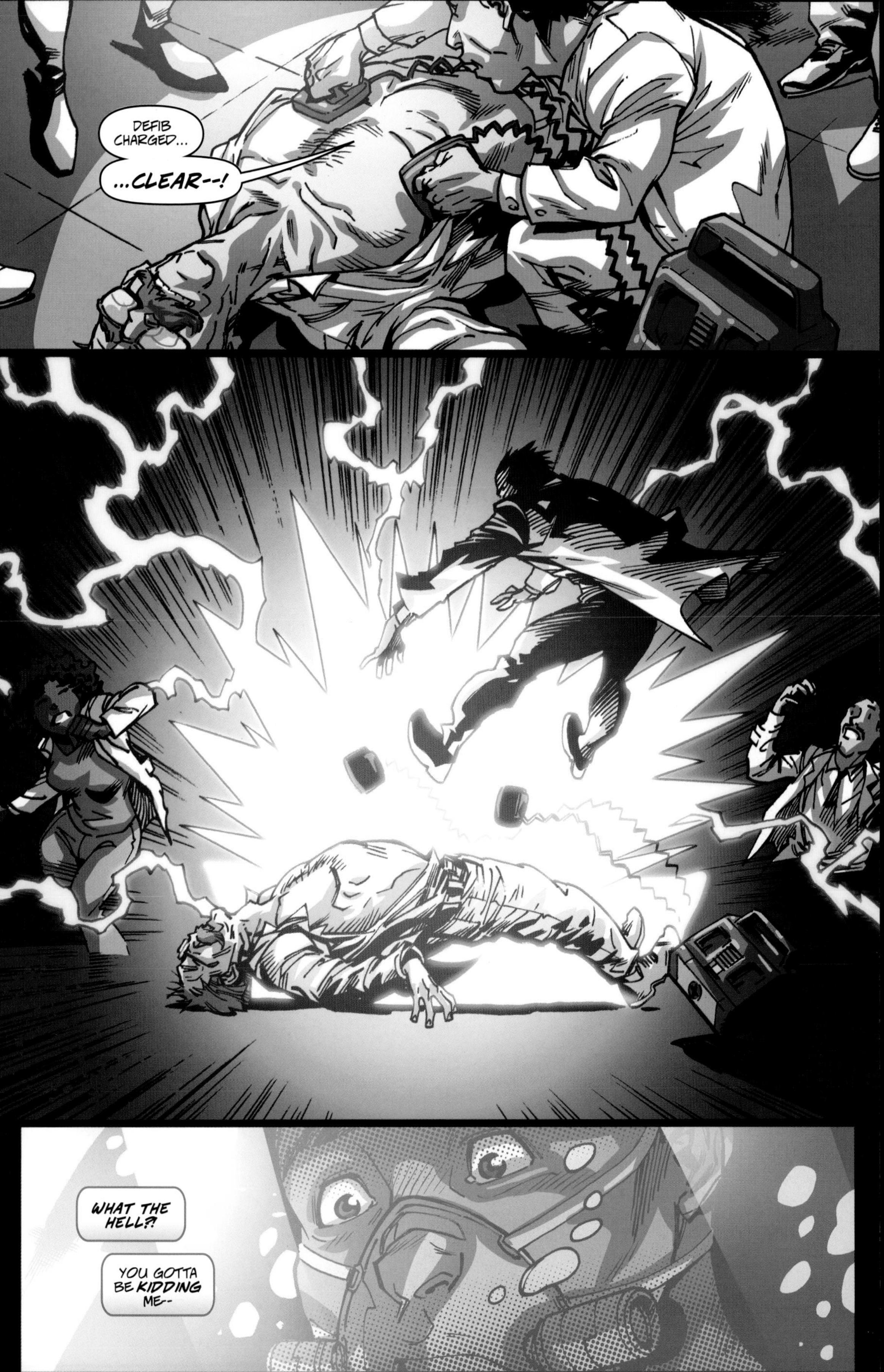
DEFIB CHARGED...
...CLEAR--!
WHAT THE HELL?!
YOU GOTTA BE KIDDING ME--

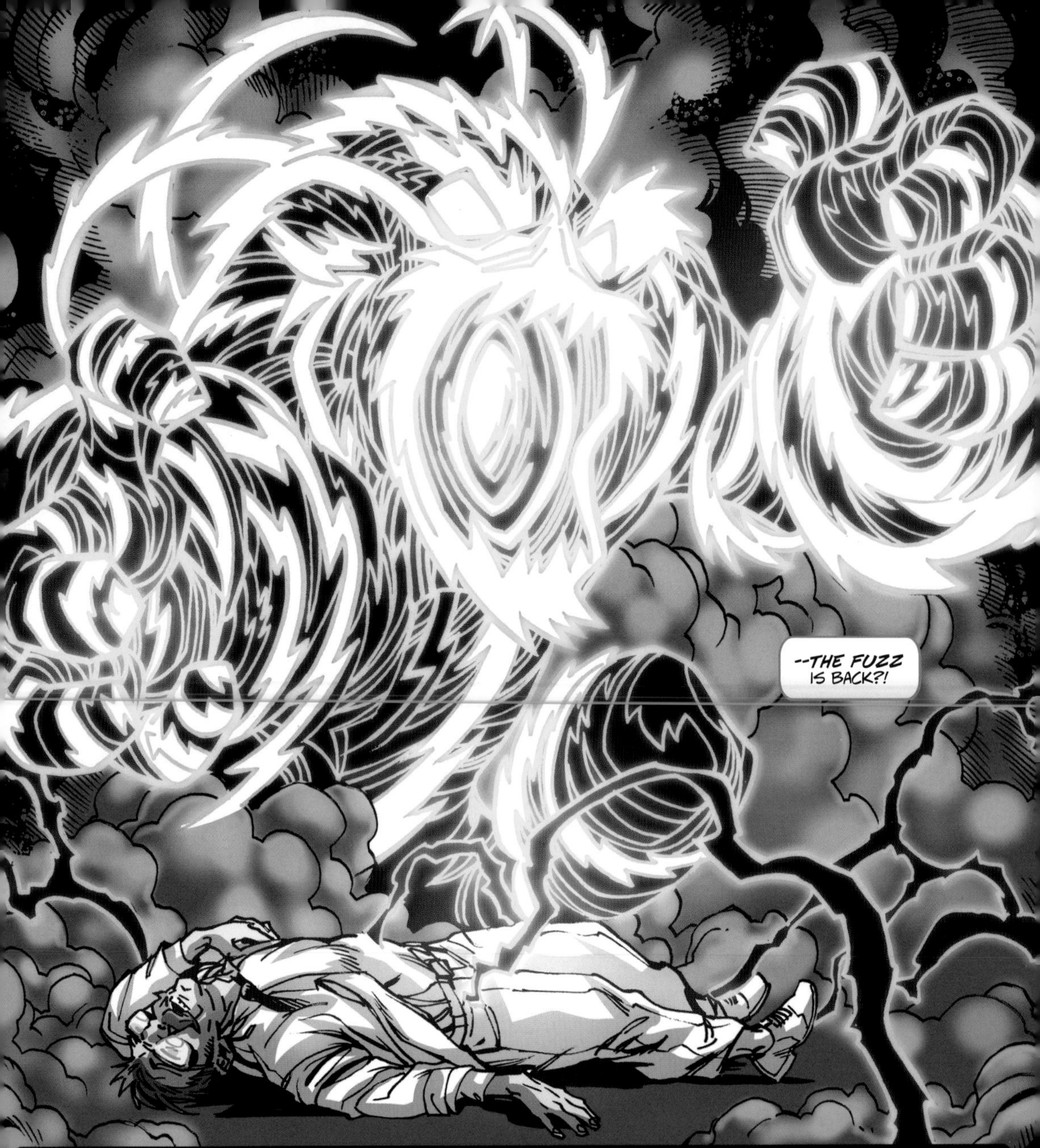
--THE FUZZ IS BACK?!

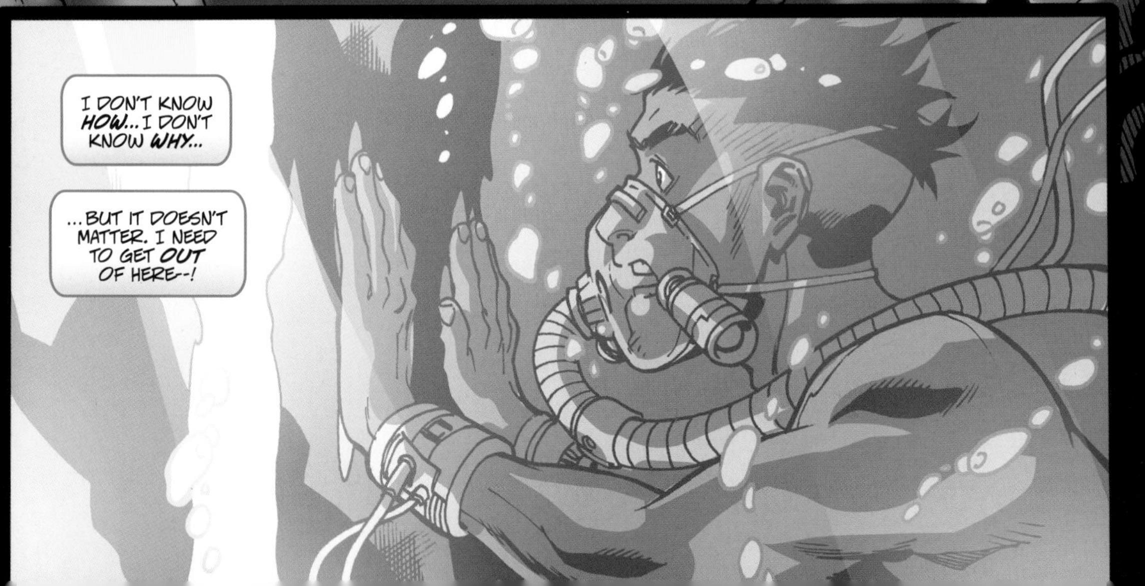
I DON'T KNOW HOW... I DON'T KNOW WHY...
...BUT IT DOESN'T MATTER. I NEED TO GET OUT OF HERE--!

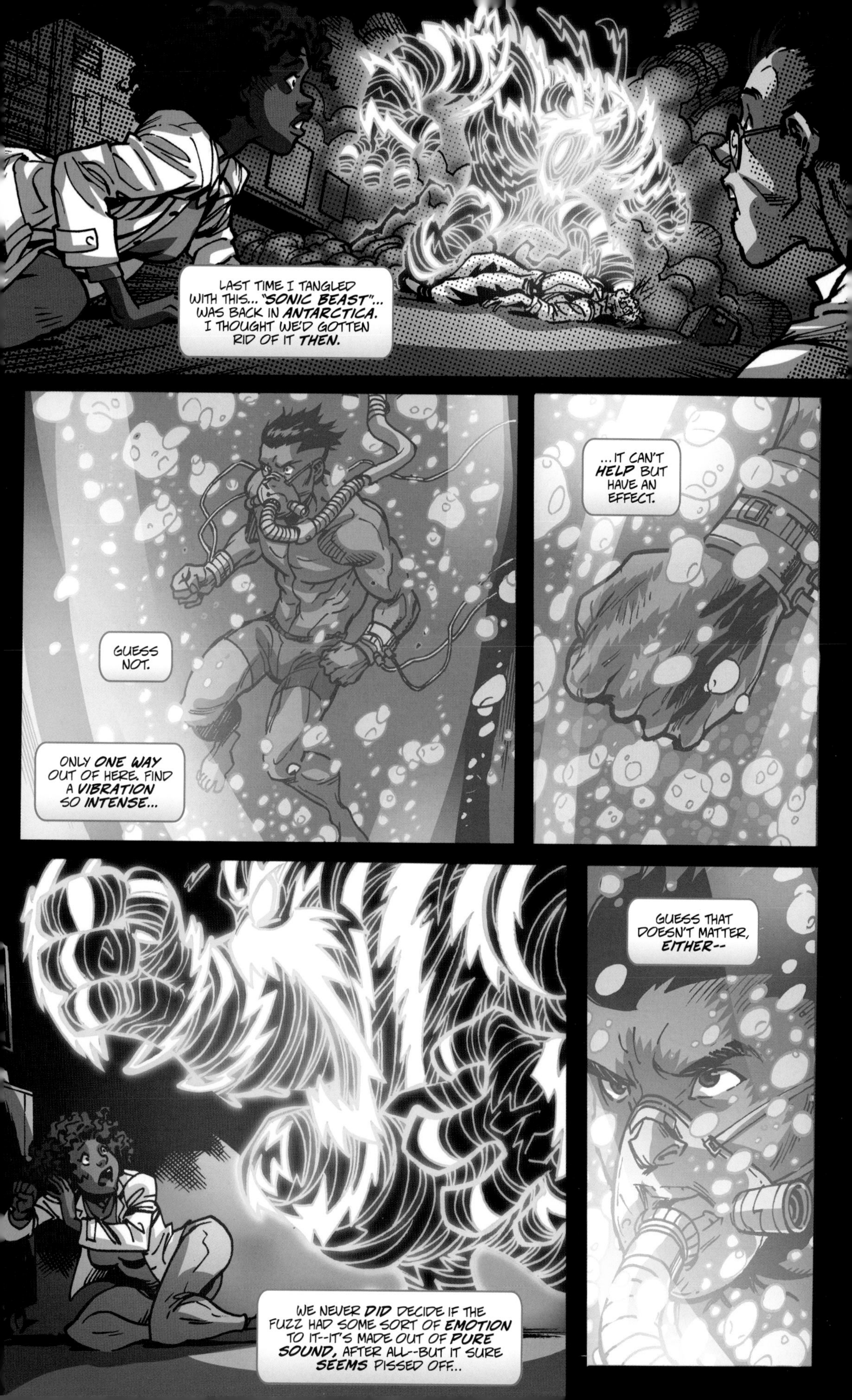
LAST TIME I TANGLED WITH THIS... "SONIC BEAST"... WAS BACK IN ANTARCTICA. I THOUGHT WE'D GOTTEN RID OF IT THEN.
GUESS NOT.
ONLY ONE WAY OUT OF HERE. FIND A VIBRATION SO INTENSE...
...IT CAN'T HELP BUT HAVE AN EFFECT.
WE NEVER DID DECIDE IF THE FUZZ HAD SOME SORT OF EMOTION TO IT--IT'S MADE OUT OF PURE SOUND, AFTER ALL--BUT IT SURE SEEMS PISSED OFF...
GUESS THAT DOESN'T MATTER, EITHER--

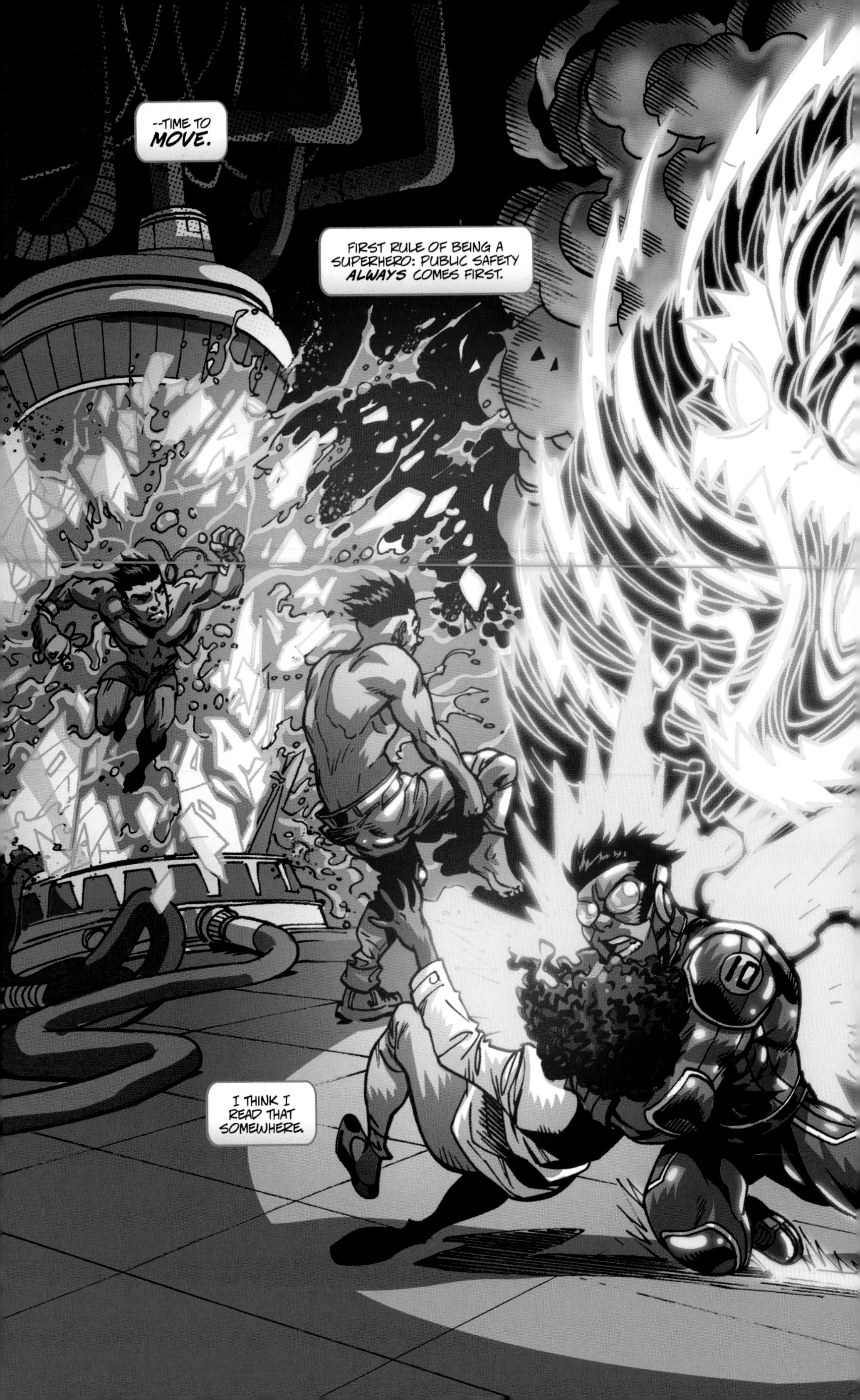
--TIME TO MOVE.
FIRST RULE OF BEING A SUPERHERO: PUBLIC SAFETY ALWAYS COMES FIRST.
I THINK I READ THAT SOMEWHERE.
10

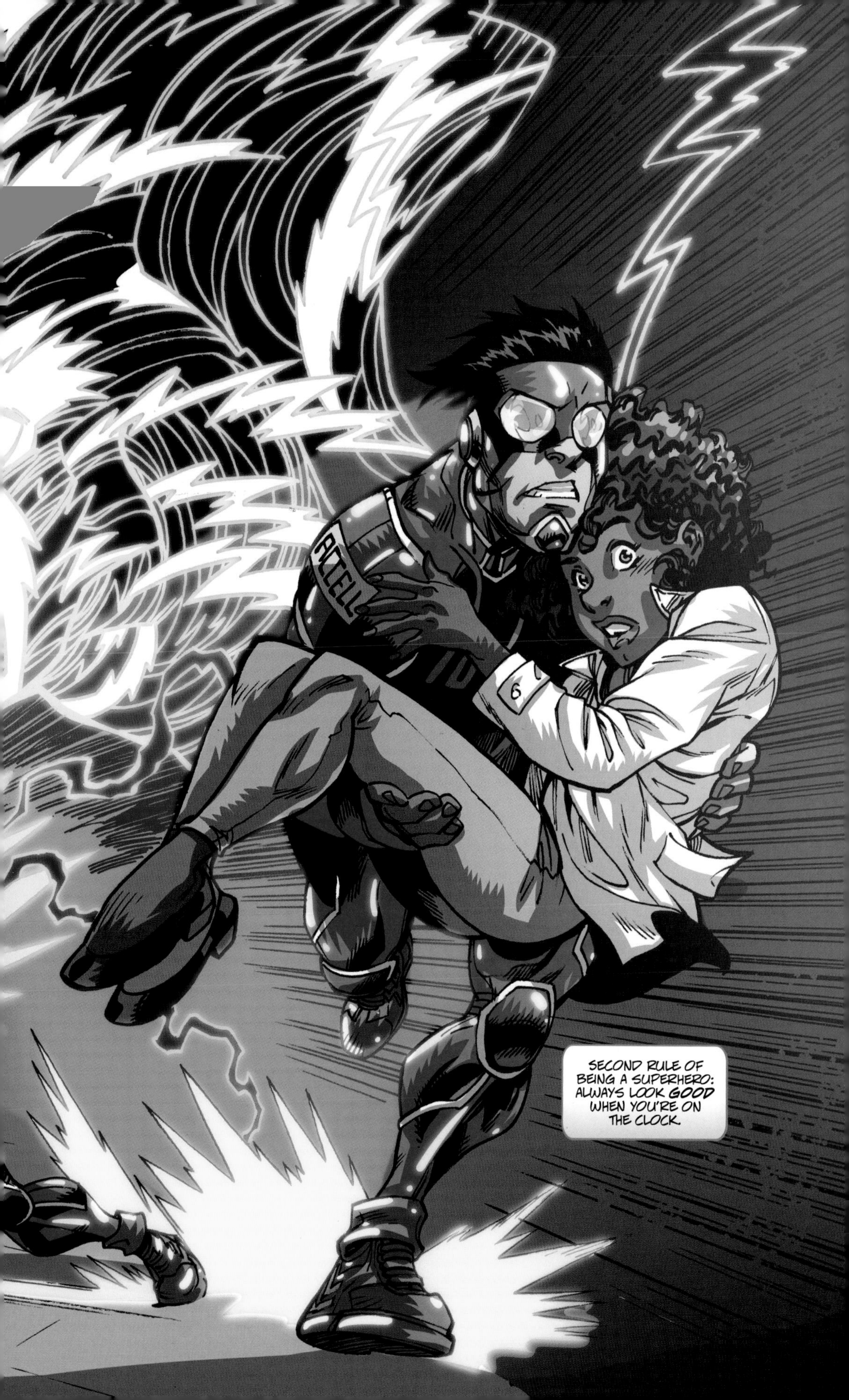
SECOND RULE OF BEING A SUPERHERO: ALWAYS LOOK GOOD WHEN YOU'RE ON THE CLOCK.

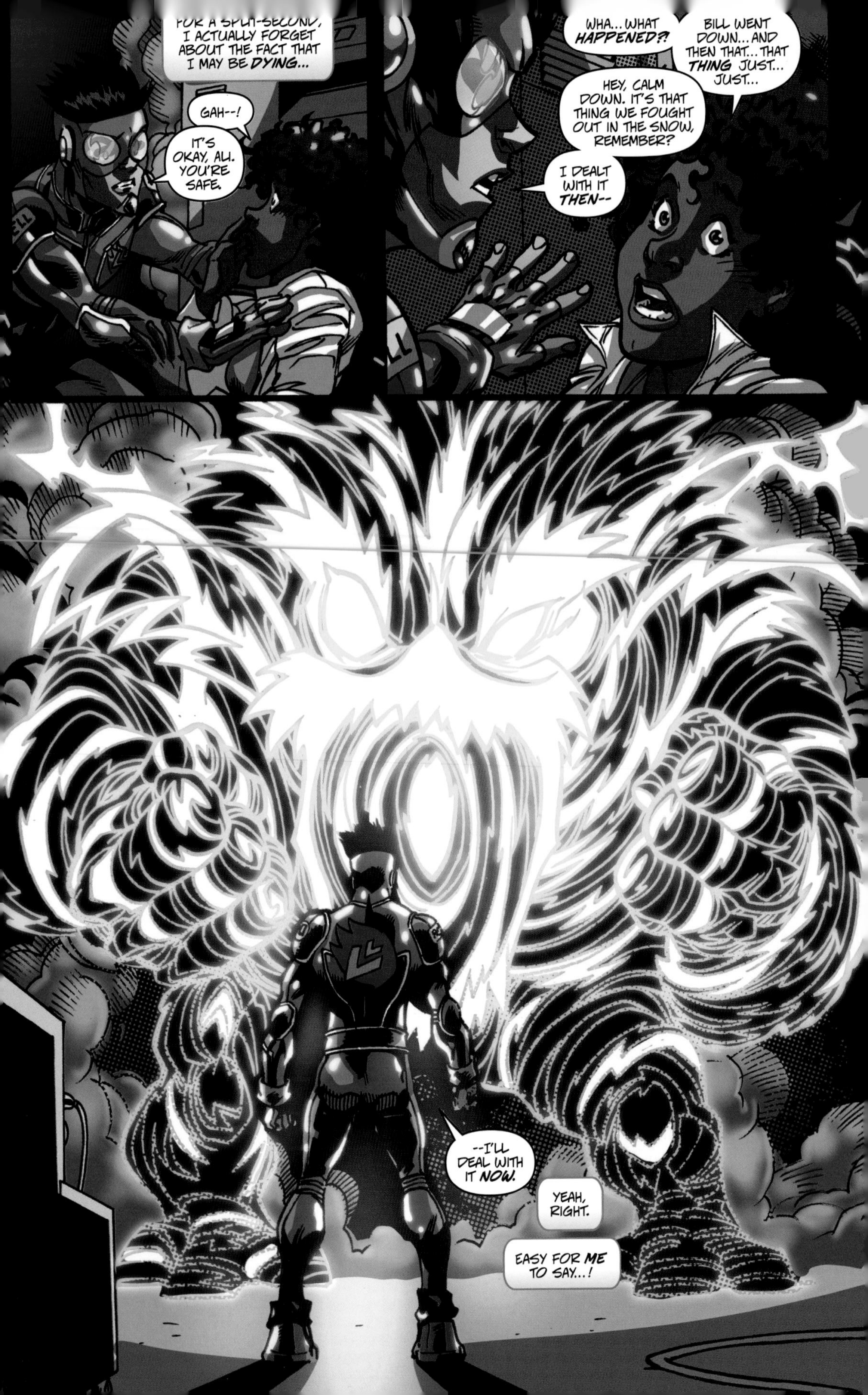
FOR A SPLIT-SECOND, I ACTUALLY FORGET ABOUT THE FACT THAT I MAY BE DYING...
GAH--!
IT'S OKAY, ALI. YOU'RE SAFE.
WHA... WHAT HAPPENED?!
BILL WENT DOWN... AND THEN THAT... THAT THING JUST... JUST...
HEY, CALM DOWN. IT'S THAT THING WE FOUGHT OUT IN THE SNOW, REMEMBER?
I DEALT WITH IT THEN--
--I'LL DEAL WITH IT NOW.
YEAH, RIGHT.
EASY FOR ME TO SAY...!

CHAPTER TWO

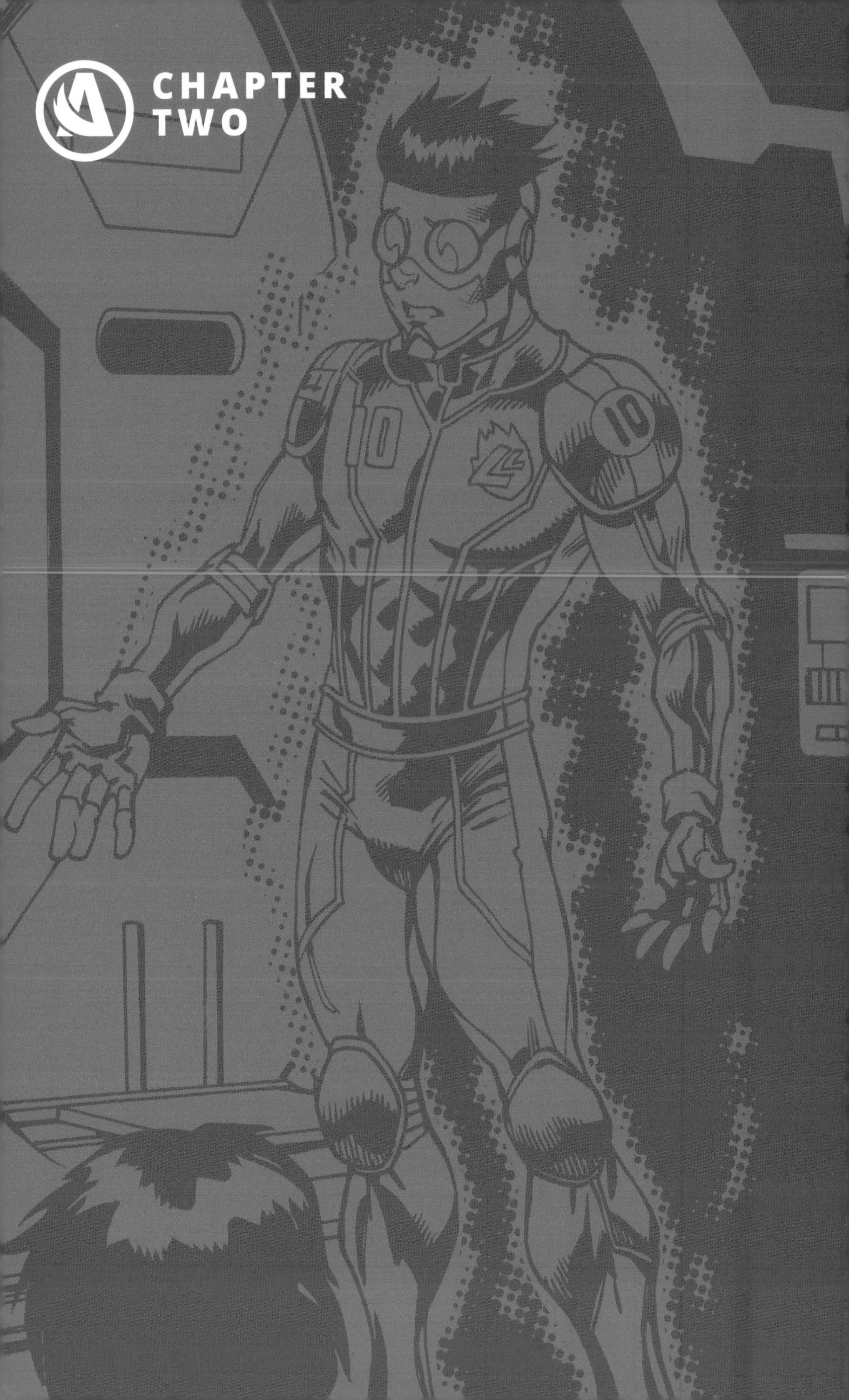

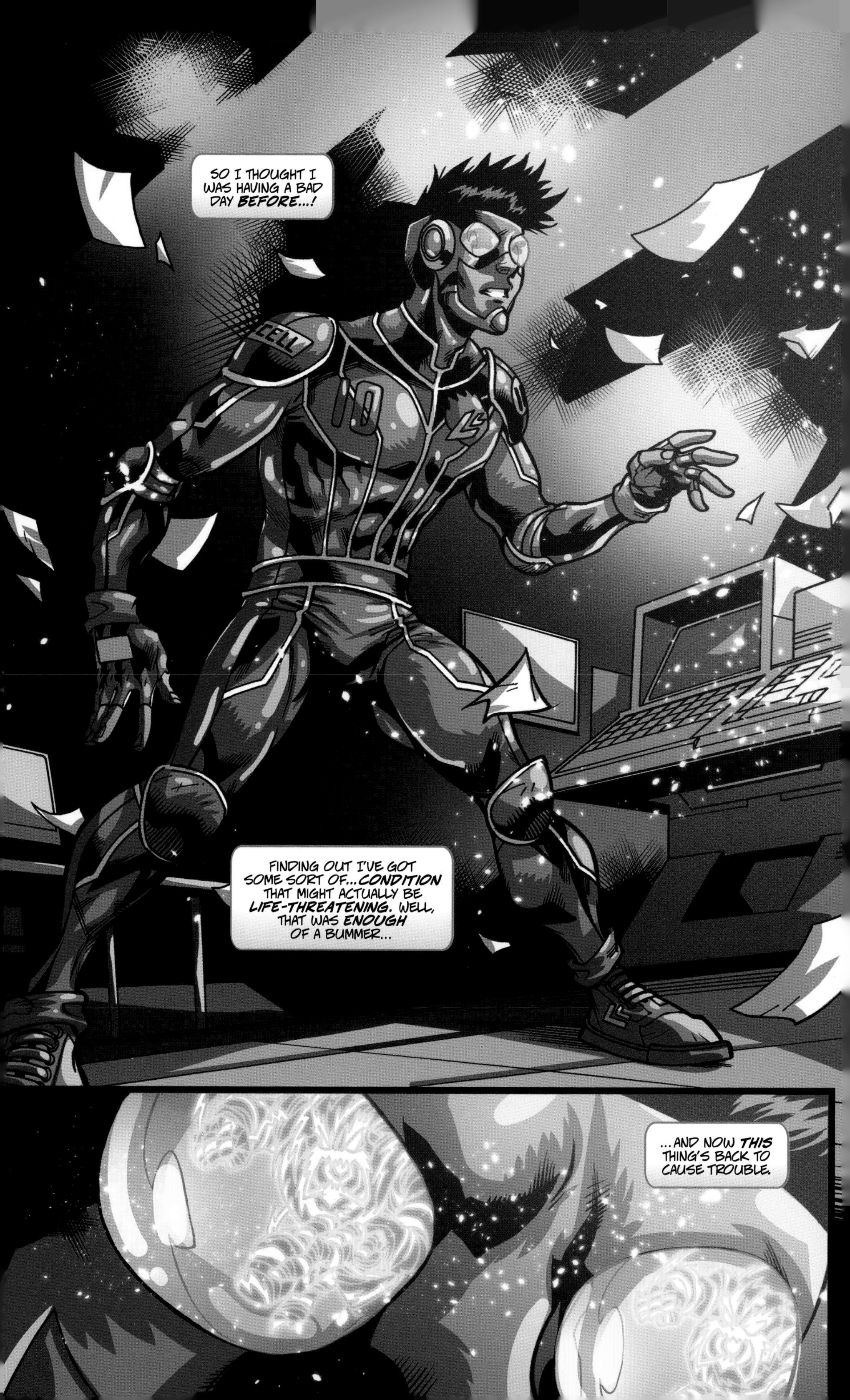
SO I THOUGHT I WAS HAVING A BAD DAY BEFORE...!
FINDING OUT I'VE GOT SOME SORT OF...CONDITION THAT MIGHT ACTUALLY BE LIFE-THREATENING. WELL, THAT WAS ENOUGH OF A BUMMER...
...AND NOW THIS THING'S BACK TO CAUSE TROUBLE.

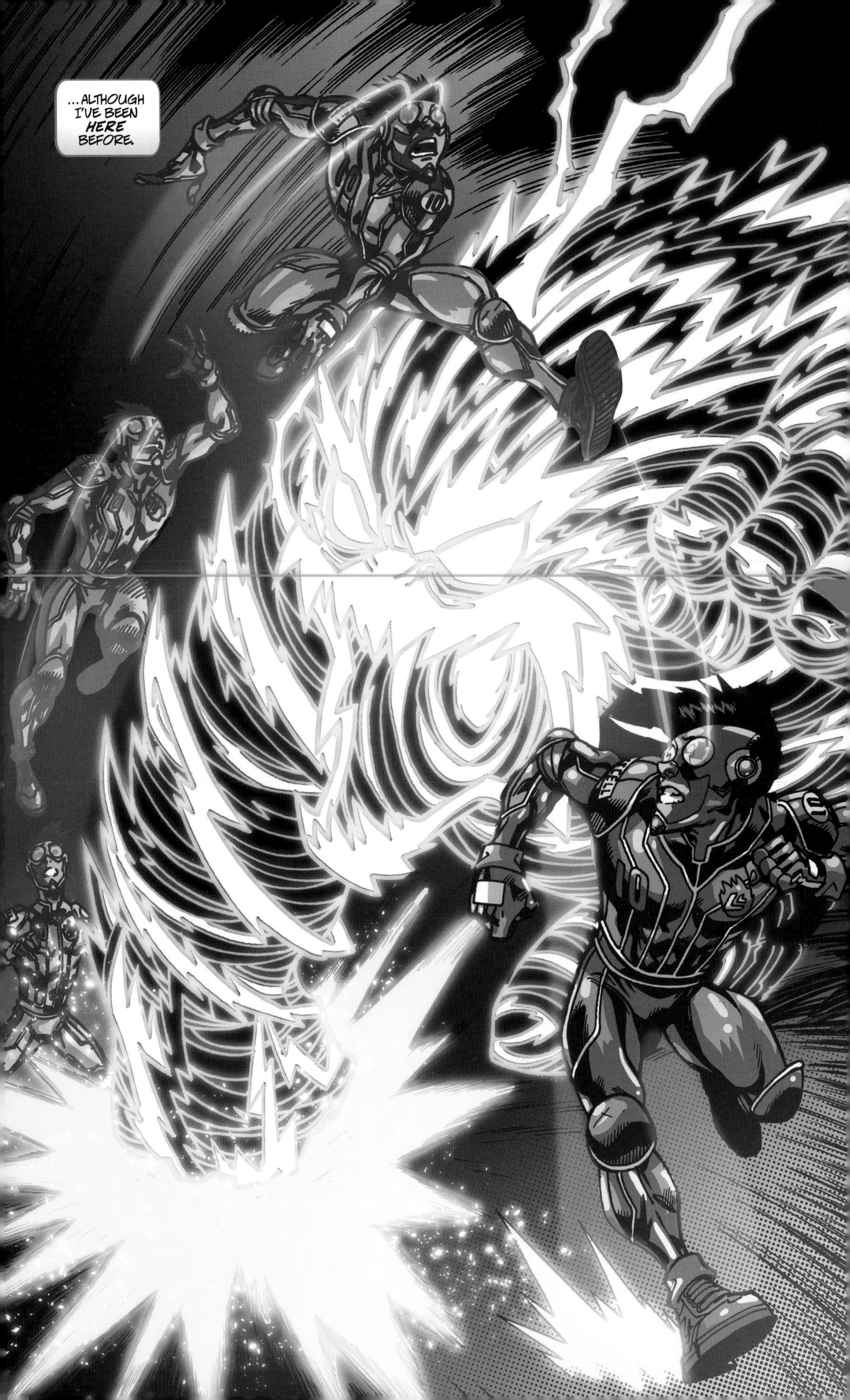
...ALTHOUGH I'VE BEEN HERE BEFORE.

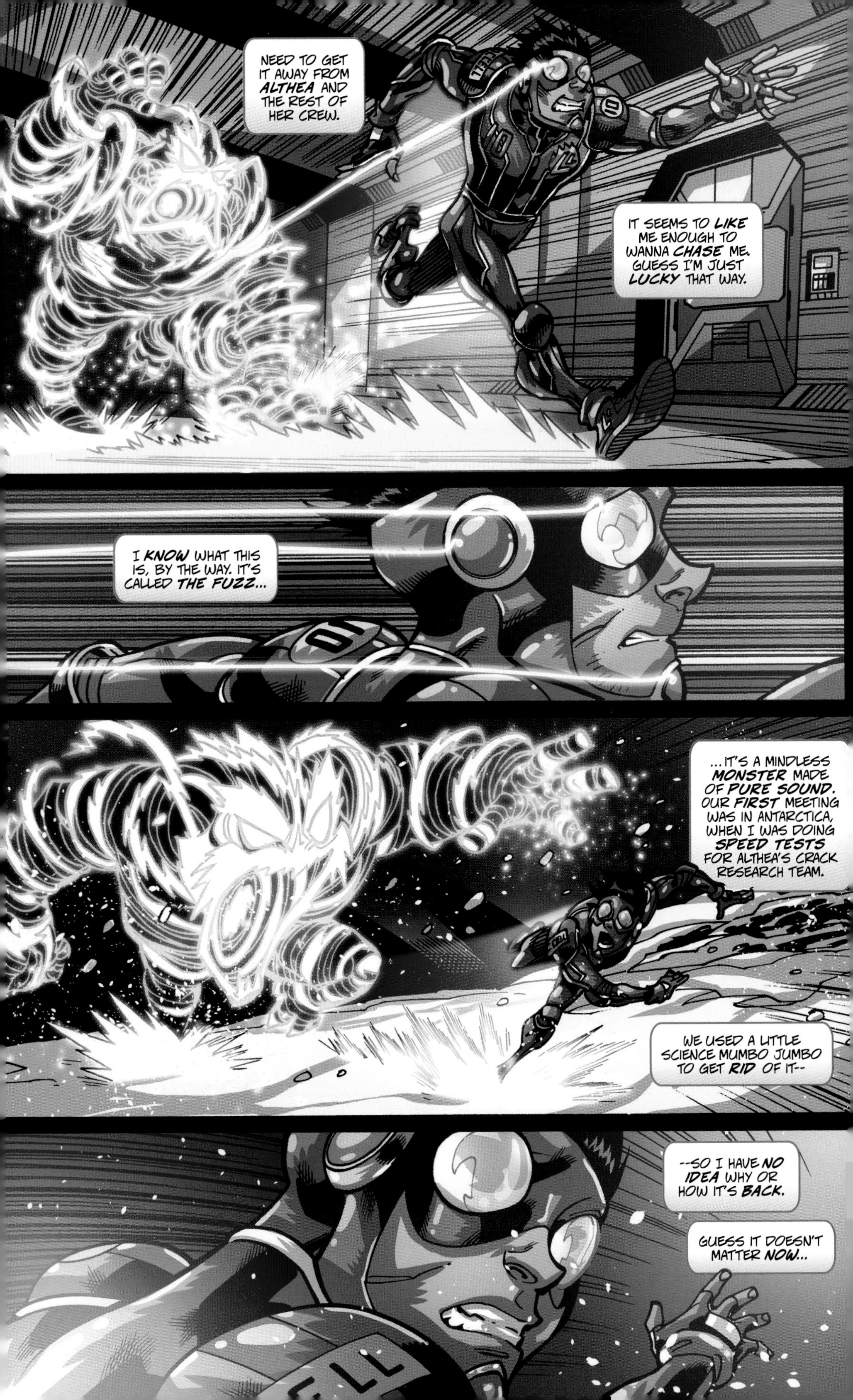
NEED TO GET IT AWAY FROM ALTHEA AND THE REST OF HER CREW.
IT SEEMS TO LIKE ME ENOUGH TO WANNA CHASE ME. GUESS I'M JUST LUCKY THAT WAY.
I KNOW WHAT THIS IS, BY THE WAY. IT'S CALLED THE FUZZ...
...IT'S A MINDLESS MONSTER MADE OF PURE SOUND. OUR FIRST MEETING WAS IN ANTARCTICA, WHEN I WAS DOING SPEED TESTS FOR ALTHEA'S CRACK RESEARCH TEAM.
WE USED A LITTLE SCIENCE MUMBO JUMBO TO GET RID OF IT--
--SO I HAVE NO IDEA WHY OR HOW IT'S BACK.
GUESS IT DOESN'T MATTER NOW...

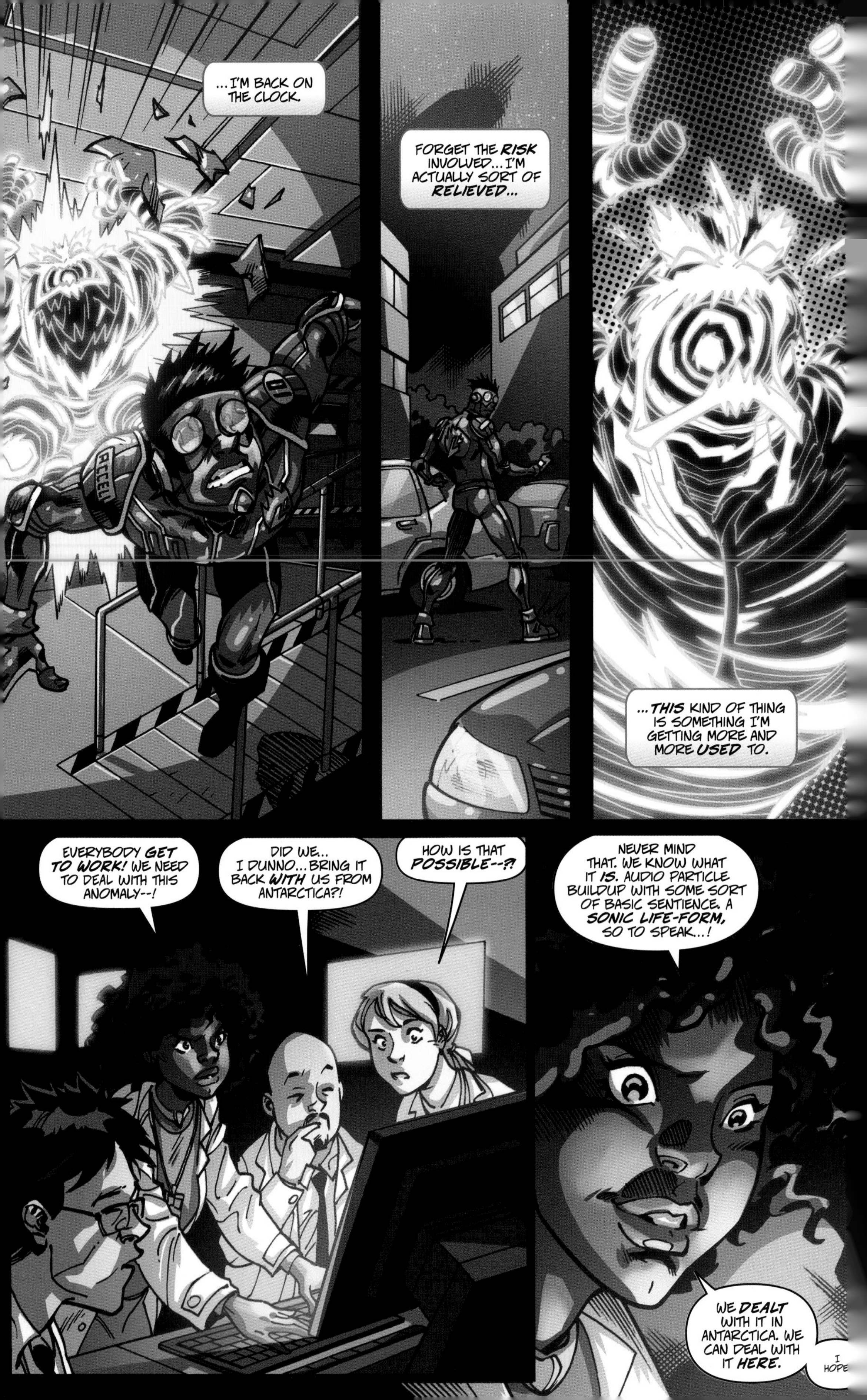
...I'M BACK ON THE CLOCK.
FORGET THE RISK INVOLVED... I'M ACTUALLY SORT OF RELIEVED...
...THIS KIND OF THING IS SOMETHING I'M GETTING MORE AND MORE USED TO.
EVERYBODY GET TO WORK! WE NEED TO DEAL WITH THIS ANOMALY--!
DID WE... I DUNNO... BRING IT BACK WITH US FROM ANTARCTICA?!
HOW IS THAT POSSIBLE--?!
NEVER MIND THAT. WE KNOW WHAT IT IS. AUDIO PARTICLE BUILDUP WITH SOME SORT OF BASIC SENTIENCE. A SONIC LIFE-FORM, SO TO SPEAK...!
WE DEALT WITH IT IN ANTARCTICA. WE CAN DEAL WITH IT HERE.
I HOPE

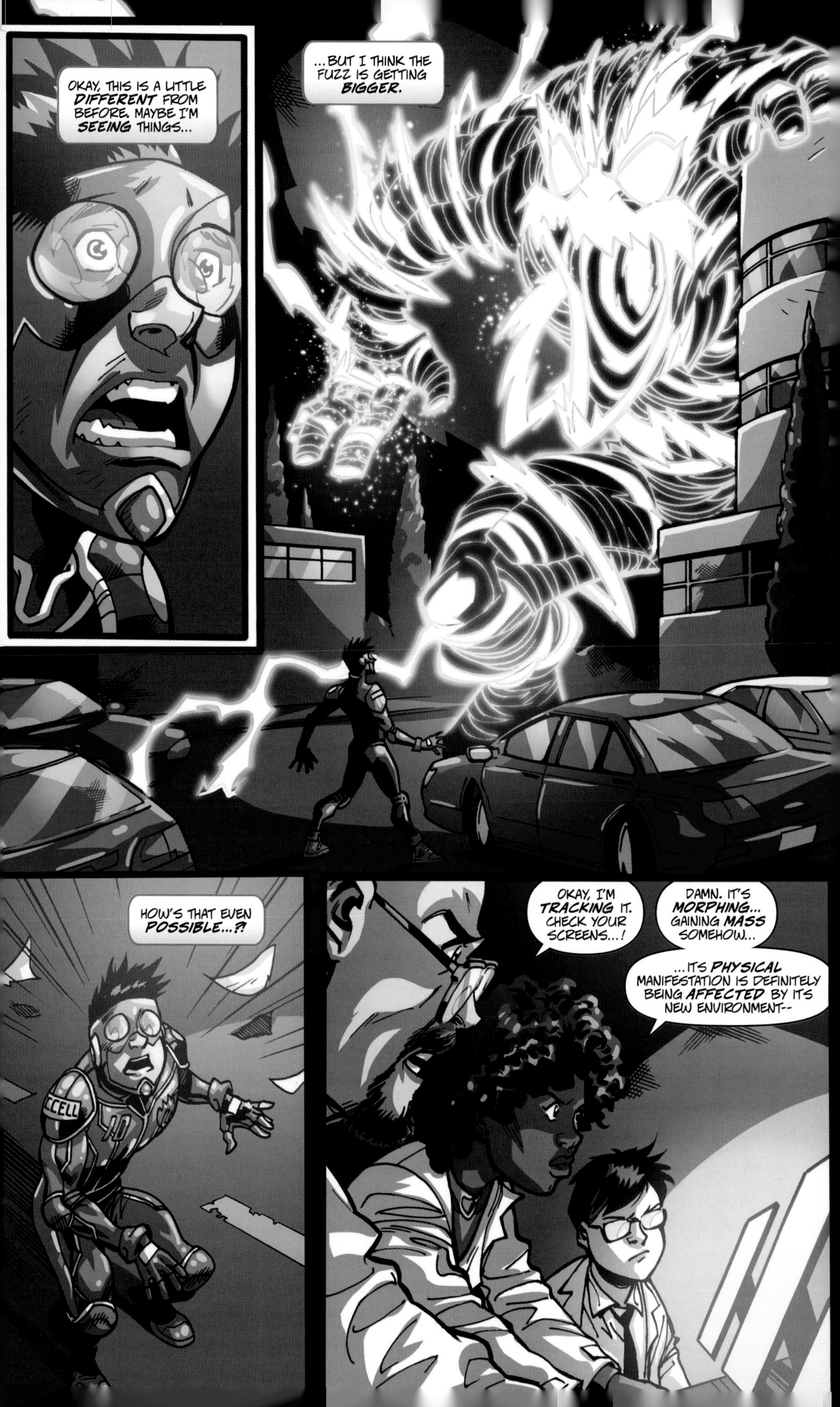
OKAY, THIS IS A LITTLE DIFFERENT FROM BEFORE. MAYBE I'M SEEING THINGS...
...BUT I THINK THE FUZZ IS GETTING BIGGER.
HOW'S THAT EVEN POSSIBLE...?!
CCELL
OKAY, I'M TRACKING IT. CHECK YOUR SCREENS...!
DAMN. IT'S MORPHING... GAINING MASS SOMEHOW...
...ITS PHYSICAL MANIFESTATION IS DEFINITELY BEING AFFECTED BY ITS NEW ENVIRONMENT--

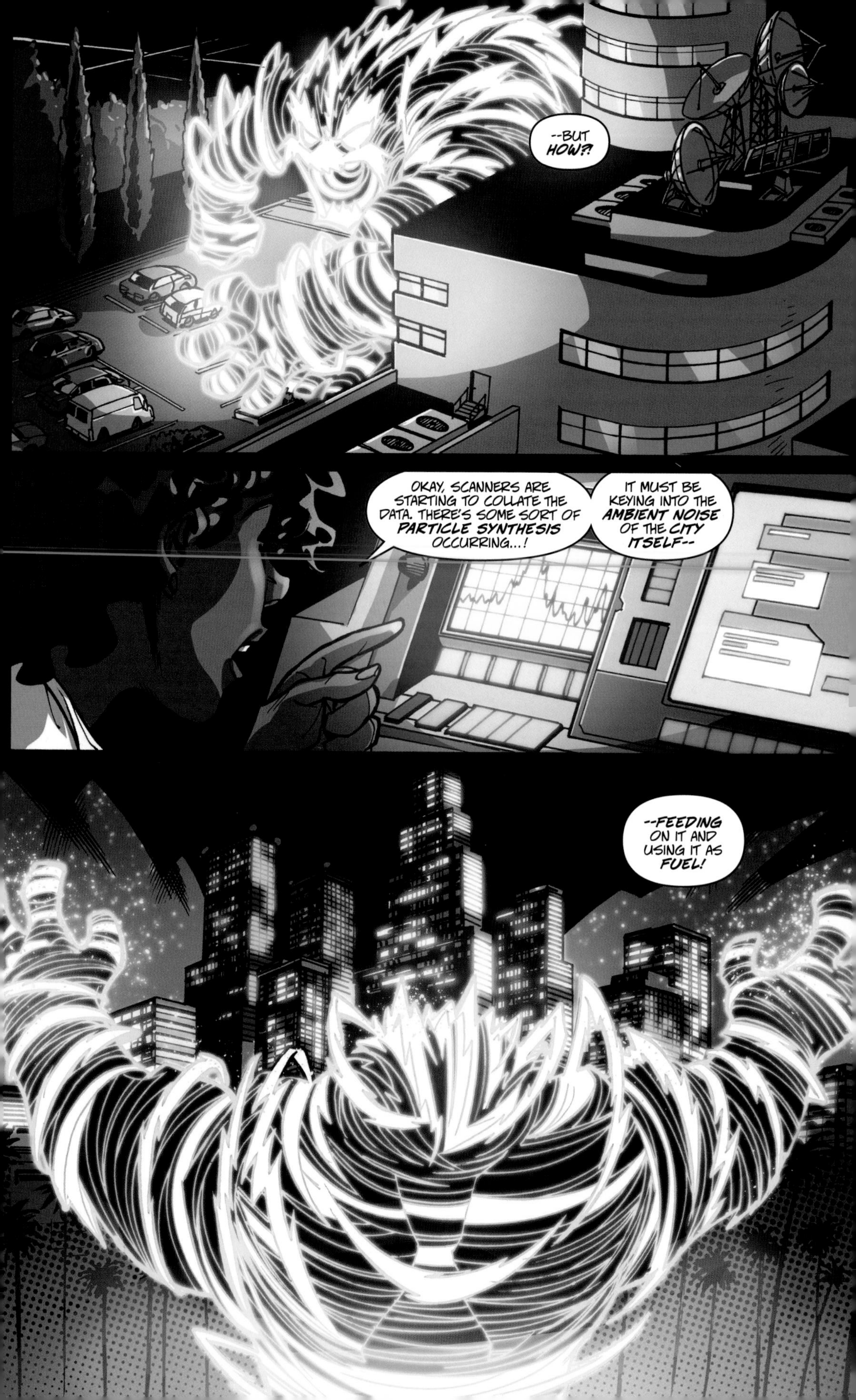
--BUT HOW?!
OKAY, SCANNERS ARE STARTING TO COLLATE THE DATA. THERE'S SOME SORT OF PARTICLE SYNTHESIS OCCURRING...!
IT MUST BE KEYING INTO THE AMBIENT NOISE OF THE CITY ITSELF--
--FEEDING ON IT AND USING IT AS FUEL!

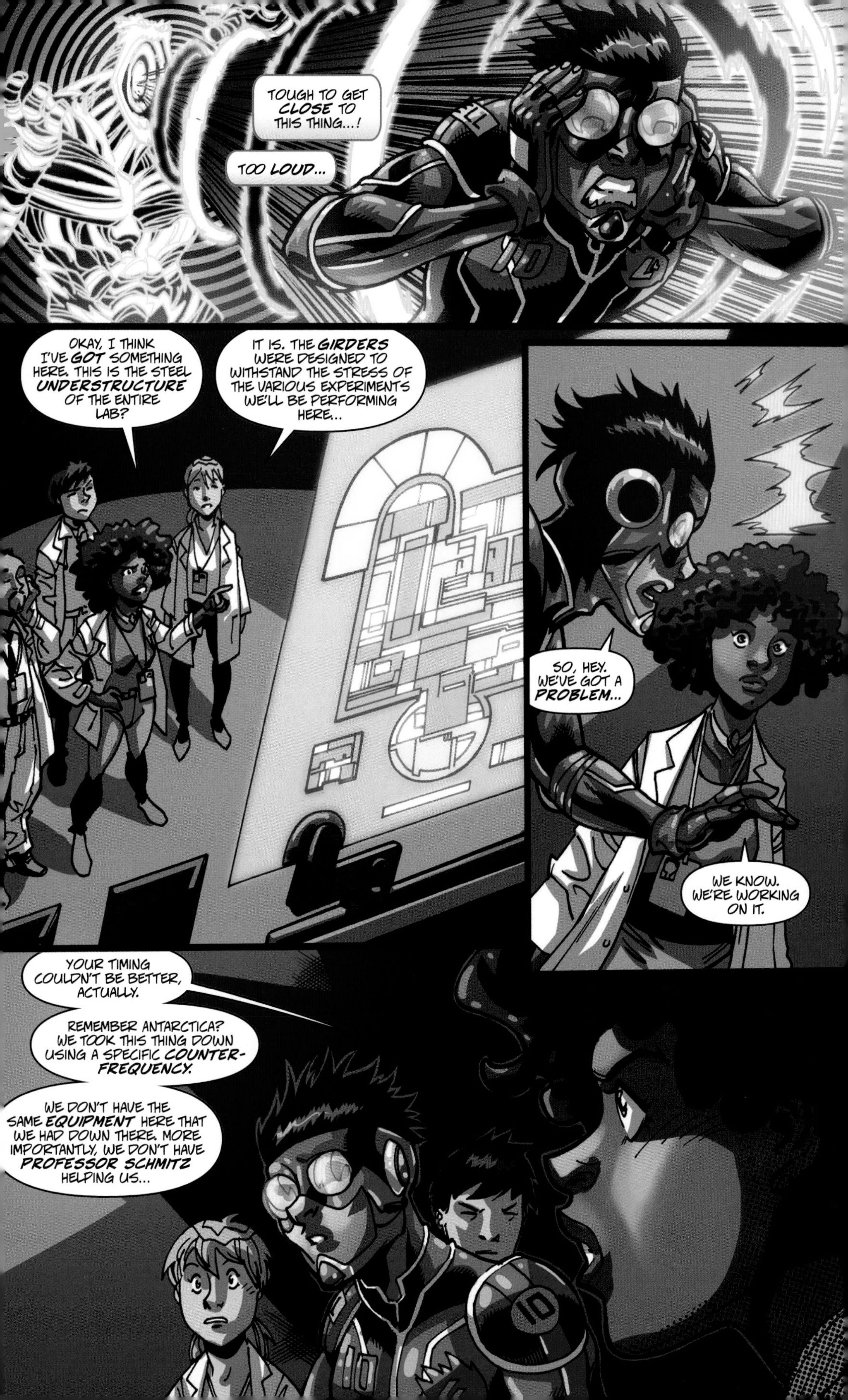
TOUGH TO GET CLOSE TO THIS THING...!
TOO LOUD...
OKAY, I THINK I'VE GOT SOMETHING HERE. THIS IS THE STEEL UNDERSTRUCTURE OF THE ENTIRE LAB?
IT IS. THE GIRDERS WERE DESIGNED TO WITHSTAND THE STRESS OF THE VARIOUS EXPERIMENTS WE'LL BE PERFORMING HERE...
SO, HEY. WE'VE GOT A PROBLEM...
WE KNOW. WE'RE WORKING ON IT.
YOUR TIMING COULDN'T BE BETTER, ACTUALLY.
REMEMBER ANTARCTICA? WE TOOK THIS THING DOWN USING A SPECIFIC COUNTER-FREQUENCY.
WE DON'T HAVE THE SAME EQUIPMENT HERE THAT WE HAD DOWN THERE. MORE IMPORTANTLY, WE DON'T HAVE PROFESSOR SCHMITZ HELPING US...

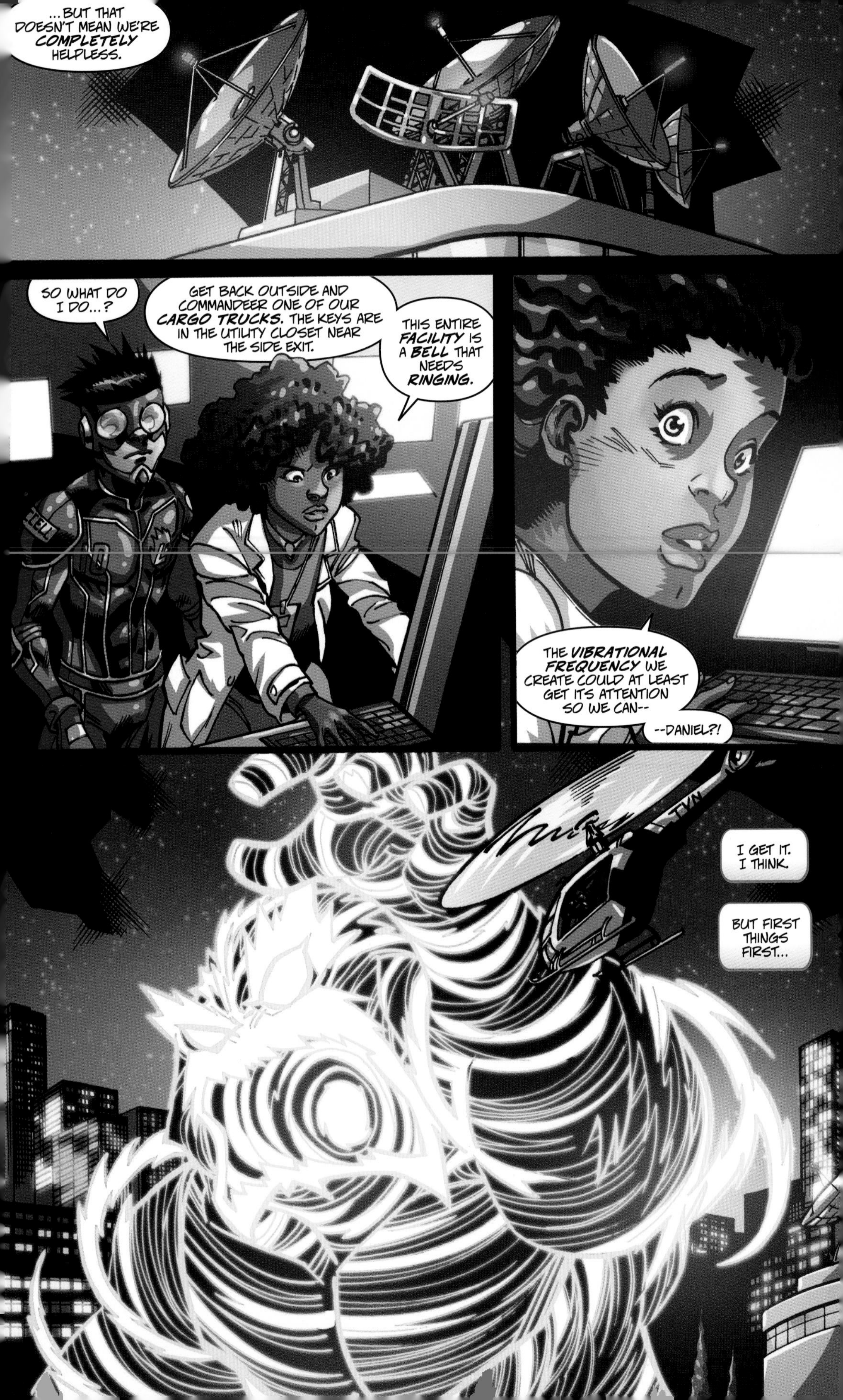
...BUT THAT DOESN'T MEAN WE'RE COMPLETELY HELPLESS.
SO WHAT DO I DO...?
GET BACK OUTSIDE AND COMMANDEER ONE OF OUR CARGO TRUCKS. THE KEYS ARE IN THE UTILITY CLOSET NEAR THE SIDE EXIT.
THIS ENTIRE FACILITY IS A BELL THAT NEEDS RINGING.
THE VIBRATIONAL FREQUENCY WE CREATE COULD AT LEAST GET ITS ATTENTION SO WE CAN--
--DANIEL?!
I GET IT. I THINK.
BUT FIRST THINGS FIRST...

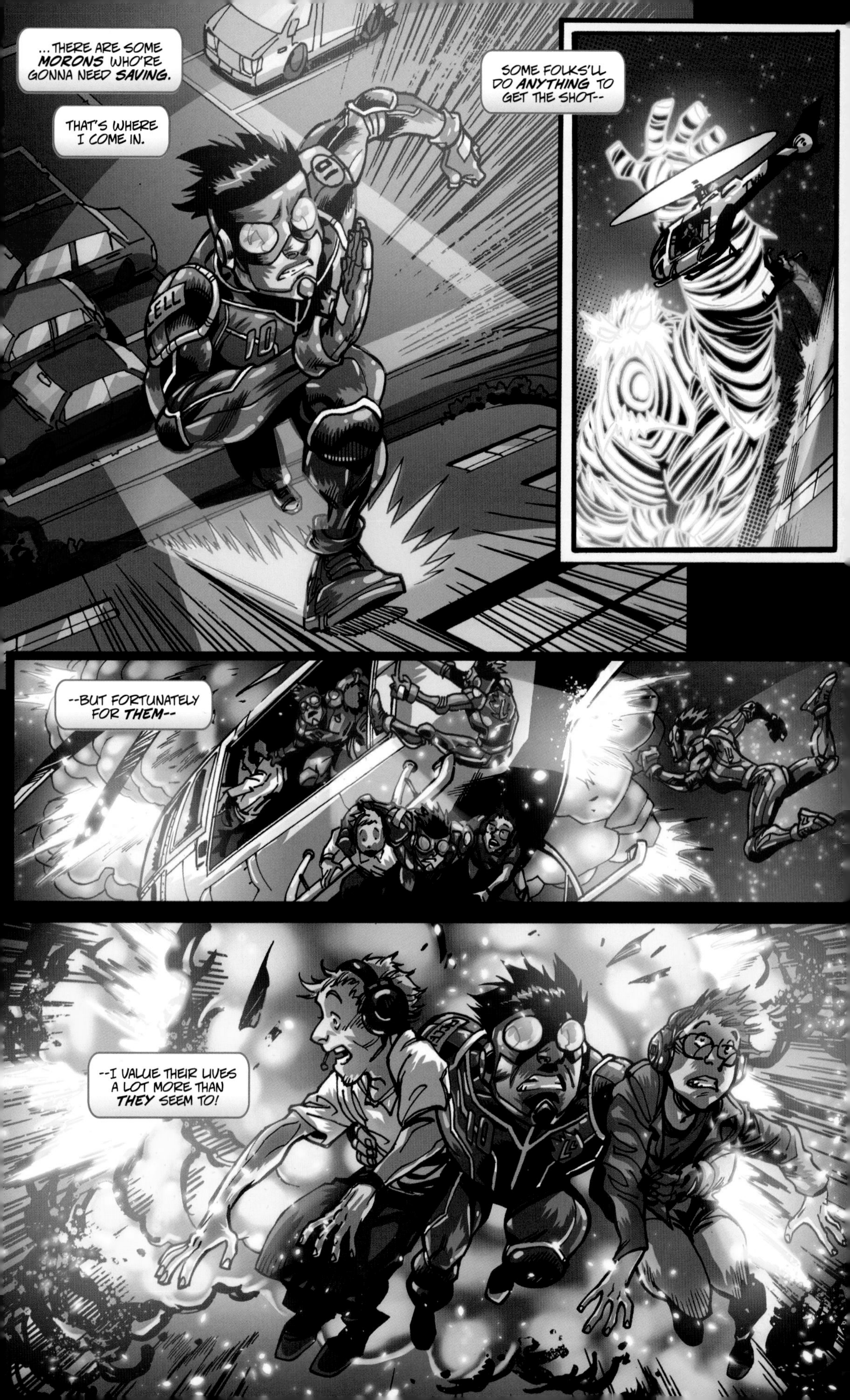
...THERE ARE SOME MORONS WHO'RE GONNA NEED SAVING.
THAT'S WHERE I COME IN.
SOME FOLKS'LL DO ANYTHING TO GET THE SHOT--
--BUT FORTUNATELY FOR THEM--
--I VALUE THEIR LIVES A LOT MORE THAN THEY SEEM TO!

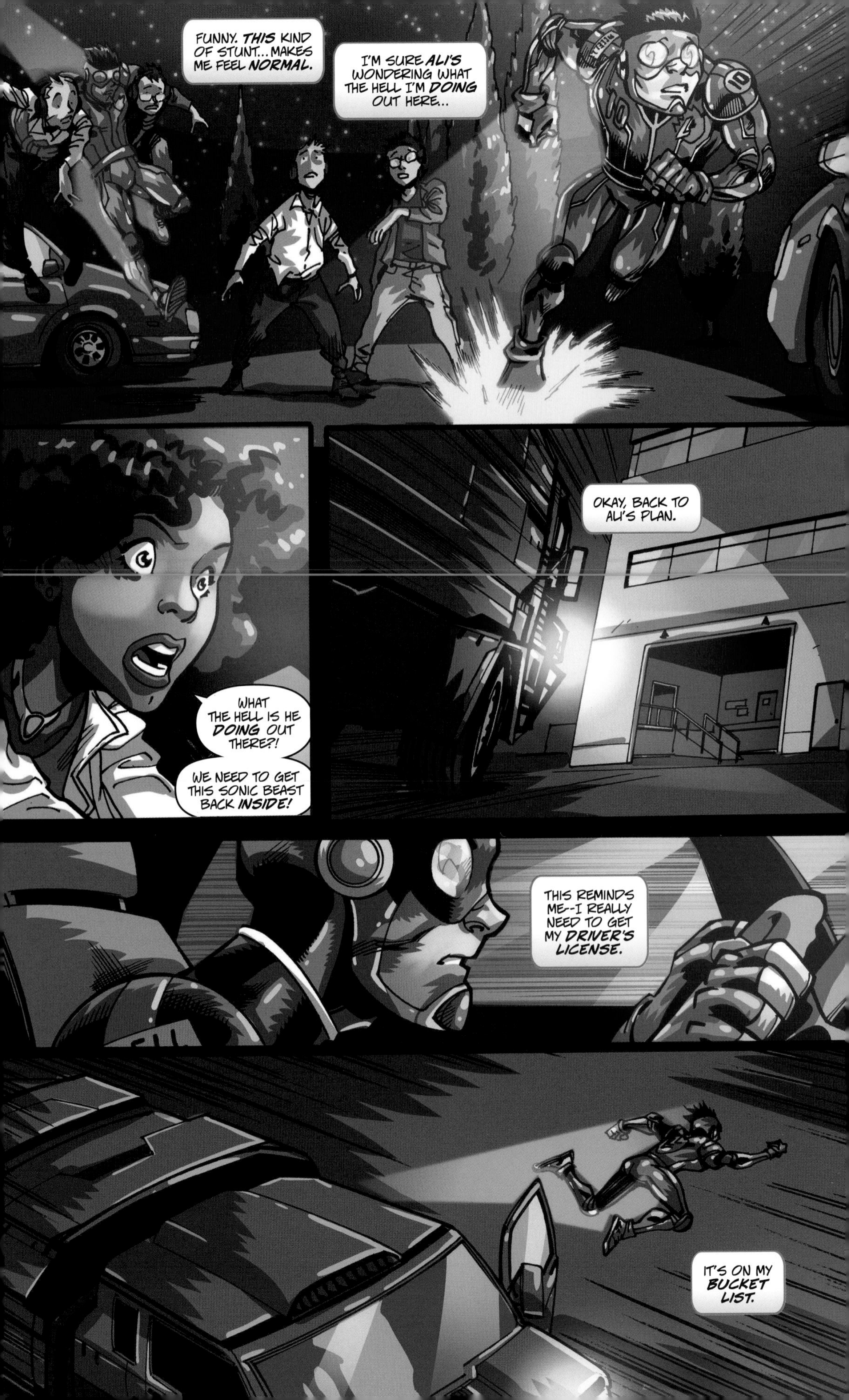
FUNNY. THIS KIND OF STUNT...MAKES ME FEEL NORMAL.
I'M SURE ALI'S WONDERING WHAT THE HELL I'M DOING OUT HERE...
WHAT THE HELL IS HE DOING OUT THERE?!
WE NEED TO GET THIS SONIC BEAST BACK INSIDE!
OKAY, BACK TO ALI'S PLAN.
THIS REMINDS ME--I REALLY NEED TO GET MY DRIVER'S LICENSE.
IT'S ON MY BUCKET LIST.

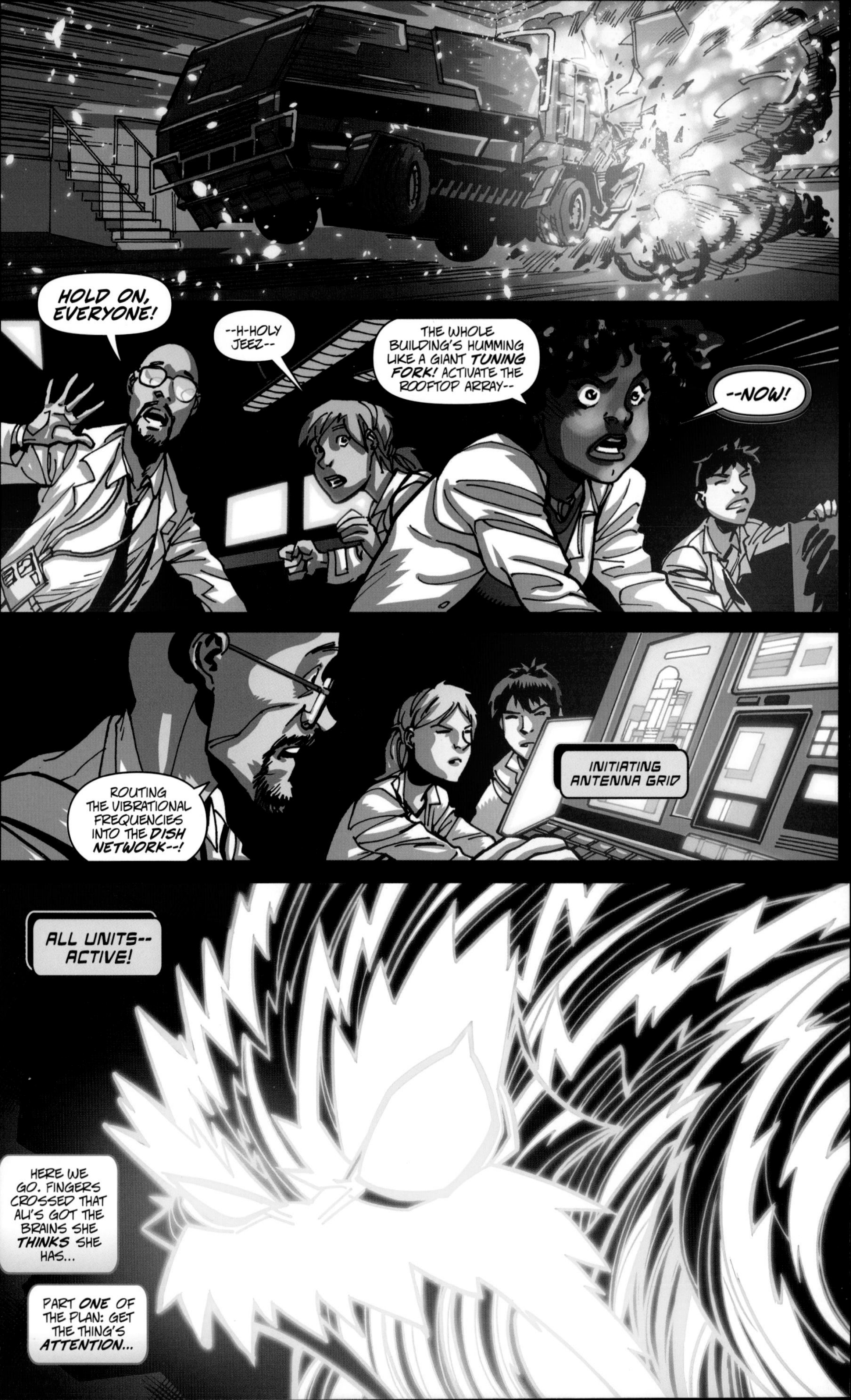

HOLD ON, EVERYONE!
--H-HOLY JEEZ--
THE WHOLE BUILDING'S HUMMING LIKE A GIANT TUNING FORK! ACTIVATE THE ROOFTOP ARRAY--
--NOW!
ROUTING THE VIBRATIONAL FREQUENCIES INTO THE DISH NETWORK--!
INITIATING ANTENNA GRID
ALL UNITS-- ACTIVE!
HERE WE GO. FINGERS CROSSED THAT ALI'S GOT THE BRAINS SHE THINKS SHE HAS...
PART ONE OF THE PLAN: GET THE THING'S ATTENTION...

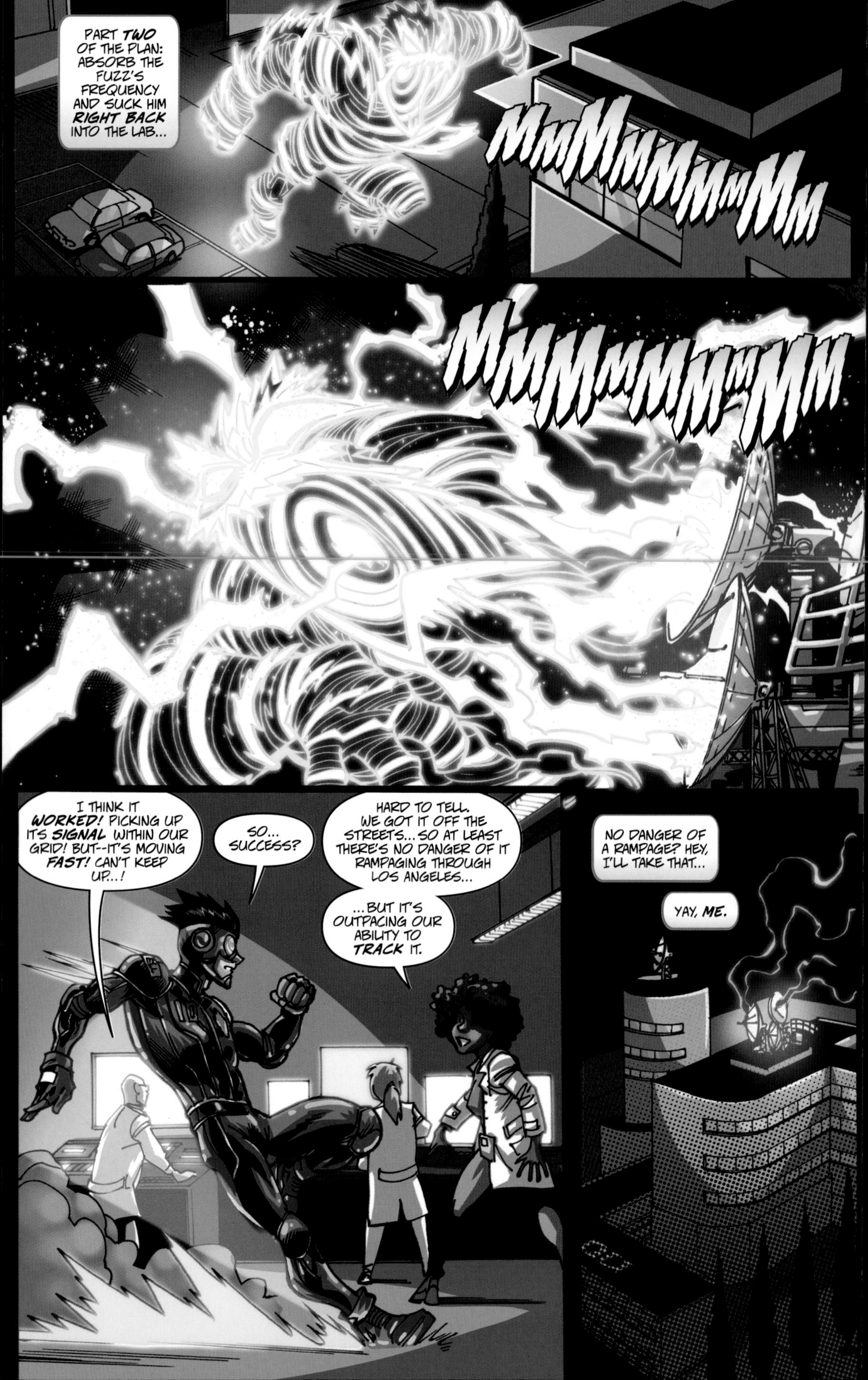

PART TWO OF THE PLAN: ABSORB THE FUZZ'S FREQUENCY AND SUCK HIM RIGHT BACK INTO THE LAB...
MMMMMMMMMMM
MMMMMMMMMMM
I THINK IT WORKED! PICKING UP ITS SIGNAL WITHIN OUR GRID! BUT--IT'S MOVING FAST! CAN'T KEEP UP...!
SO... SUCCESS?
HARD TO TELL. WE GOT IT OFF THE STREETS... SO AT LEAST THERE'S NO DANGER OF IT RAMPAGING THROUGH LOS ANGELES...
...BUT IT'S OUTPACING OUR ABILITY TO TRACK IT.
NO DANGER OF A RAMPAGE? HEY, I'LL TAKE THAT...
YAY, ME.

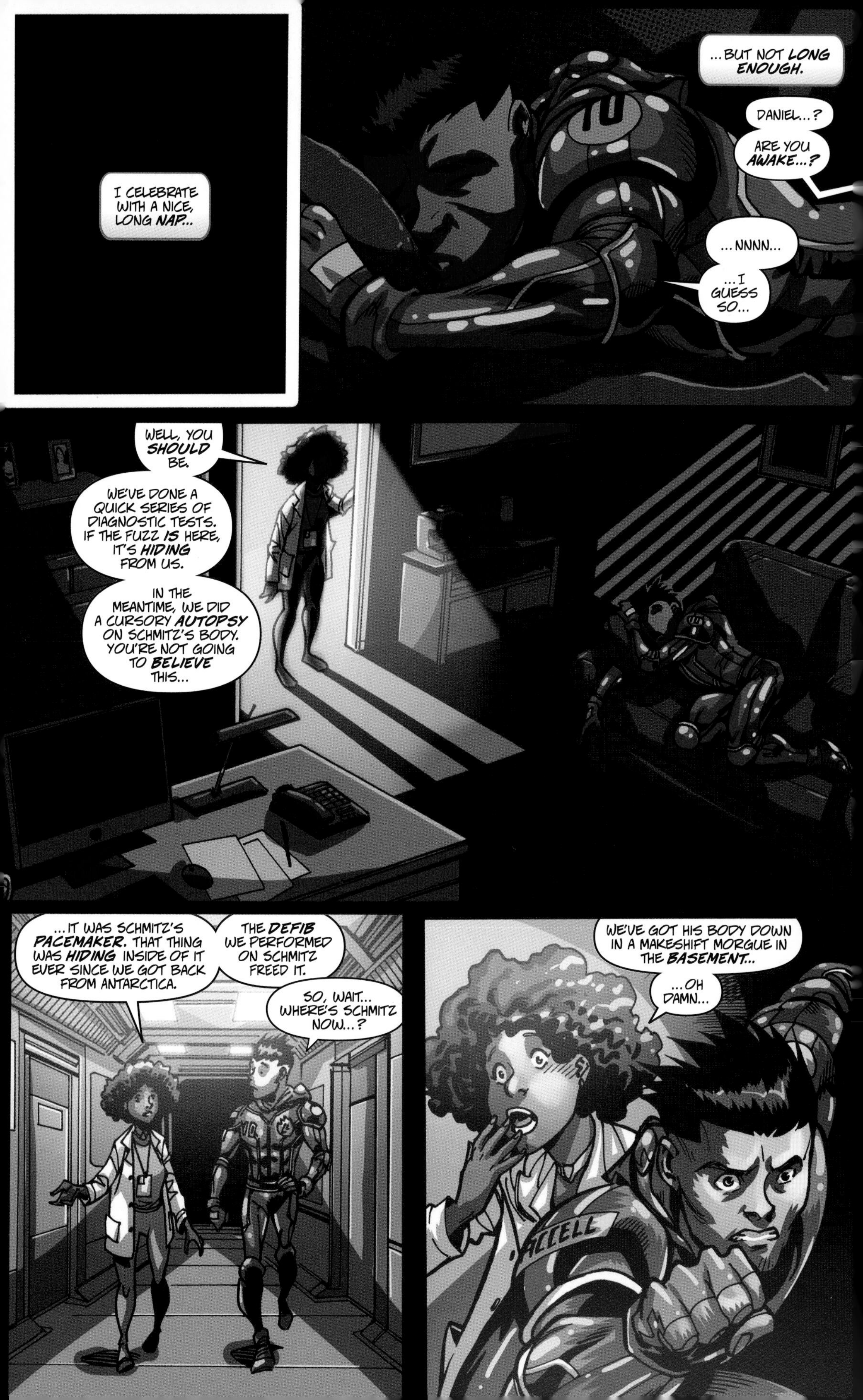
I CELEBRATE WITH A NICE, LONG NAP...
...BUT NOT LONG ENOUGH.
DANIEL...?
ARE YOU AWAKE...?
...NNNN...
...I GUESS SO...
WELL, YOU SHOULD BE.
WE'VE DONE A QUICK SERIES OF DIAGNOSTIC TESTS. IF THE FUZZ IS HERE, IT'S HIDING FROM US.
IN THE MEANTIME, WE DID A CURSORY AUTOPSY ON SCHMITZ'S BODY. YOU'RE NOT GOING TO BELIEVE THIS...
...IT WAS SCHMITZ'S PACEMAKER. THAT THING WAS HIDING INSIDE OF IT EVER SINCE WE GOT BACK FROM ANTARCTICA.
THE DEFIB WE PERFORMED ON SCHMITZ FREED IT.
SO, WAIT... WHERE'S SCHMITZ NOW...?
WE'VE GOT HIS BODY DOWN IN A MAKESHIFT MORGUE IN THE BASEMENT...
...OH DAMN...

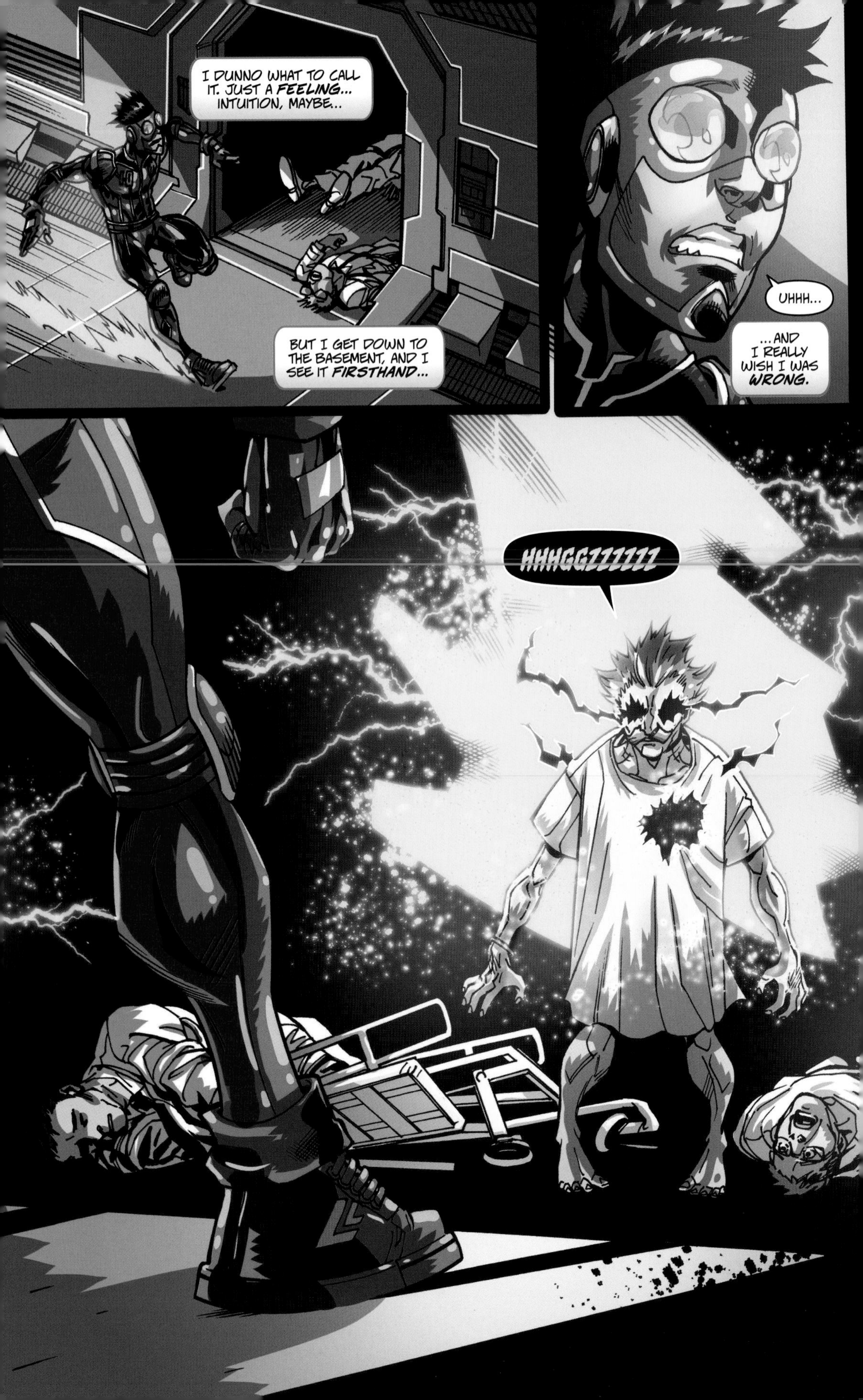
I DUNNO WHAT TO CALL IT. JUST A FEELING... INTUITION, MAYBE...
BUT I GET DOWN TO THE BASEMENT, AND I SEE IT FIRSTHAND...
UHHH...
...AND I REALLY WISH I WAS WRONG.
HHHGGZZZZZZ

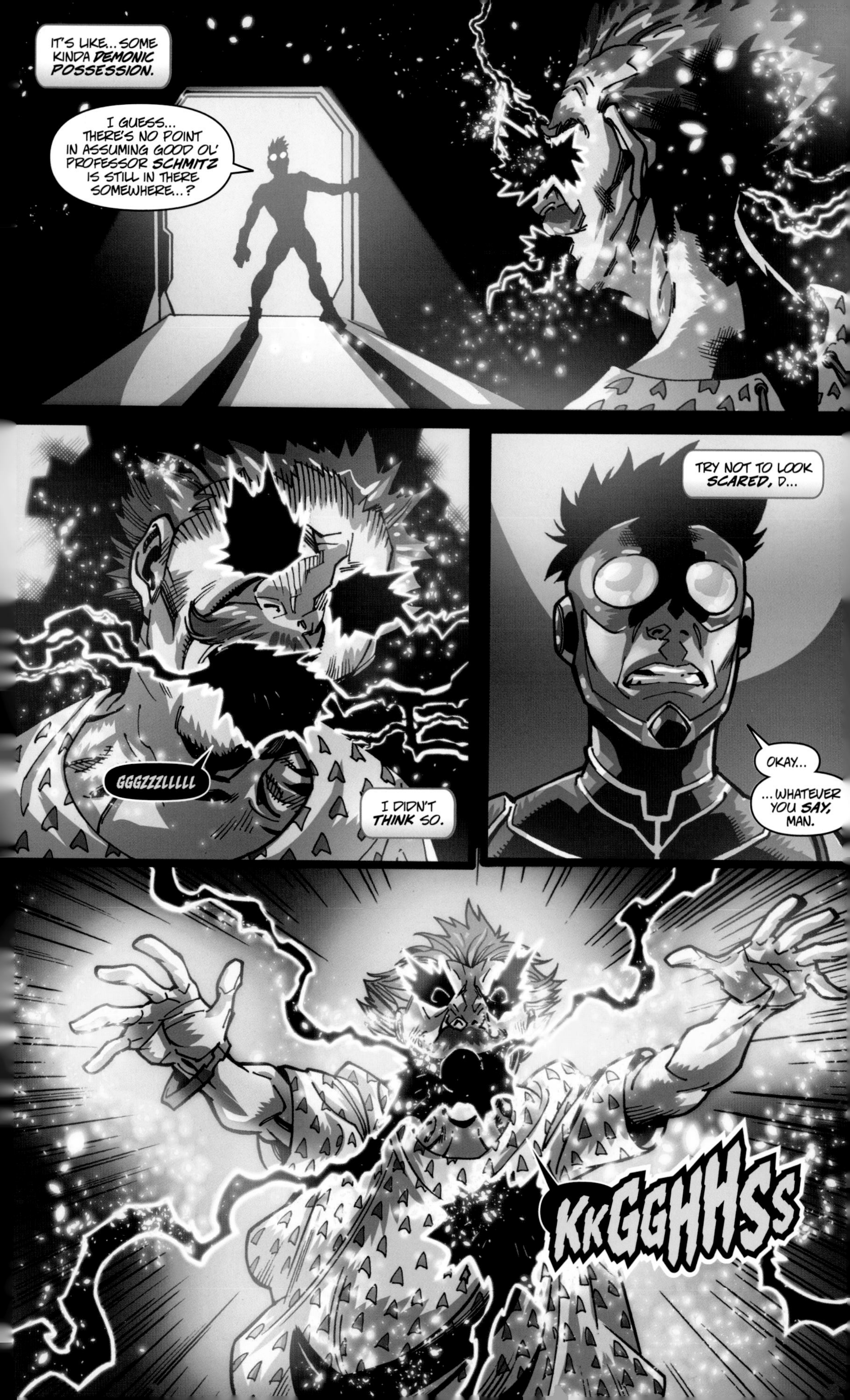
IT'S LIKE... SOME KINDA DEMONIC POSSESSION.
I GUESS... THERE'S NO POINT IN ASSUMING GOOD OL' PROFESSOR SCHMITZ IS STILL IN THERE SOMEWHERE...?
GGGZZZLLLLL
I DIDN'T THINK SO.
TRY NOT TO LOOK SCARED, D...
OKAY...
...WHATEVER YOU SAY, MAN.
KKGGHHSS

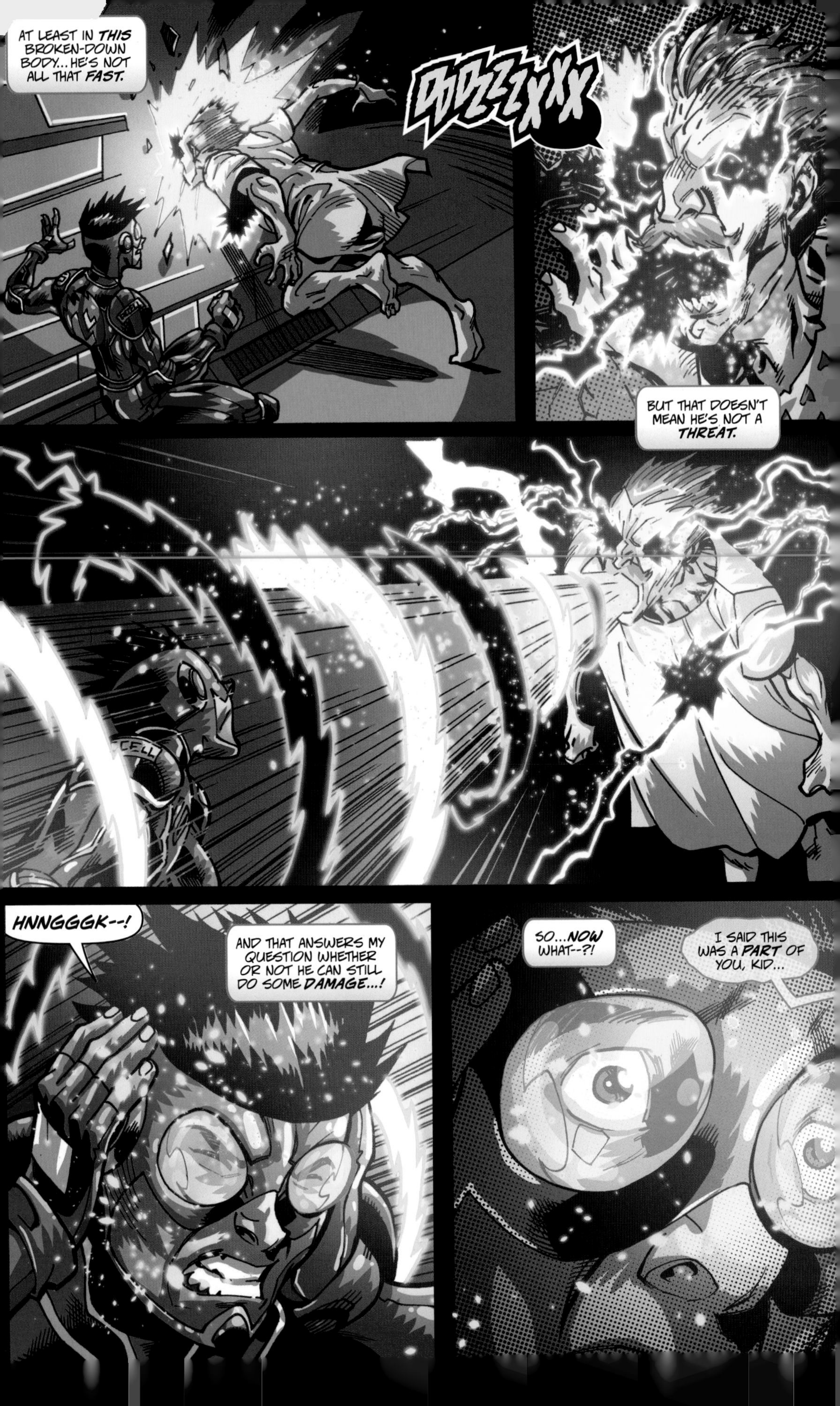
AT LEAST IN THIS BROKEN-DOWN BODY... HE'S NOT ALL THAT FAST.
BUT THAT DOESN'T MEAN HE'S NOT A THREAT.
HNNGGGK--!
AND THAT ANSWERS MY QUESTION WHETHER OR NOT HE CAN STILL DO SOME DAMAGE...!
SO...NOW WHAT--?!
I SAID THIS WAS A PART OF YOU, KID...

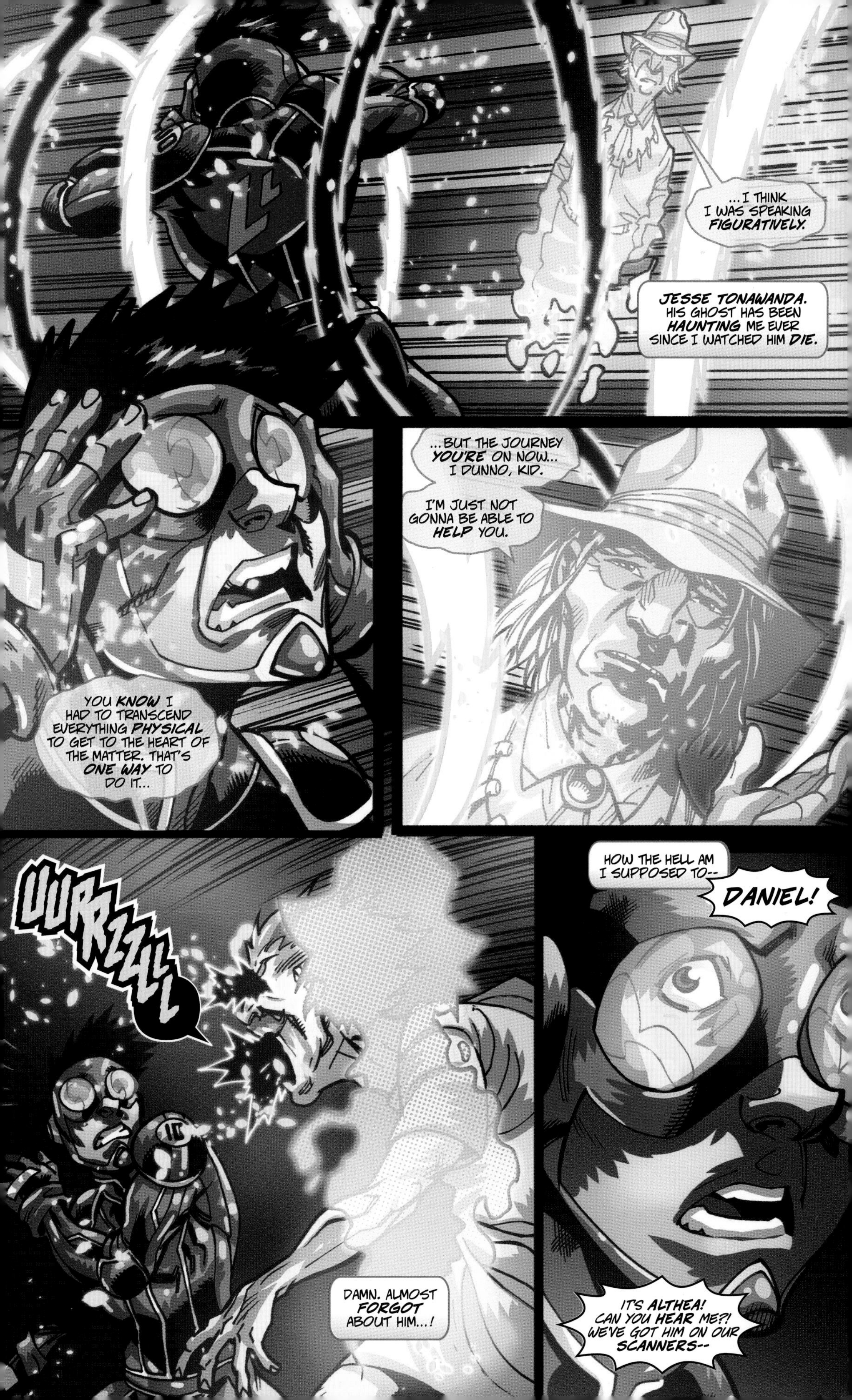
...I THINK I WAS SPEAKING FIGURATIVELY.
JESSE TONAWANDA. HIS GHOST HAS BEEN HAUNTING ME EVER SINCE I WATCHED HIM DIE.
YOU KNOW I HAD TO TRANSCEND EVERYTHING PHYSICAL TO GET TO THE HEART OF THE MATTER. THAT'S ONE WAY TO DO IT...
...BUT THE JOURNEY YOU'RE ON NOW... I DUNNO, KID.
I'M JUST NOT GONNA BE ABLE TO HELP YOU.
UURRZZLLL
DAMN. ALMOST FORGOT ABOUT HIM...!
HOW THE HELL AM I SUPPOSED TO--
DANIEL!
IT'S ALTHEA! CAN YOU HEAR ME?! WE'VE GOT HIM ON OUR SCANNERS--

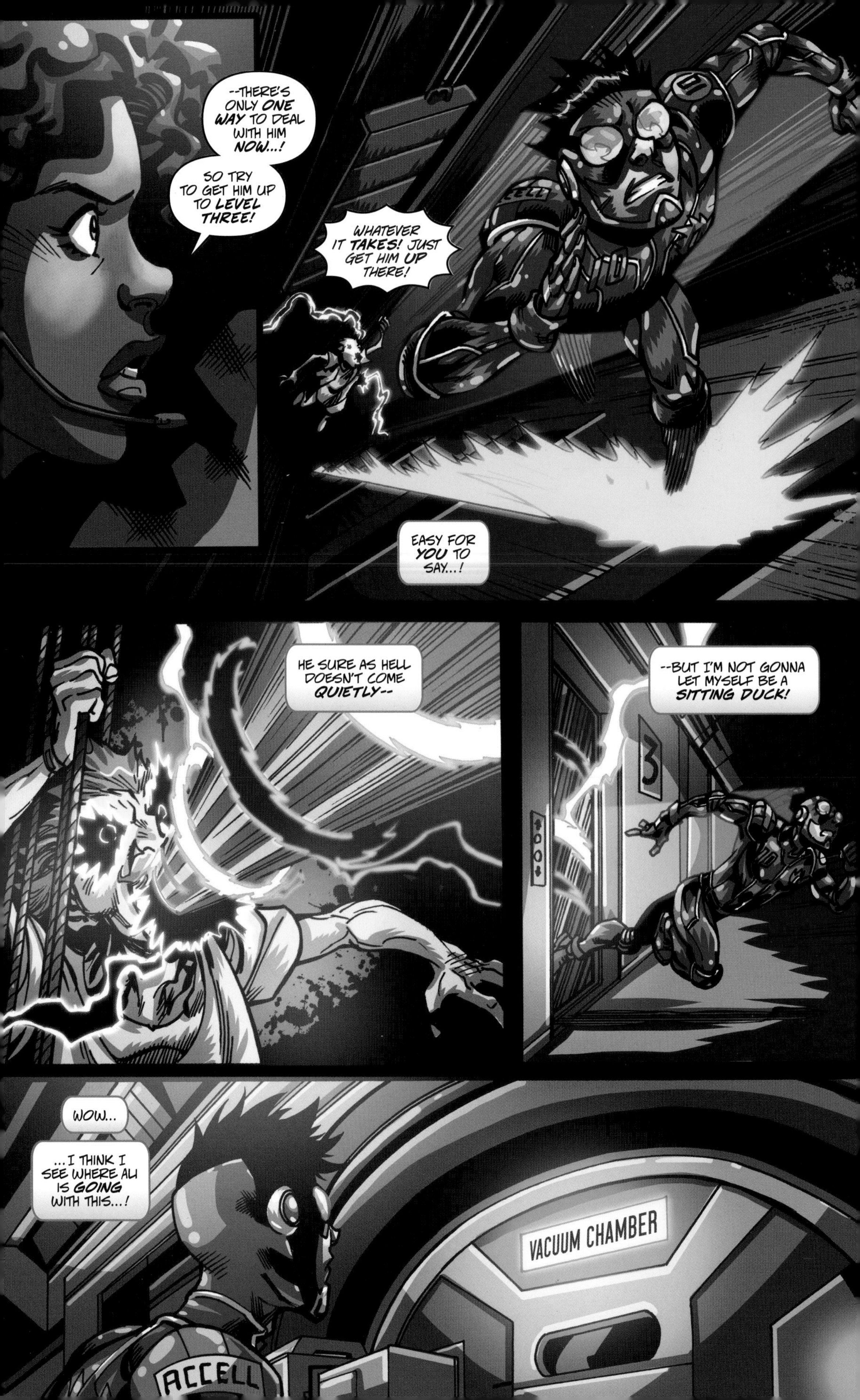
--THERE'S ONLY ONE WAY TO DEAL WITH HIM NOW...!
SO TRY TO GET HIM UP TO LEVEL THREE!
WHATEVER IT TAKES! JUST GET HIM UP THERE!
EASY FOR YOU TO SAY...!
HE SURE AS HELL DOESN'T COME QUIETLY--
--BUT I'M NOT GONNA LET MYSELF BE A SITTING DUCK!
3
WOW...
...I THINK I SEE WHERE ALI IS GOING WITH THIS...!
VACUUM CHAMBER
ACCELL

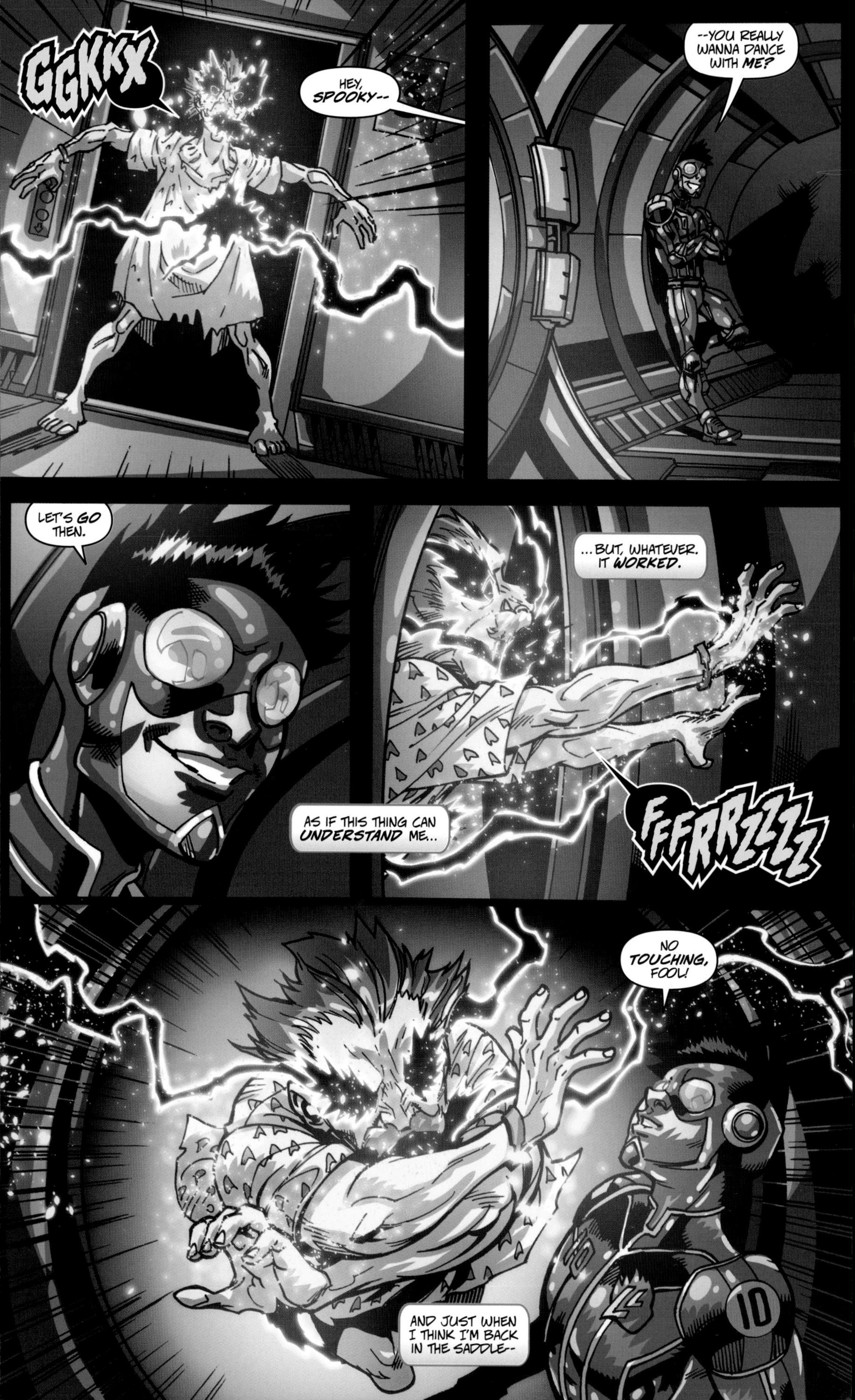
GGKKX
HEY, SPOOKY--
--YOU REALLY WANNA DANCE WITH ME?
LET'S GO THEN.
...BUT, WHATEVER. IT WORKED.
AS IF THIS THING CAN UNDERSTAND ME...
FFFRRZZZZ
NO TOUCHING, FOOL!
AND JUST WHEN I THINK I'M BACK IN THE SADDLE--
10

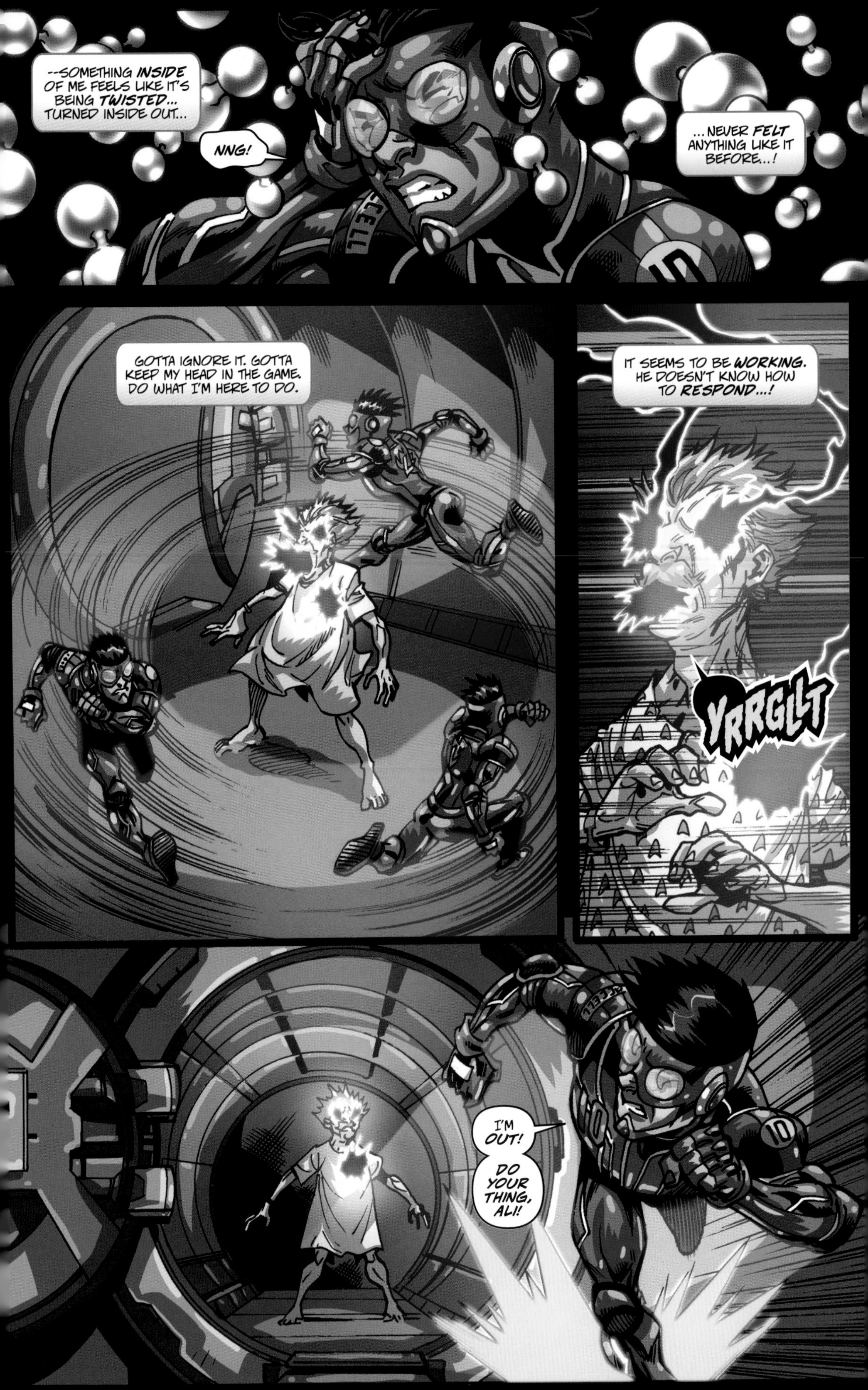
--SOMETHING INSIDE OF ME FEELS LIKE IT'S BEING TWISTED... TURNED INSIDE OUT...
NNG!
...NEVER FELT ANYTHING LIKE IT BEFORE...!
GOTTA IGNORE IT. GOTTA KEEP MY HEAD IN THE GAME. DO WHAT I'M HERE TO DO.
IT SEEMS TO BE WORKING. HE DOESN'T KNOW HOW TO RESPOND...!
YRRGLLT
I'M OUT!
DO YOUR THING, ALI!

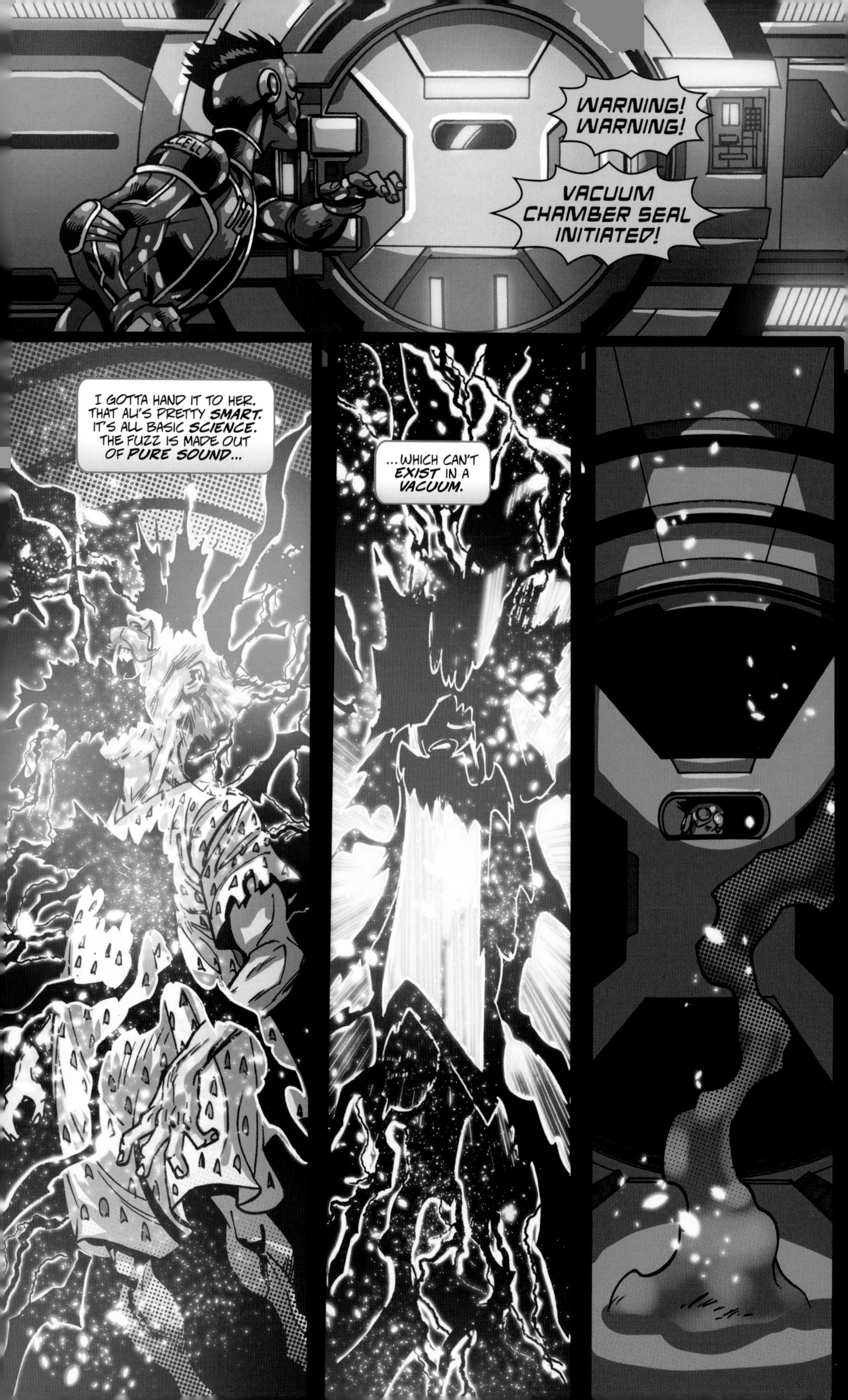
WARNING! WARNING!
VACUUM CHAMBER SEAL INITIATED!
I GOTTA HAND IT TO HER. THAT ALI'S PRETTY SMART. IT'S ALL BASIC SCIENCE. THE FUZZ IS MADE OUT OF PURE SOUND...
...WHICH CAN'T EXIST IN A VACUUM.

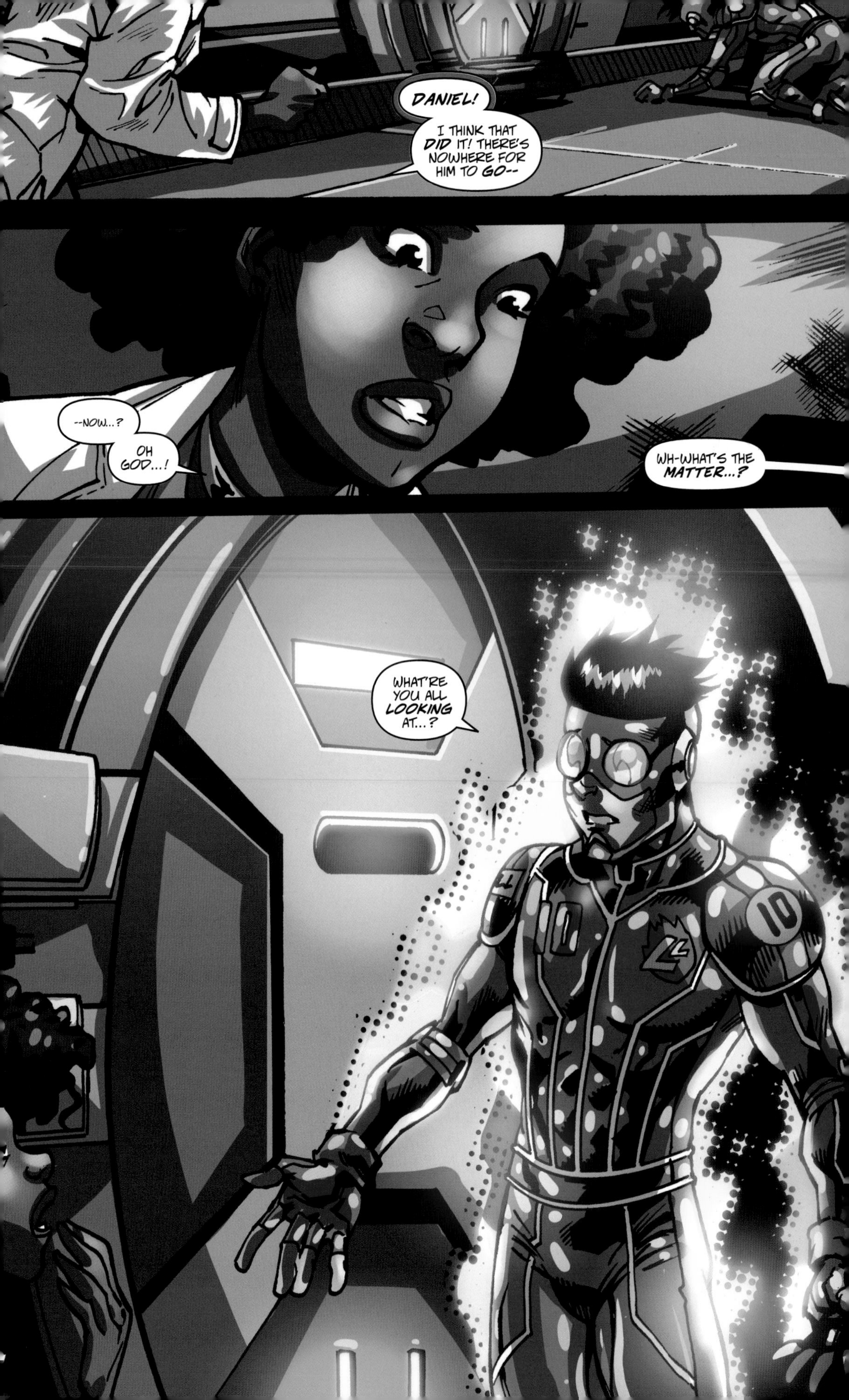
DANIEL!
I THINK THAT DID IT! THERE'S NOWHERE FOR HIM TO GO--
--NOW...?
OH GOD...!
WH-WHAT'S THE MATTER...?
WHAT'RE YOU ALL LOOKING AT...?

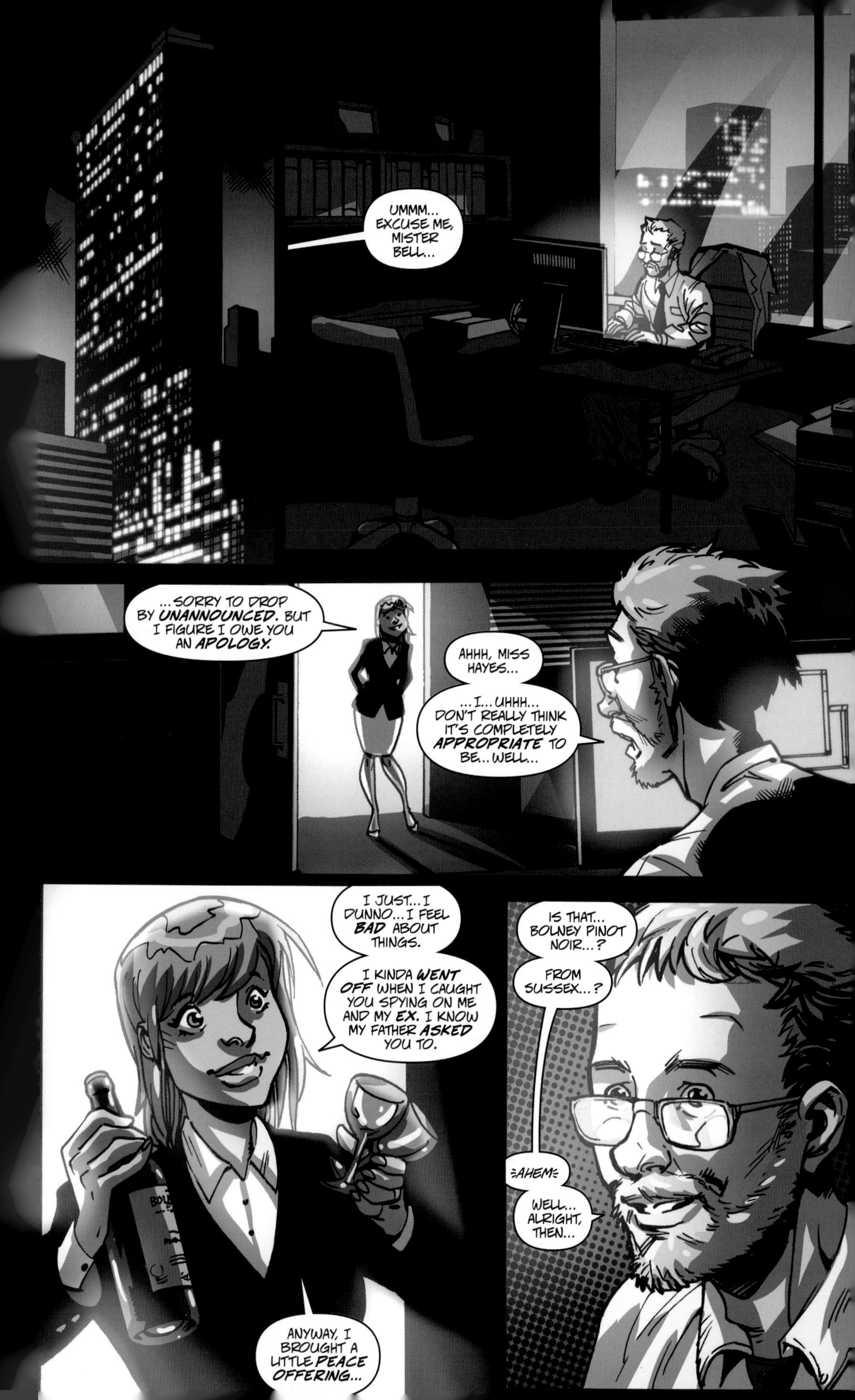
UMMM... EXCUSE ME, MISTER BELL...
...SORRY TO DROP BY UNANNOUNCED. BUT I FIGURE I OWE YOU AN APOLOGY.
AHHH, MISS HAYES...
...I...UHHH... DON'T REALLY THINK IT'S COMPLETELY APPROPRIATE TO BE...WELL...
I JUST...I DUNNO...I FEEL BAD ABOUT THINGS.
I KINDA WENT OFF WHEN I CAUGHT YOU SPYING ON ME AND MY EX. I KNOW MY FATHER ASKED YOU TO.
ANYWAY, I BROUGHT A LITTLE PEACE OFFERING...
IS THAT... BOLNEY PINOT NOIR...?
FROM SUSSEX...?
AHEM
WELL... ALRIGHT, THEN...

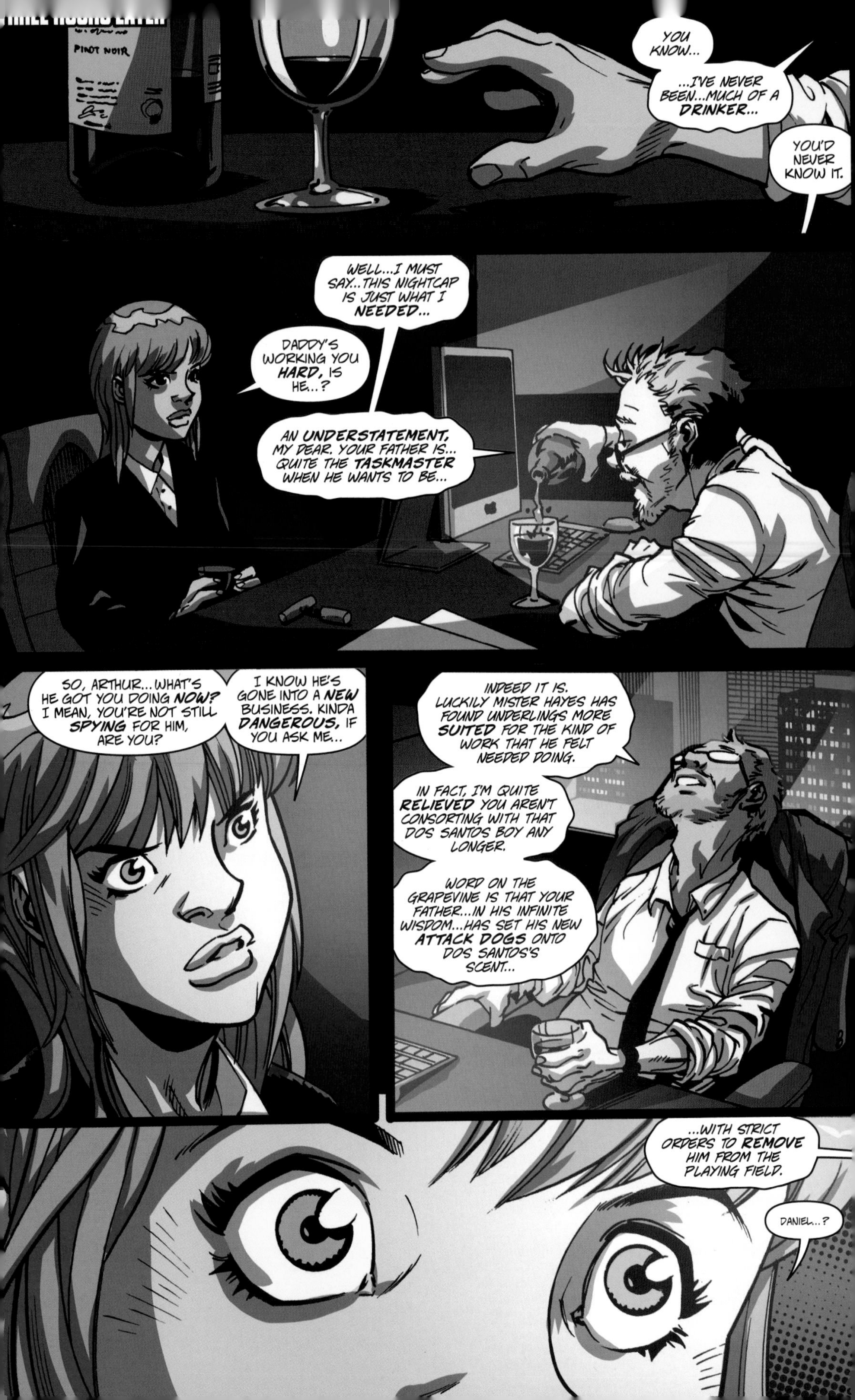

YOU KNOW...
...I'VE NEVER BEEN...MUCH OF A DRINKER...
YOU'D NEVER KNOW IT.
WELL...I MUST SAY...THIS NIGHTCAP IS JUST WHAT I NEEDED...
DADDY'S WORKING YOU HARD, IS HE...?
AN UNDERSTATEMENT, MY DEAR. YOUR FATHER IS... QUITE THE TASKMASTER WHEN HE WANTS TO BE...
SO, ARTHUR... WHAT'S HE GOT YOU DOING NOW? I MEAN, YOU'RE NOT STILL SPYING FOR HIM, ARE YOU?
I KNOW HE'S GONE INTO A NEW BUSINESS. KINDA DANGEROUS, IF YOU ASK ME...
INDEED IT IS. LUCKILY MISTER HAYES HAS FOUND UNDERLINGS MORE SUITED FOR THE KIND OF WORK THAT HE FELT NEEDED DOING.
IN FACT, I'M QUITE RELIEVED YOU AREN'T CONSORTING WITH THAT DOS SANTOS BOY ANY LONGER.
WORD ON THE GRAPEVINE IS THAT YOUR FATHER...IN HIS INFINITE WISDOM...HAS SET HIS NEW ATTACK DOGS ONTO DOS SANTOS'S SCENT...
...WITH STRICT ORDERS TO REMOVE HIM FROM THE PLAYING FIELD.
DANIEL...?

CHAPTER THREE

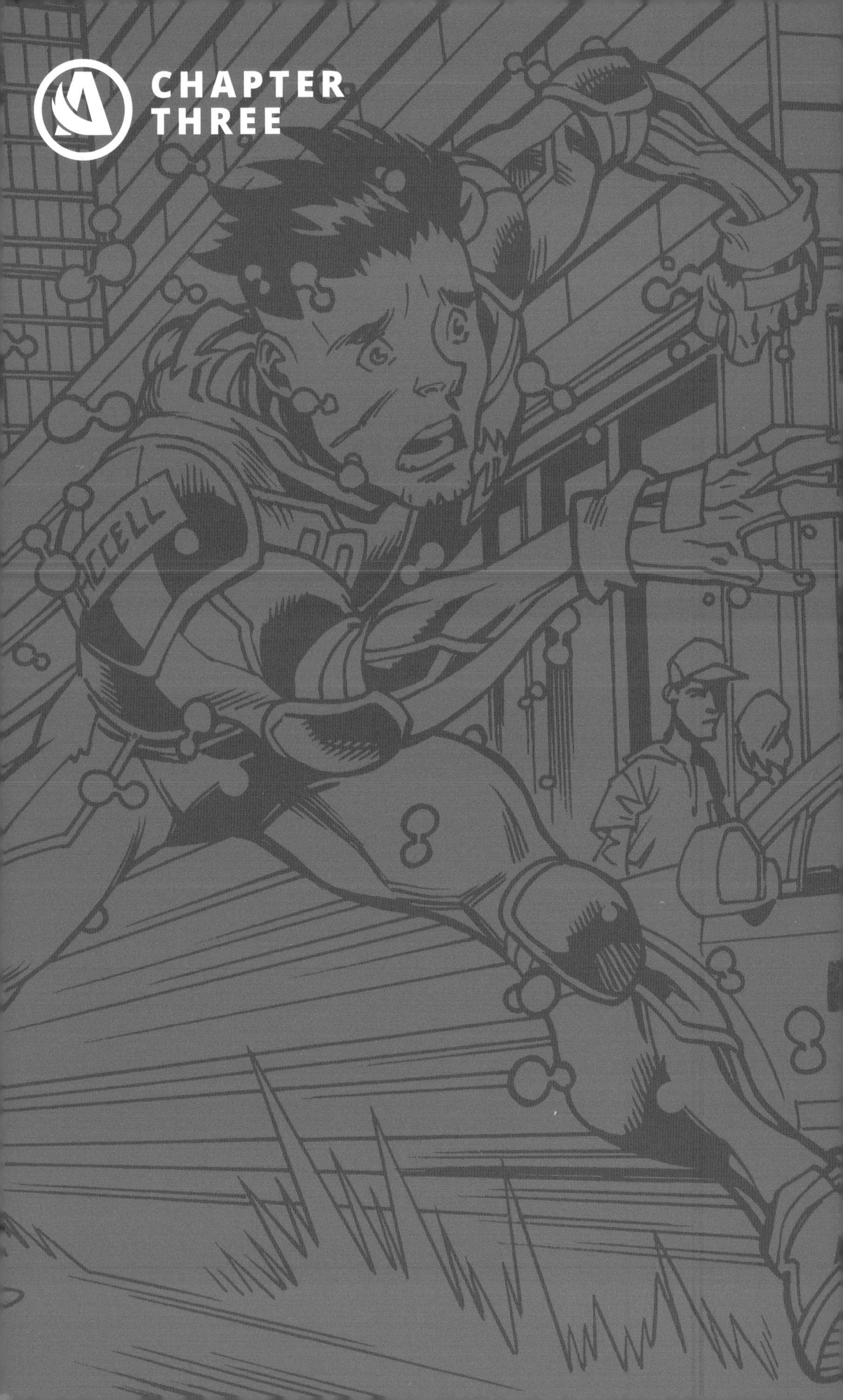

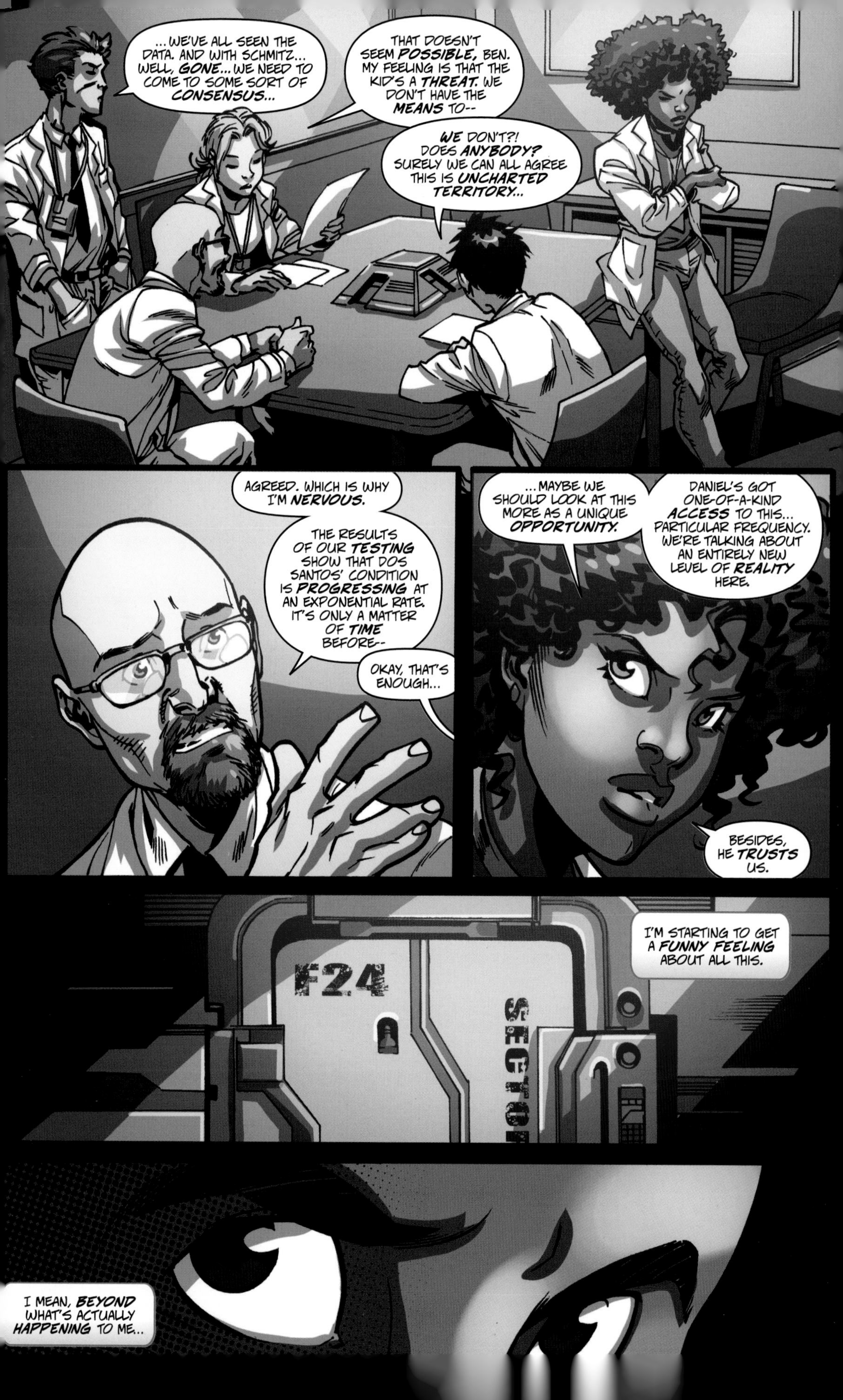
...WE'VE ALL SEEN THE DATA. AND WITH SCHMITZ... WELL, GONE... WE NEED TO COME TO SOME SORT OF CONSENSUS...
THAT DOESN'T SEEM POSSIBLE, BEN. MY FEELING IS THAT THE KID'S A THREAT. WE DON'T HAVE THE MEANS TO--
WE DON'T?! DOES ANYBODY? SURELY WE CAN ALL AGREE THIS IS UNCHARTED TERRITORY...
AGREED. WHICH IS WHY I'M NERVOUS.
THE RESULTS OF OUR TESTING SHOW THAT DOS SANTOS' CONDITION IS PROGRESSING AT AN EXPONENTIAL RATE. IT'S ONLY A MATTER OF TIME BEFORE--
OKAY, THAT'S ENOUGH...
...MAYBE WE SHOULD LOOK AT THIS MORE AS A UNIQUE OPPORTUNITY.
DANIEL'S GOT ONE-OF-A-KIND ACCESS TO THIS... PARTICULAR FREQUENCY. WE'RE TALKING ABOUT AN ENTIRELY NEW LEVEL OF REALITY HERE.
BESIDES, HE TRUSTS US.
F24
SECTOR
I'M STARTING TO GET A FUNNY FEELING ABOUT ALL THIS.
I MEAN, BEYOND WHAT'S ACTUALLY HAPPENING TO ME...

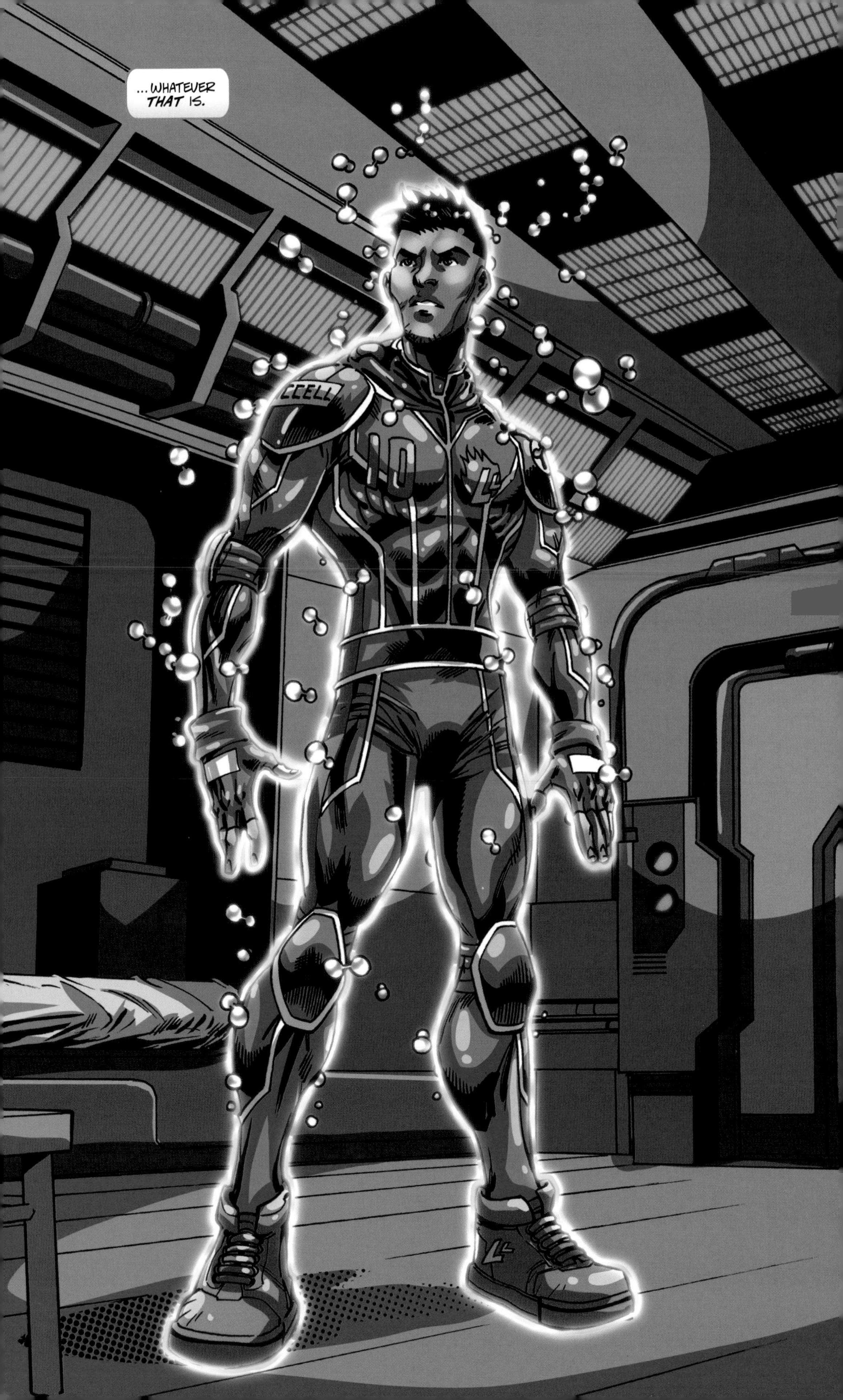
...WHATEVER THAT IS.

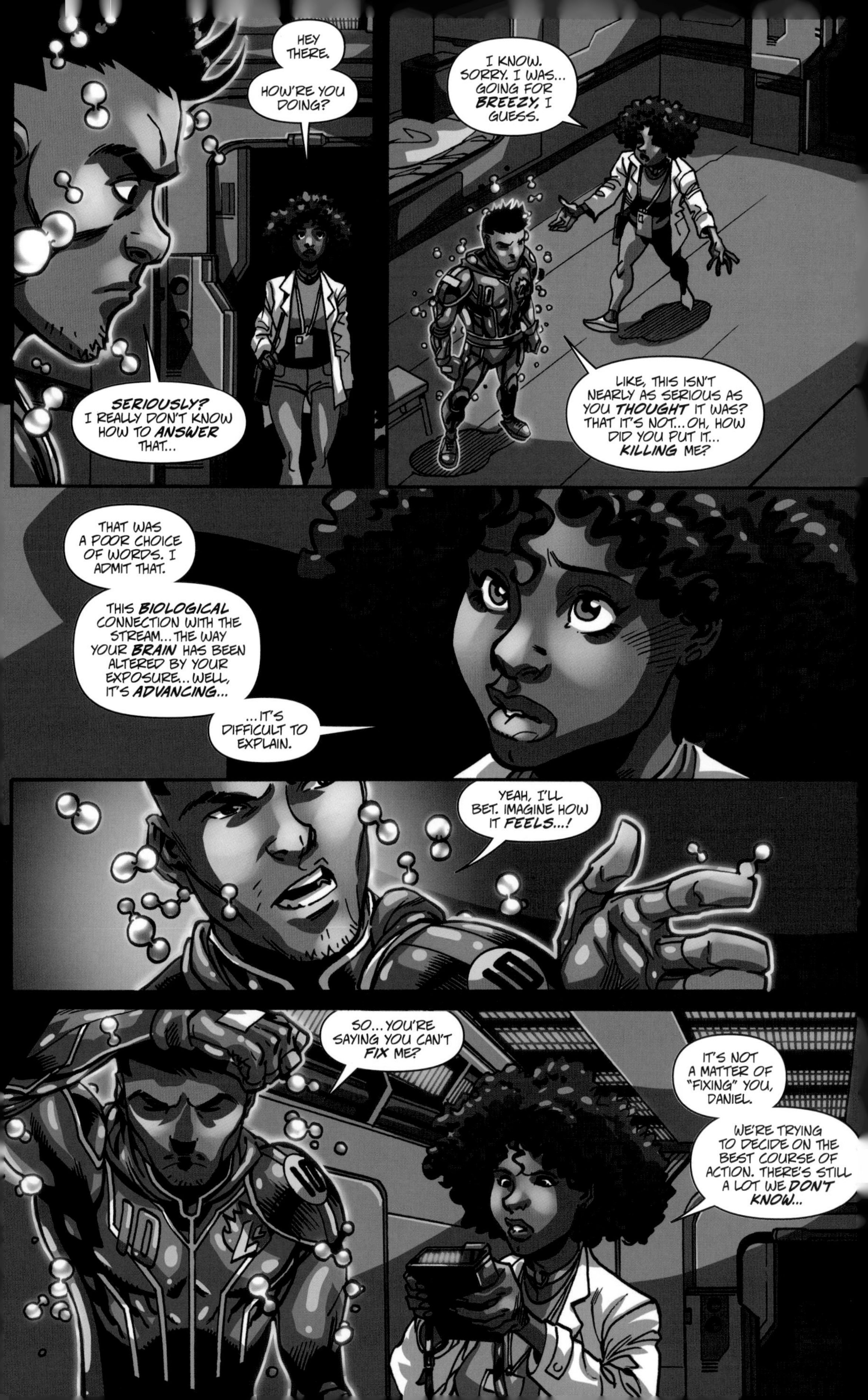
HEY THERE.
HOW'RE YOU DOING?
SERIOUSLY? I REALLY DON'T KNOW HOW TO ANSWER THAT...
I KNOW. SORRY. I WAS... GOING FOR BREEZY, I GUESS.
LIKE, THIS ISN'T NEARLY AS SERIOUS AS YOU THOUGHT IT WAS? THAT IT'S NOT...OH, HOW DID YOU PUT IT... KILLING ME?
THAT WAS A POOR CHOICE OF WORDS. I ADMIT THAT.
THIS BIOLOGICAL CONNECTION WITH THE STREAM... THE WAY YOUR BRAIN HAS BEEN ALTERED BY YOUR EXPOSURE...WELL, IT'S ADVANCING...
...IT'S DIFFICULT TO EXPLAIN.
YEAH, I'LL BET. IMAGINE HOW IT FEELS...!
SO... YOU'RE SAYING YOU CAN'T FIX ME?
IT'S NOT A MATTER OF "FIXING" YOU, DANIEL.
WE'RE TRYING TO DECIDE ON THE BEST COURSE OF ACTION. THERE'S STILL A LOT WE DON'T KNOW...

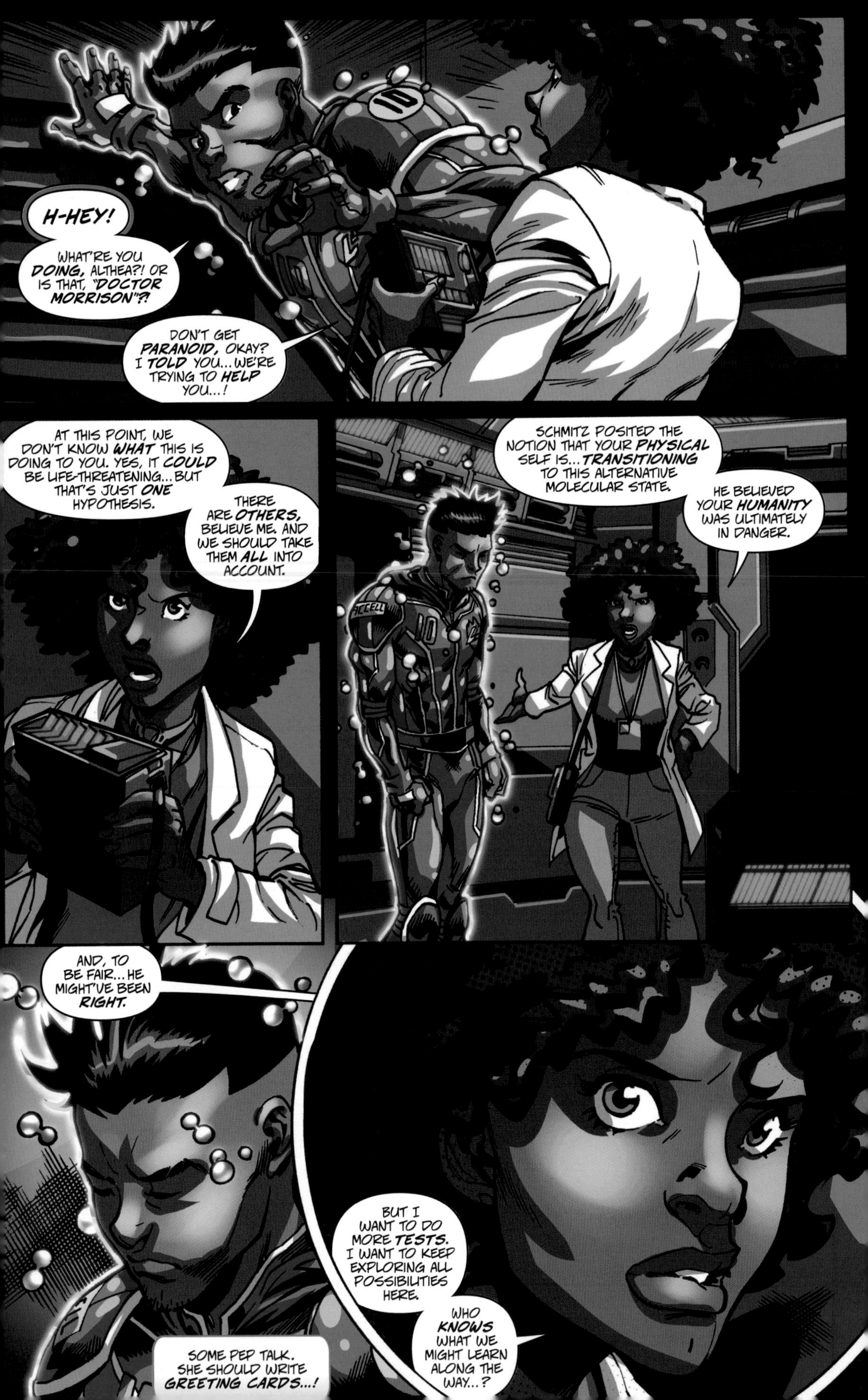
H-HEY!
WHAT'RE YOU DOING, ALTHEA?! OR IS THAT, "DOCTOR MORRISON"?!
DON'T GET PARANOID, OKAY? I TOLD YOU... WE'RE TRYING TO HELP YOU...!
AT THIS POINT, WE DON'T KNOW WHAT THIS IS DOING TO YOU. YES, IT COULD BE LIFE-THREATENING... BUT THAT'S JUST ONE HYPOTHESIS.
THERE ARE OTHERS, BELIEVE ME. AND WE SHOULD TAKE THEM ALL INTO ACCOUNT.
SCHMITZ POSITED THE NOTION THAT YOUR PHYSICAL SELF IS... TRANSITIONING TO THIS ALTERNATIVE MOLECULAR STATE.
HE BELIEVED YOUR HUMANITY WAS ULTIMATELY IN DANGER.
ACCELL
10
AND, TO BE FAIR... HE MIGHT'VE BEEN RIGHT.
BUT I WANT TO DO MORE TESTS. I WANT TO KEEP EXPLORING ALL POSSIBILITIES HERE.
WHO KNOWS WHAT WE MIGHT LEARN ALONG THE WAY...?
SOME PEP TALK. SHE SHOULD WRITE GREETING CARDS...!

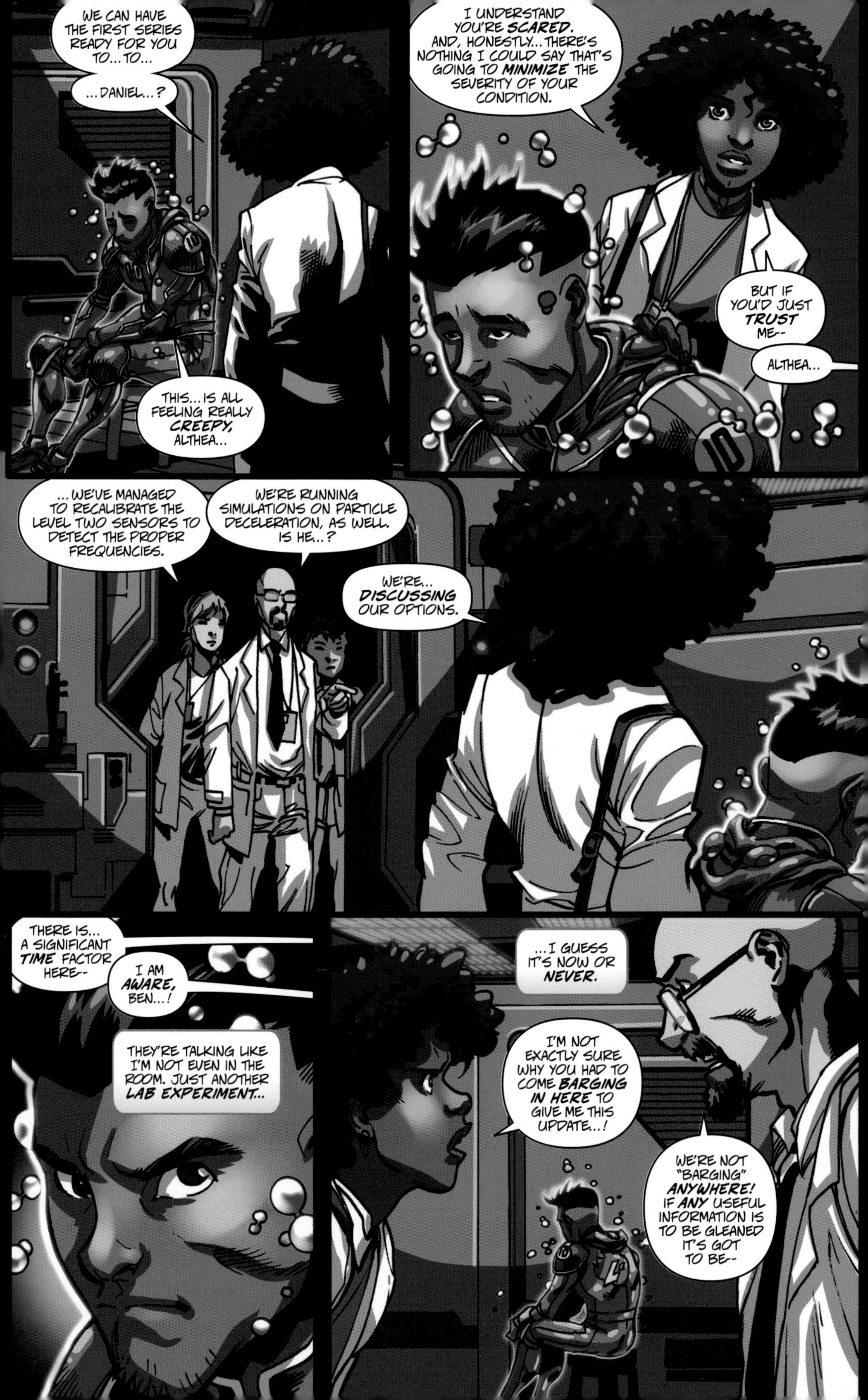

WE CAN HAVE THE FIRST SERIES READY FOR YOU TO... TO...
...DANIEL...?
THIS... IS ALL FEELING REALLY CREEPY, ALTHEA...
I UNDERSTAND YOU'RE SCARED. AND, HONESTLY... THERE'S NOTHING I COULD SAY THAT'S GOING TO MINIMIZE THE SEVERITY OF YOUR CONDITION.
BUT IF YOU'D JUST TRUST ME--
ALTHEA...
...WE'VE MANAGED TO RECALIBRATE THE LEVEL TWO SENSORS TO DETECT THE PROPER FREQUENCIES.
WE'RE RUNNING SIMULATIONS ON PARTICLE DECELERATION, AS WELL. IS HE...?
WE'RE... DISCUSSING OUR OPTIONS.
THERE IS... A SIGNIFICANT TIME FACTOR HERE--
I AM AWARE, BEN...!
THEY'RE TALKING LIKE I'M NOT EVEN IN THE ROOM. JUST ANOTHER LAB EXPERIMENT...
...I GUESS IT'S NOW OR NEVER.
I'M NOT EXACTLY SURE WHY YOU HAD TO COME BARGING IN HERE TO GIVE ME THIS UPDATE...!
WE'RE NOT "BARGING" ANYWHERE! IF ANY USEFUL INFORMATION IS TO BE GLEANED IT'S GOT TO BE--

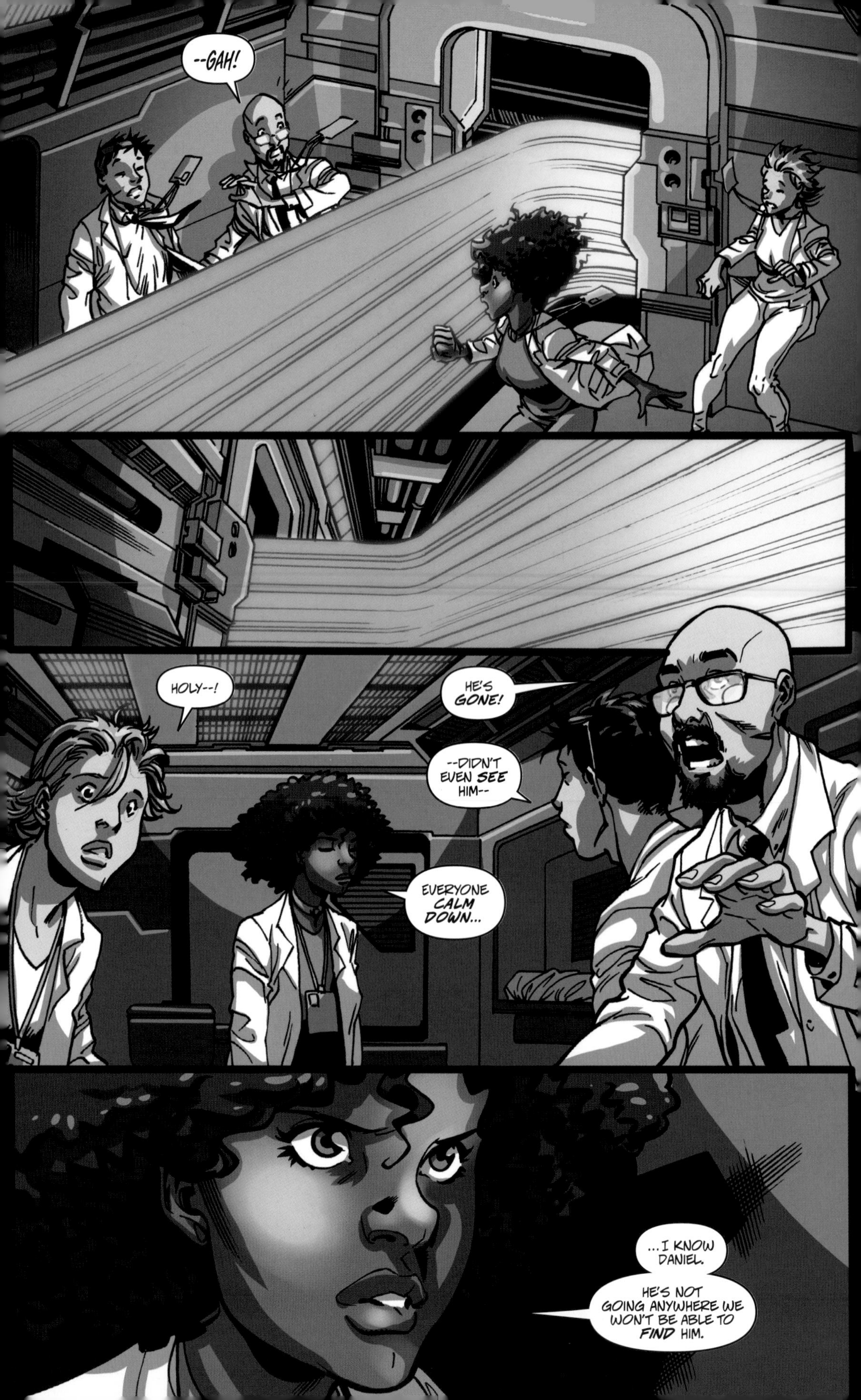
--GAH!
HOLY--!
HE'S GONE!
--DIDN'T EVEN SEE HIM--
EVERYONE CALM DOWN...
...I KNOW DANIEL.
HE'S NOT GOING ANYWHERE WE WON'T BE ABLE TO FIND HIM.

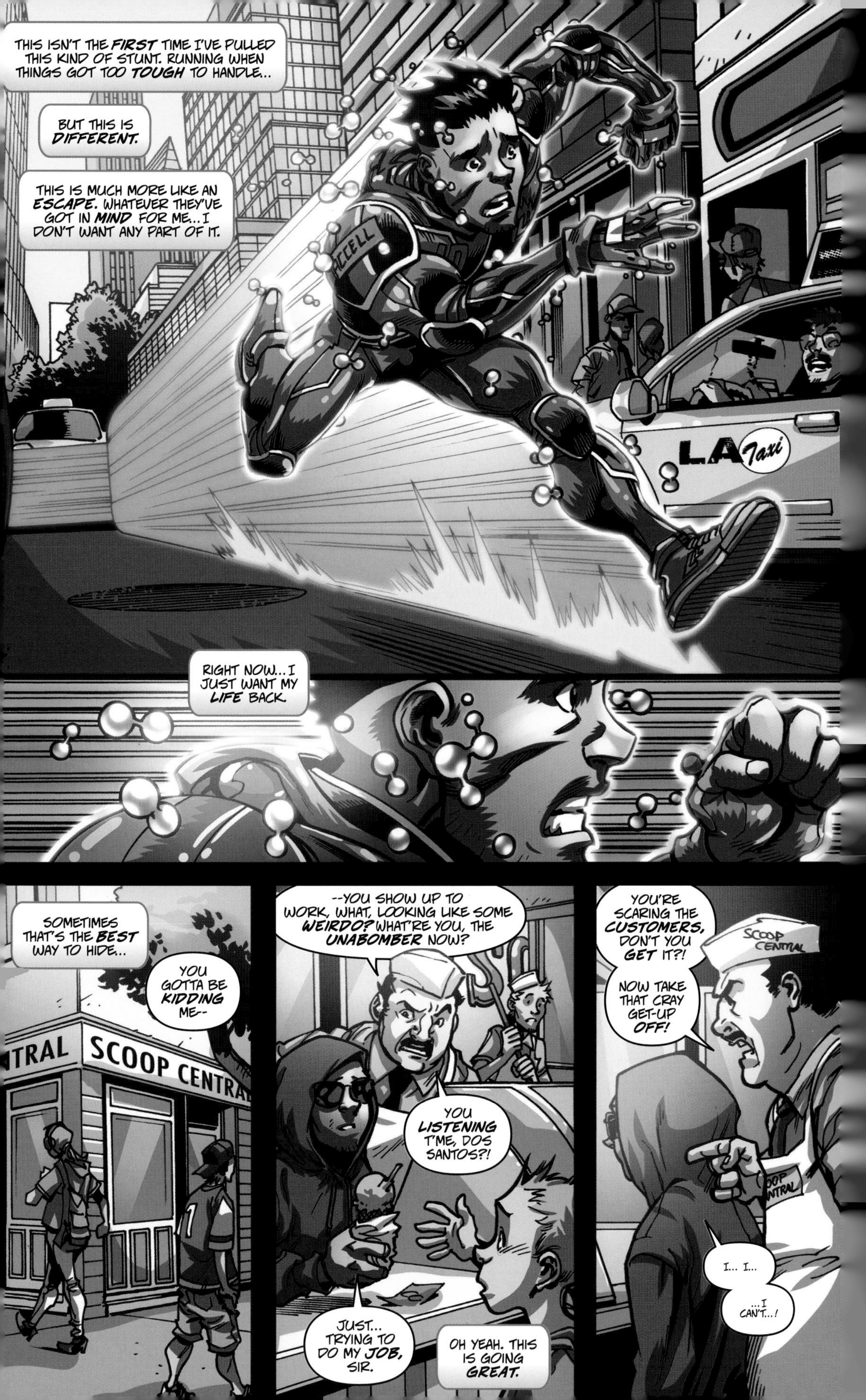
THIS ISN'T THE FIRST TIME I'VE PULLED THIS KIND OF STUNT. RUNNING WHEN THINGS GOT TOO TOUGH TO HANDLE...
BUT THIS IS DIFFERENT.
THIS IS MUCH MORE LIKE AN ESCAPE. WHATEVER THEY'VE GOT IN MIND FOR ME... I DON'T WANT ANY PART OF IT.
LA Taxi
RIGHT NOW... I JUST WANT MY LIFE BACK.
SOMETIMES THAT'S THE BEST WAY TO HIDE...
YOU GOTTA BE KIDDING ME--
SCOOP CENTRAL
--YOU SHOW UP TO WORK, WHAT, LOOKING LIKE SOME WEIRDO? WHAT'RE YOU, THE UNABOMBER NOW?
YOU LISTENING T'ME, DOS SANTOS?!
JUST... TRYING TO DO MY JOB, SIR.
OH YEAH. THIS IS GOING GREAT.
YOU'RE SCARING THE CUSTOMERS, DON'T YOU GET IT?!
NOW TAKE THAT CRAY GET-UP OFF!
I... I...
...I CAN'T...!

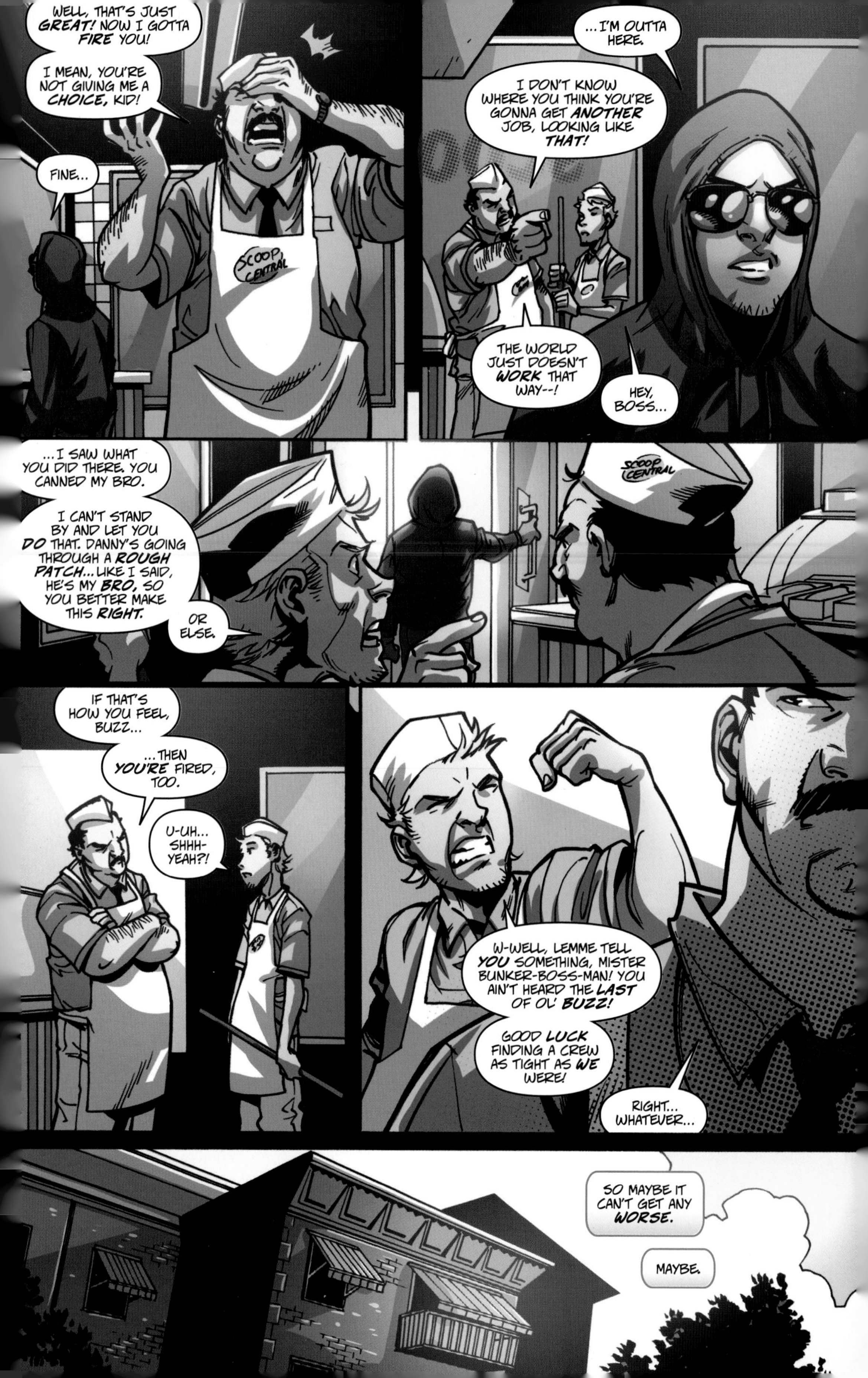
WELL, THAT'S JUST GREAT! NOW I GOTTA FIRE YOU!
I MEAN, YOU'RE NOT GIVING ME A CHOICE, KID!
FINE...
...I'M OUTTA HERE.
I DON'T KNOW WHERE YOU THINK YOU'RE GONNA GET ANOTHER JOB, LOOKING LIKE THAT!
THE WORLD JUST DOESN'T WORK THAT WAY--!
HEY, BOSS...
...I SAW WHAT YOU DID THERE. YOU CANNED MY BRO.
I CAN'T STAND BY AND LET YOU DO THAT. DANNY'S GOING THROUGH A ROUGH PATCH... LIKE I SAID, HE'S MY BRO, SO YOU BETTER MAKE THIS RIGHT.
OR ELSE.
IF THAT'S HOW YOU FEEL, BUZZ...
...THEN YOU'RE FIRED, TOO.
U-UH... SHHH-YEAH?!
W-WELL, LEMME TELL YOU SOMETHING, MISTER BUNKER-BOSS-MAN! YOU AIN'T HEARD THE LAST OF OL' BUZZ!
GOOD LUCK FINDING A CREW AS TIGHT AS WE WERE!
RIGHT... WHATEVER...
SO MAYBE IT CAN'T GET ANY WORSE.
MAYBE.

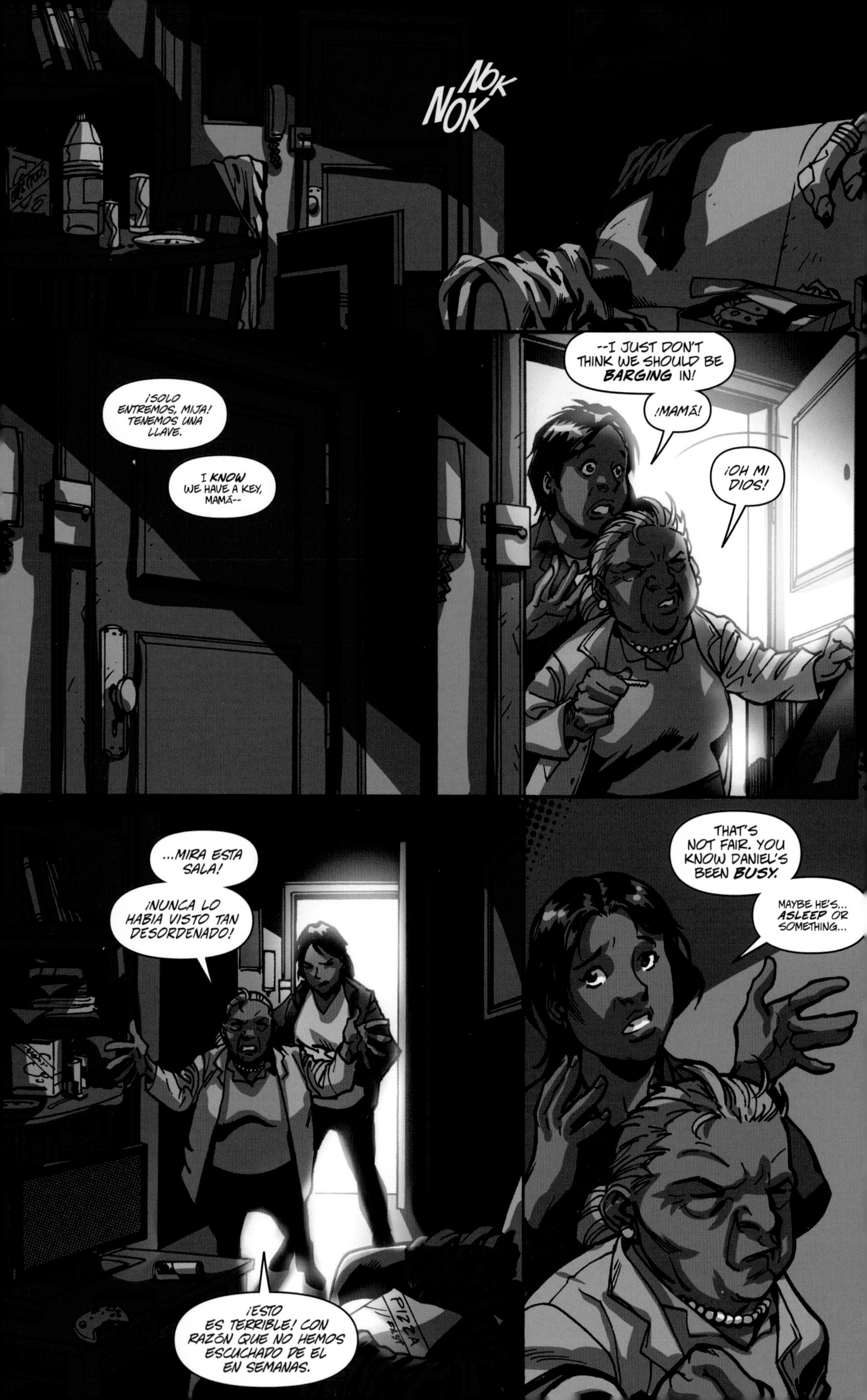
NOK NOK
¡SOLO ENTREMOS, MIJA! TENEMOS UNA LLAVE.
I KNOW WE HAVE A KEY, MAMÁ--
--I JUST DON'T THINK WE SHOULD BE BARGING IN!
¡MAMÁ!
¡OH MI DIOS!
...MIRA ESTA SALA!
¡NUNCA LO HABIA VISTO TAN DESORDENADO!
¡ESTO ES TERRIBLE! CON RAZÓN QUE NO HEMOS ESCUCHADO DE EL EN SEMANAS.
PIZZA
THAT'S NOT FAIR. YOU KNOW DANIEL'S BEEN BUSY.
MAYBE HE'S... ASLEEP OR SOMETHING...

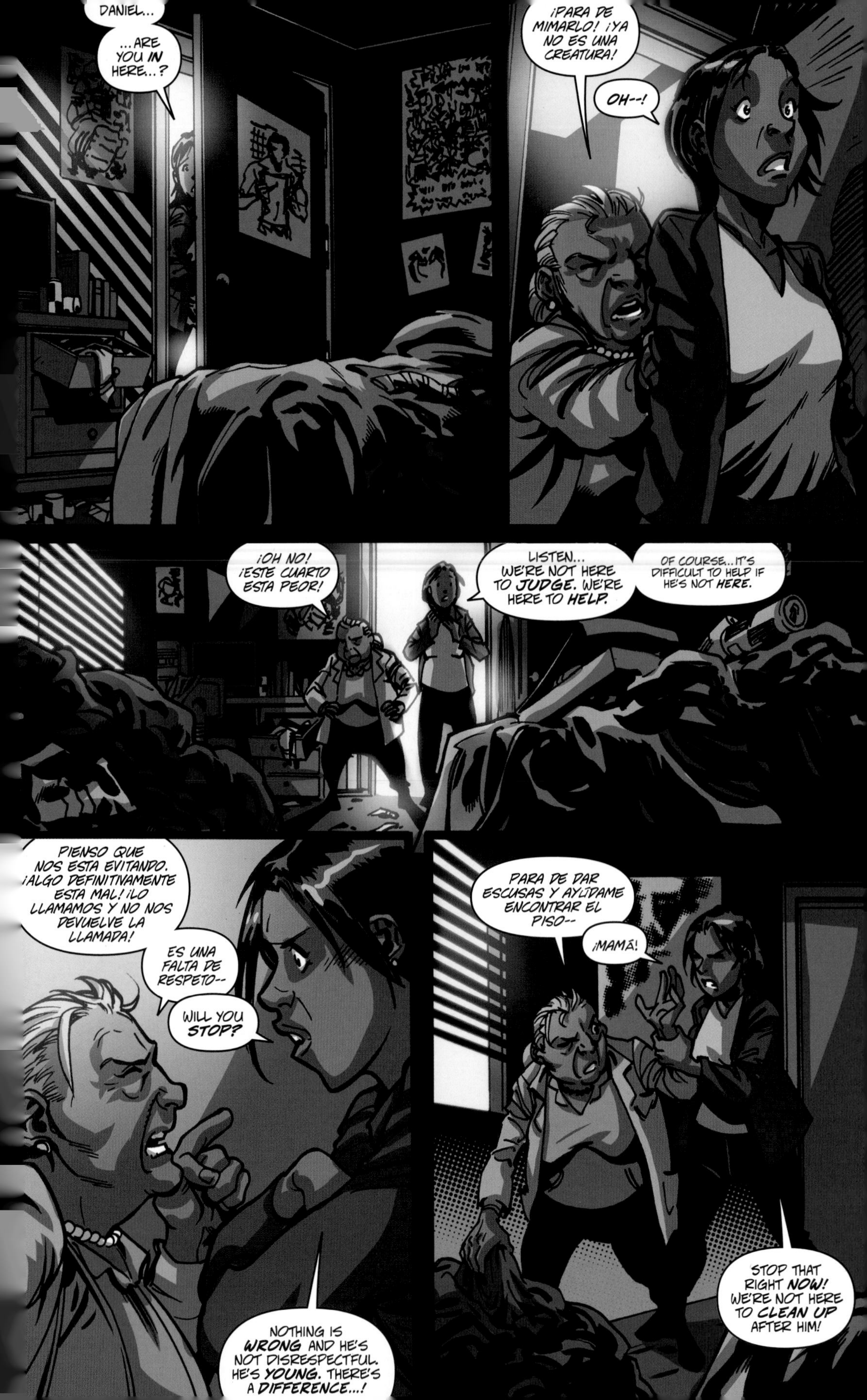
DANIEL...
...ARE YOU IN HERE...?
¡PARA DE MIMARLO! ¡YA NO ES UNA CREATURA!
OH--!
¡OH NO! ¡ESTE CUARTO ESTA PEOR!
LISTEN... WE'RE NOT HERE TO JUDGE. WE'RE HERE TO HELP.
OF COURSE... IT'S DIFFICULT TO HELP IF HE'S NOT HERE.
PIENSO QUE NOS ESTA EVITANDO. ¡ALGO DEFINITIVAMENTE ESTA MAL! ¡LO LLAMAMOS Y NO NOS DEVUELVE LA LLAMADA!
ES UNA FALTA DE RESPETO--
WILL YOU STOP?
NOTHING IS WRONG AND HE'S NOT DISRESPECTFUL. HE'S YOUNG. THERE'S A DIFFERENCE...!
PARA DE DAR ESCUSAS Y AYÚDAME ENCONTRAR EL PISO--
¡MAMÁ!
STOP THAT RIGHT NOW! WE'RE NOT HERE TO CLEAN UP AFTER HIM!

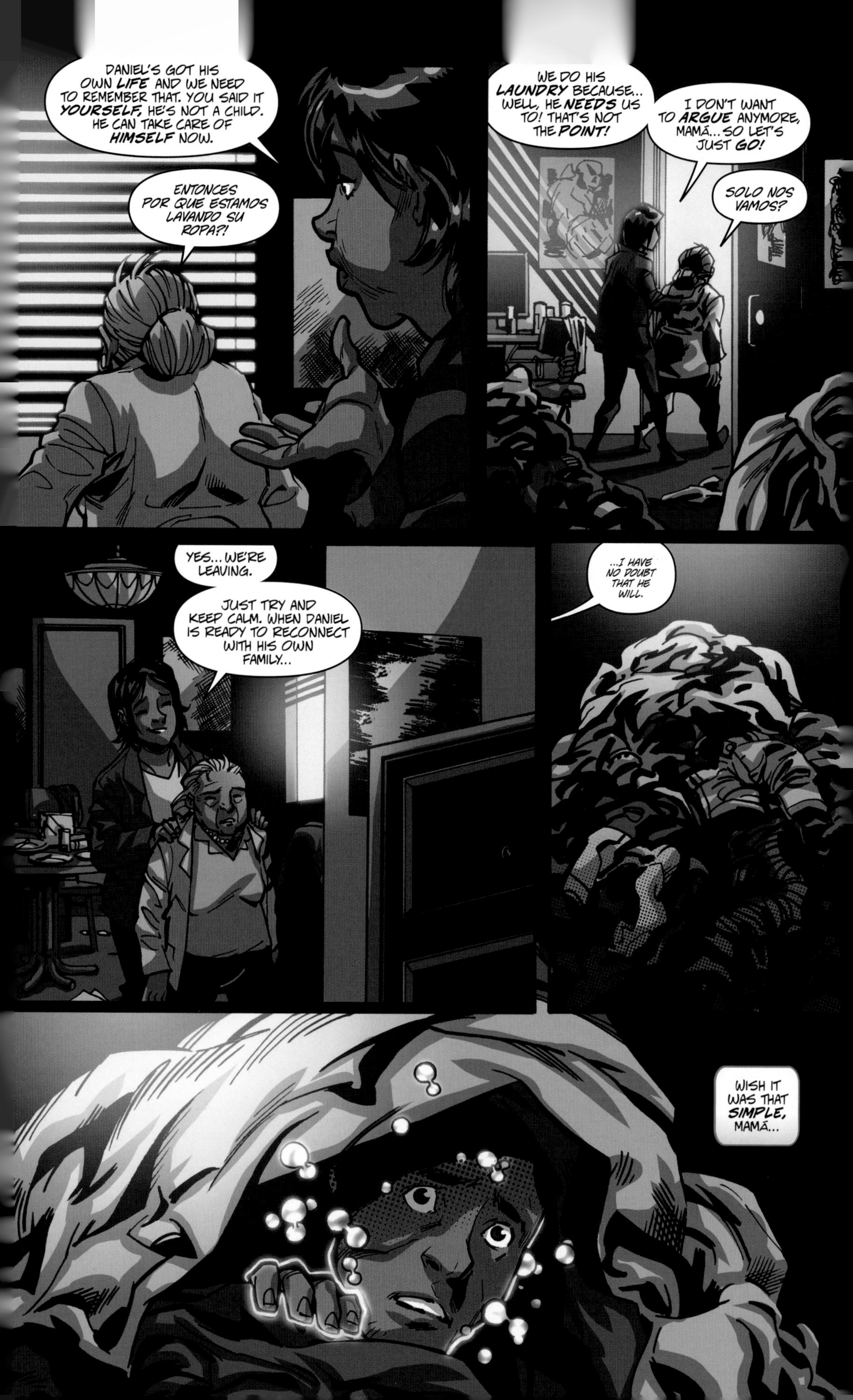
DANIEL'S GOT HIS OWN LIFE AND WE NEED TO REMEMBER THAT. YOU SAID IT YOURSELF, HE'S NOT A CHILD. HE CAN TAKE CARE OF HIMSELF NOW.
ENTONCES POR QUE ESTAMOS LAVANDO SU ROPA?!
WE DO HIS LAUNDRY BECAUSE... WELL, HE NEEDS US TO! THAT'S NOT THE POINT!
I DON'T WANT TO ARGUE ANYMORE, MAMÁ... SO LET'S JUST GO!
SOLO NOS VAMOS?
YES... WE'RE LEAVING.
JUST TRY AND KEEP CALM. WHEN DANIEL IS READY TO RECONNECT WITH HIS OWN FAMILY...
...I HAVE NO DOUBT THAT HE WILL.
WISH IT WAS THAT SIMPLE, MAMÁ...

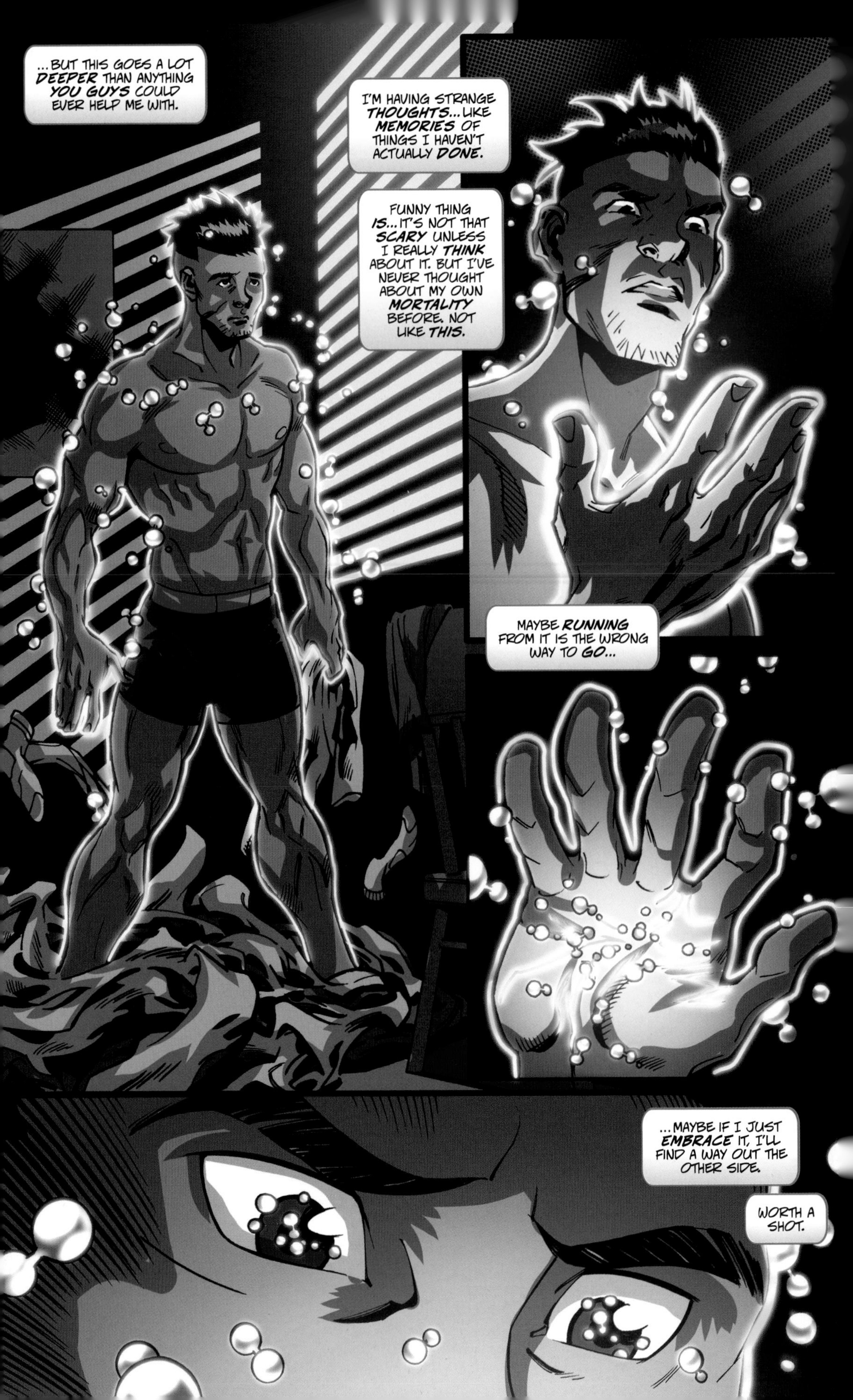
...BUT THIS GOES A LOT DEEPER THAN ANYTHING YOU GUYS COULD EVER HELP ME WITH.
I'M HAVING STRANGE THOUGHTS...LIKE MEMORIES OF THINGS I HAVEN'T ACTUALLY DONE.
FUNNY THING IS...IT'S NOT THAT SCARY UNLESS I REALLY THINK ABOUT IT. BUT I'VE NEVER THOUGHT ABOUT MY OWN MORTALITY BEFORE. NOT LIKE THIS.
MAYBE RUNNING FROM IT IS THE WRONG WAY TO GO...
...MAYBE IF I JUST EMBRACE IT, I'LL FIND A WAY OUT THE OTHER SIDE.
WORTH A SHOT.

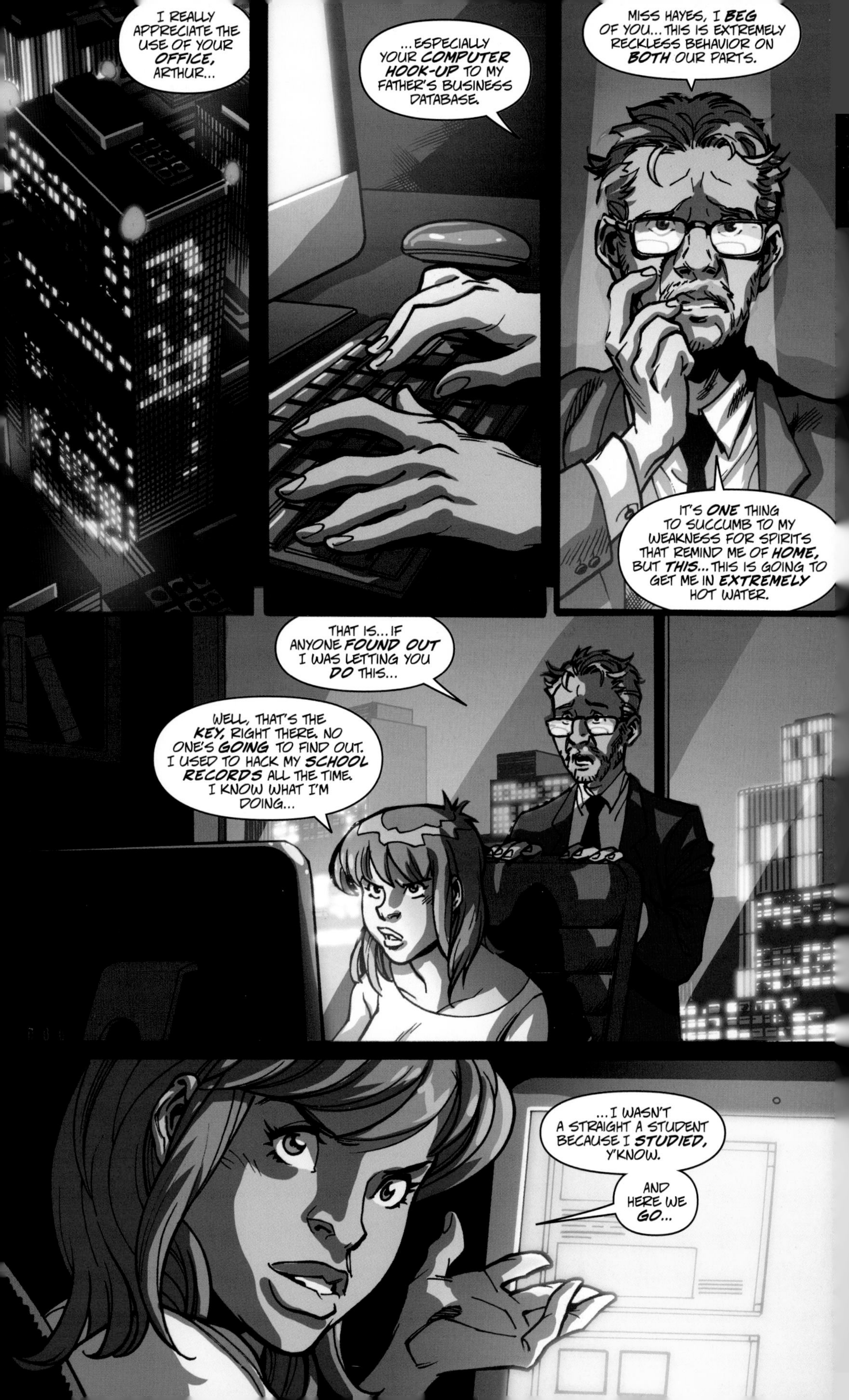
I REALLY APPRECIATE THE USE OF YOUR OFFICE, ARTHUR...
...ESPECIALLY YOUR COMPUTER HOOK-UP TO MY FATHER'S BUSINESS DATABASE.
MISS HAYES, I BEG OF YOU... THIS IS EXTREMELY RECKLESS BEHAVIOR ON BOTH OUR PARTS.
IT'S ONE THING TO SUCCUMB TO MY WEAKNESS FOR SPIRITS THAT REMIND ME OF HOME, BUT THIS... THIS IS GOING TO GET ME IN EXTREMELY HOT WATER.
THAT IS... IF ANYONE FOUND OUT I WAS LETTING YOU DO THIS...
WELL, THAT'S THE KEY, RIGHT THERE. NO ONE'S GOING TO FIND OUT. I USED TO HACK MY SCHOOL RECORDS ALL THE TIME. I KNOW WHAT I'M DOING...
...I WASN'T A STRAIGHT A STUDENT BECAUSE I STUDIED, Y'KNOW.
AND HERE WE GO...

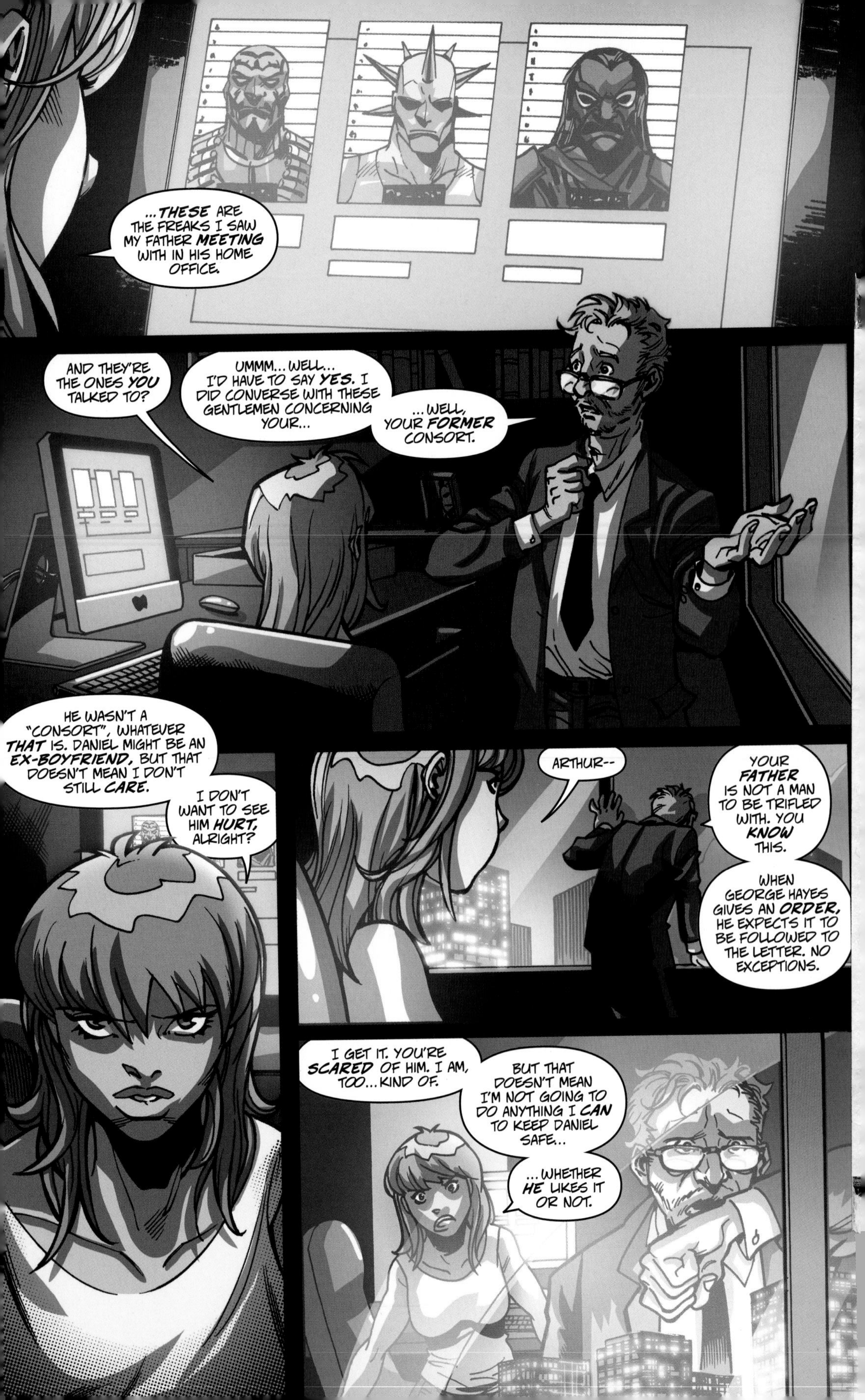
...THESE ARE THE FREAKS I SAW MY FATHER MEETING WITH IN HIS HOME OFFICE.
AND THEY'RE THE ONES YOU TALKED TO?
UMMM... WELL... I'D HAVE TO SAY YES. I DID CONVERSE WITH THESE GENTLEMEN CONCERNING YOUR...
...WELL, YOUR FORMER CONSORT.
HE WASN'T A "CONSORT", WHATEVER THAT IS. DANIEL MIGHT BE AN EX-BOYFRIEND, BUT THAT DOESN'T MEAN I DON'T STILL CARE.
I DON'T WANT TO SEE HIM HURT, ALRIGHT?
ARTHUR--
YOUR FATHER IS NOT A MAN TO BE TRIFLED WITH. YOU KNOW THIS.
WHEN GEORGE HAYES GIVES AN ORDER, HE EXPECTS IT TO BE FOLLOWED TO THE LETTER. NO EXCEPTIONS.
I GET IT. YOU'RE SCARED OF HIM. I AM, TOO... KIND OF.
BUT THAT DOESN'T MEAN I'M NOT GOING TO DO ANYTHING I CAN TO KEEP DANIEL SAFE...
...WHETHER HE LIKES IT OR NOT.

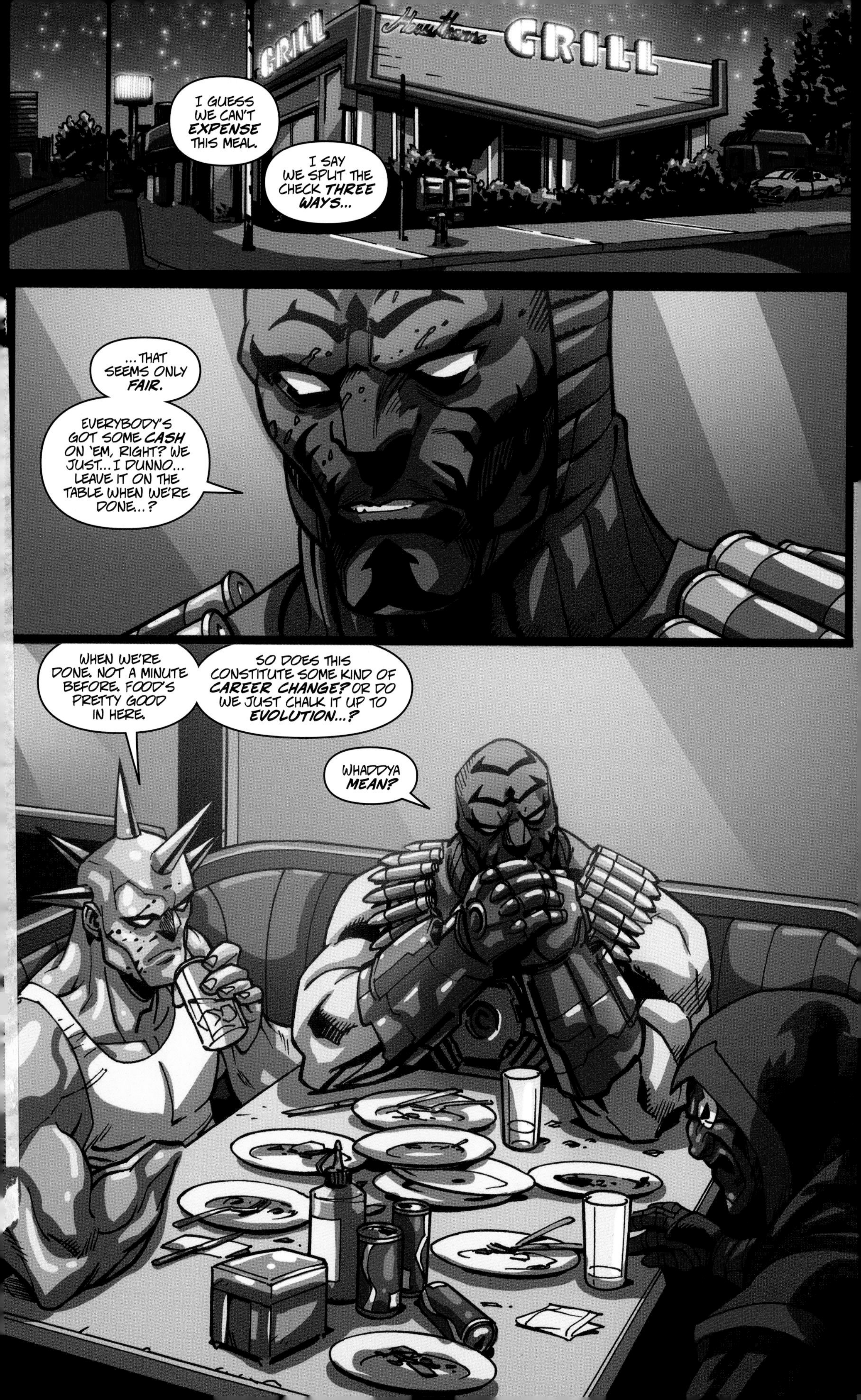
Hawthorne GRILL
GRILL
I GUESS WE CAN'T EXPENSE THIS MEAL.
I SAY WE SPLIT THE CHECK THREE WAYS...
...THAT SEEMS ONLY FAIR.
EVERYBODY'S GOT SOME CASH ON 'EM, RIGHT? WE JUST...I DUNNO... LEAVE IT ON THE TABLE WHEN WE'RE DONE...?
WHEN WE'RE DONE. NOT A MINUTE BEFORE. FOOD'S PRETTY GOOD IN HERE.
SO DOES THIS CONSTITUTE SOME KIND OF CAREER CHANGE? OR DO WE JUST CHALK IT UP TO EVOLUTION...?
WHADDYA MEAN?

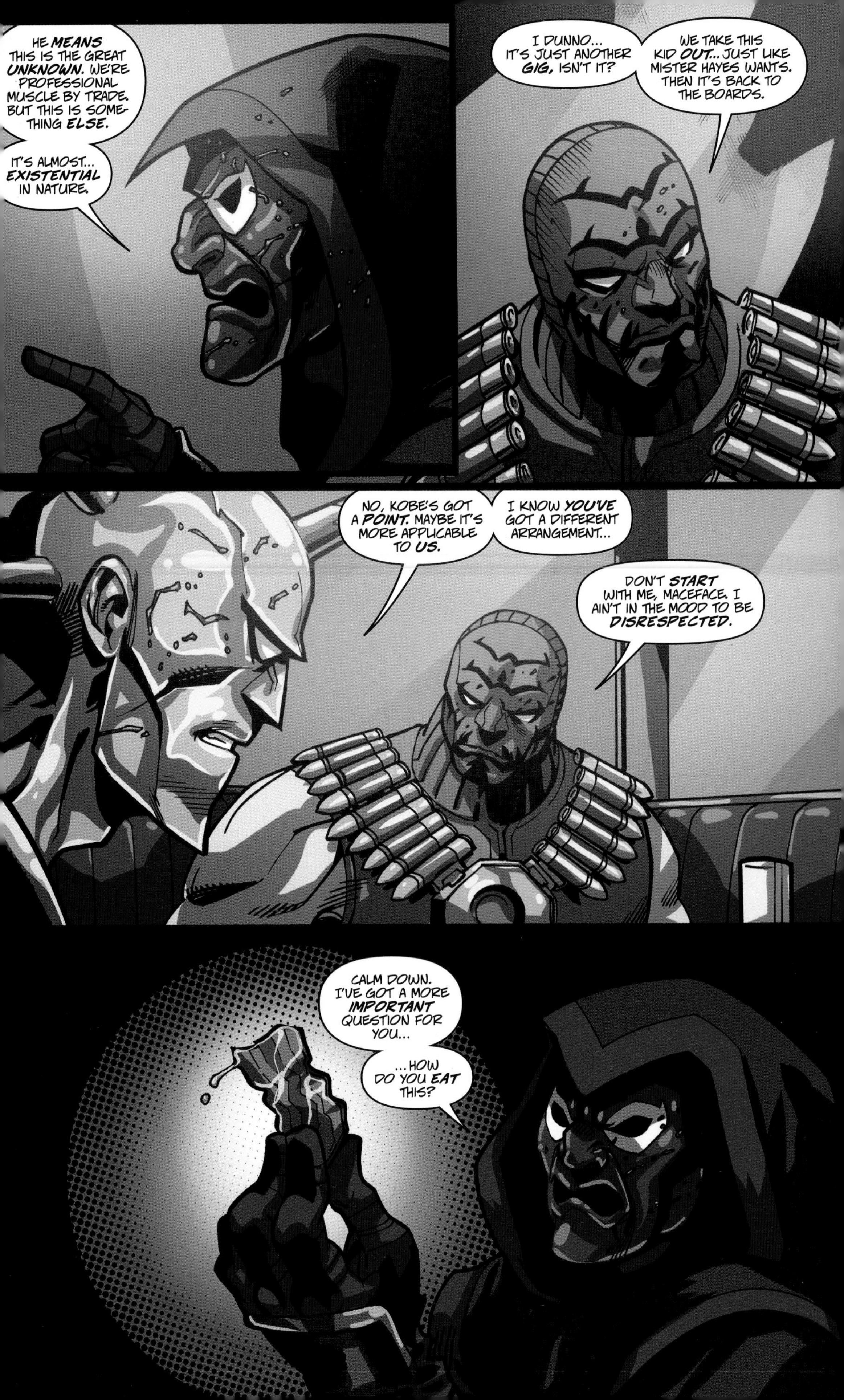
HE MEANS THIS IS THE GREAT UNKNOWN. WE'RE PROFESSIONAL MUSCLE BY TRADE. BUT THIS IS SOMETHING ELSE.
IT'S ALMOST... EXISTENTIAL IN NATURE.
I DUNNO... IT'S JUST ANOTHER GIG, ISN'T IT?
WE TAKE THIS KID OUT... JUST LIKE MISTER HAYES WANTS. THEN IT'S BACK TO THE BOARDS.
NO, KOBE'S GOT A POINT. MAYBE IT'S MORE APPLICABLE TO US.
I KNOW YOU'VE GOT A DIFFERENT ARRANGEMENT...
DON'T START WITH ME, MACEFACE. I AIN'T IN THE MOOD TO BE DISRESPECTED.
CALM DOWN. I'VE GOT A MORE IMPORTANT QUESTION FOR YOU...
...HOW DO YOU EAT THIS?

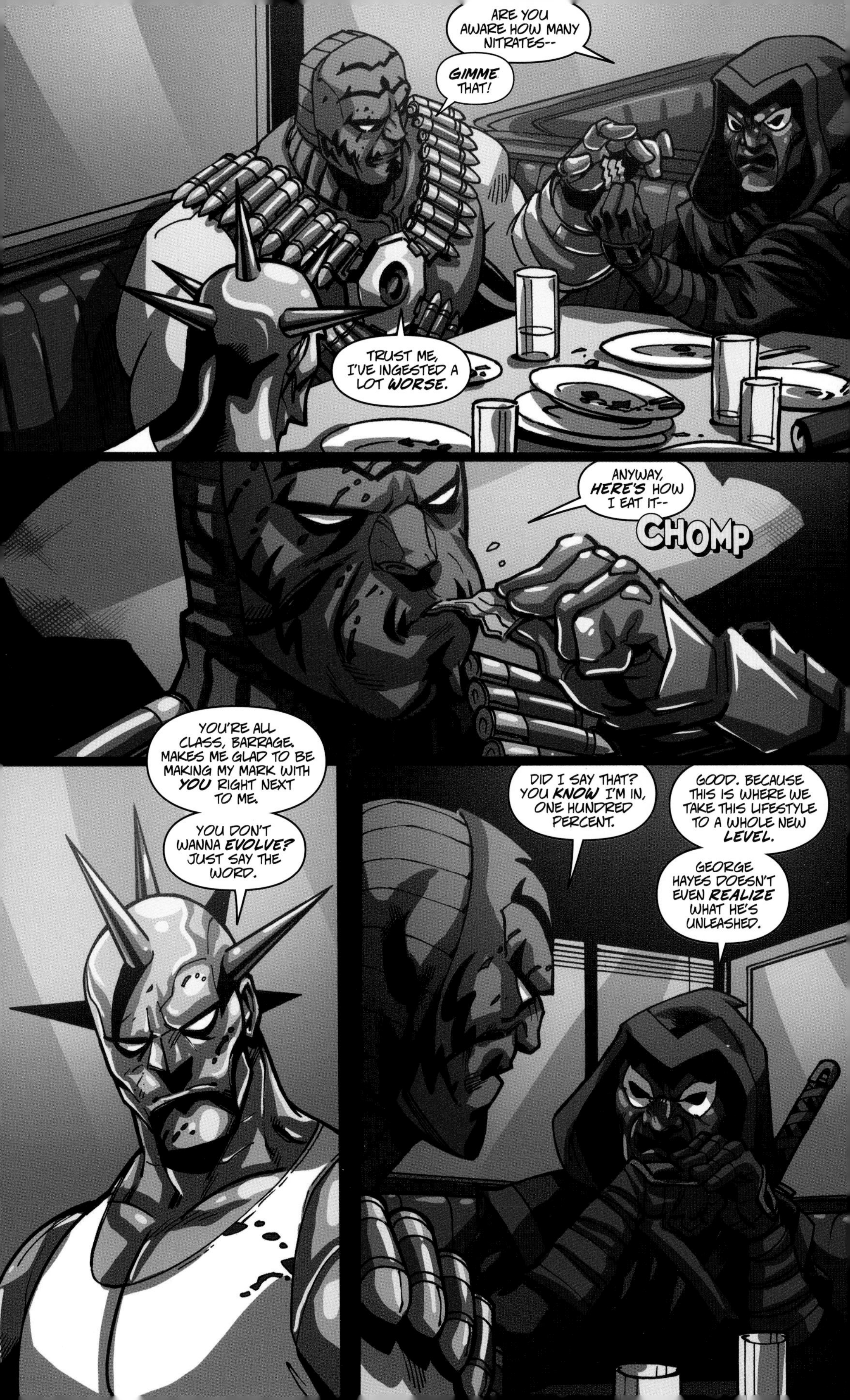

ARE YOU AWARE HOW MANY NITRATES--
GIMME THAT!
TRUST ME, I'VE INGESTED A LOT WORSE.
ANYWAY, HERE'S HOW I EAT IT--
CHOMP
YOU'RE ALL CLASS, BARRAGE. MAKES ME GLAD TO BE MAKING MY MARK WITH YOU RIGHT NEXT TO ME.
YOU DON'T WANNA EVOLVE? JUST SAY THE WORD.
DID I SAY THAT? YOU KNOW I'M IN, ONE HUNDRED PERCENT.
GOOD. BECAUSE THIS IS WHERE WE TAKE THIS LIFESTYLE TO A WHOLE NEW LEVEL.
GEORGE HAYES DOESN'T EVEN REALIZE WHAT HE'S UNLEASHED.

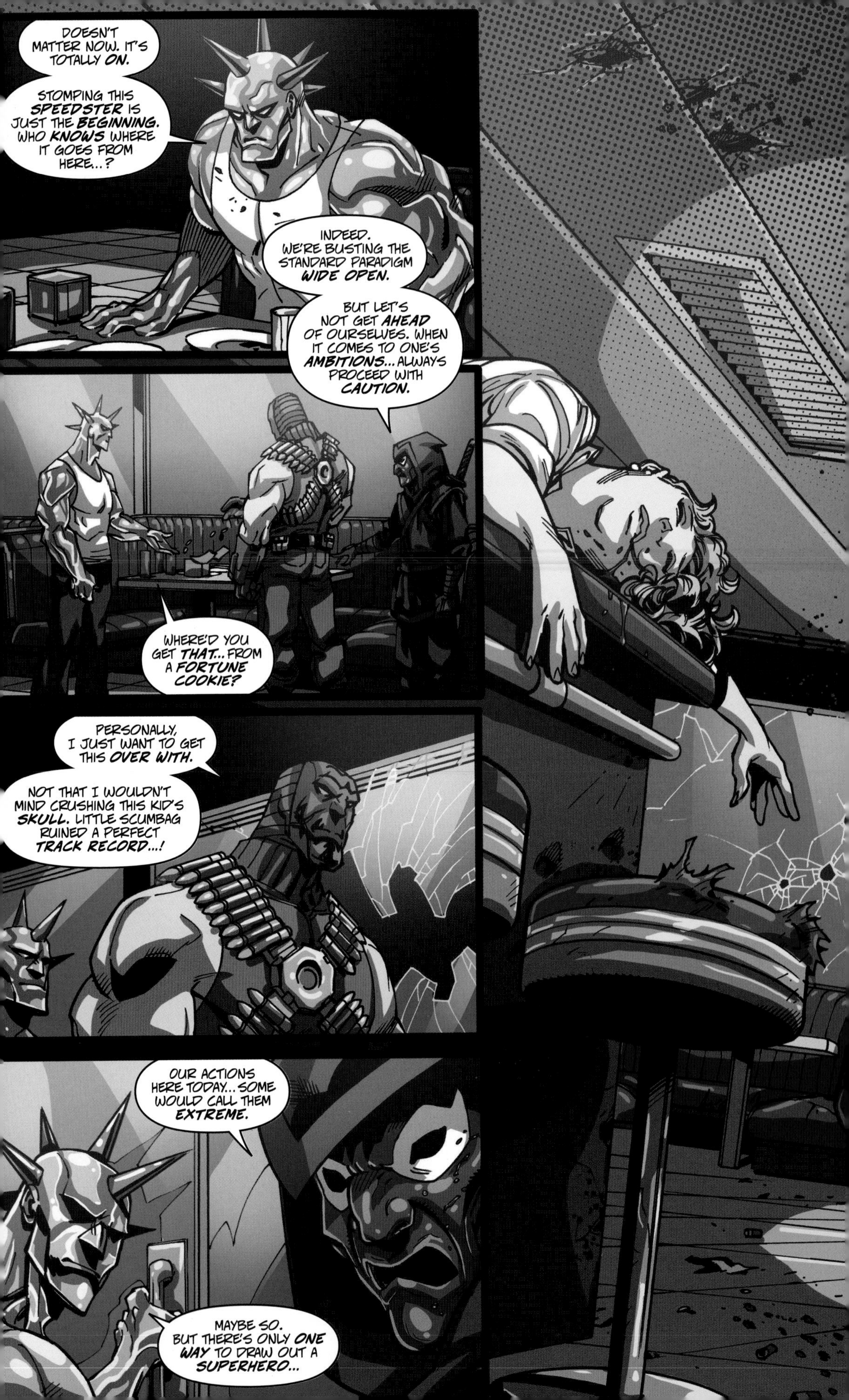
DOESN'T MATTER NOW. IT'S TOTALLY ON.
STOMPING THIS SPEEDSTER IS JUST THE BEGINNING. WHO KNOWS WHERE IT GOES FROM HERE...?
INDEED. WE'RE BUSTING THE STANDARD PARADIGM WIDE OPEN.
BUT LET'S NOT GET AHEAD OF OURSELVES. WHEN IT COMES TO ONE'S AMBITIONS... ALWAYS PROCEED WITH CAUTION.
WHERE'D YOU GET THAT... FROM A FORTUNE COOKIE?
PERSONALLY, I JUST WANT TO GET THIS OVER WITH.
NOT THAT I WOULDN'T MIND CRUSHING THIS KID'S SKULL. LITTLE SCUMBAG RUINED A PERFECT TRACK RECORD...!
OUR ACTIONS HERE TODAY... SOME WOULD CALL THEM EXTREME.
MAYBE SO. BUT THERE'S ONLY ONE WAY TO DRAW OUT A SUPERHERO...

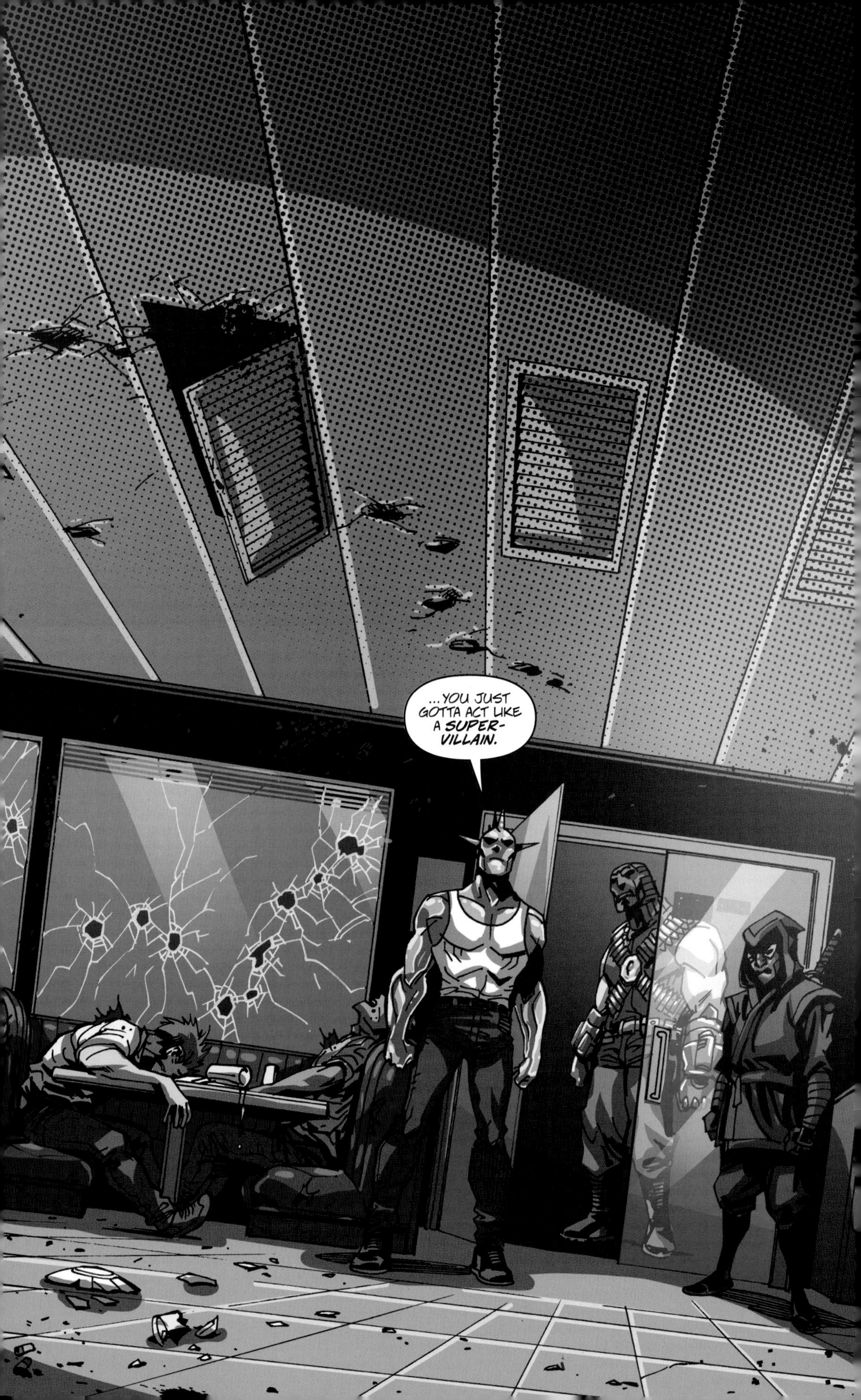
...YOU JUST GOTTA ACT LIKE A SUPER-VILLAIN.

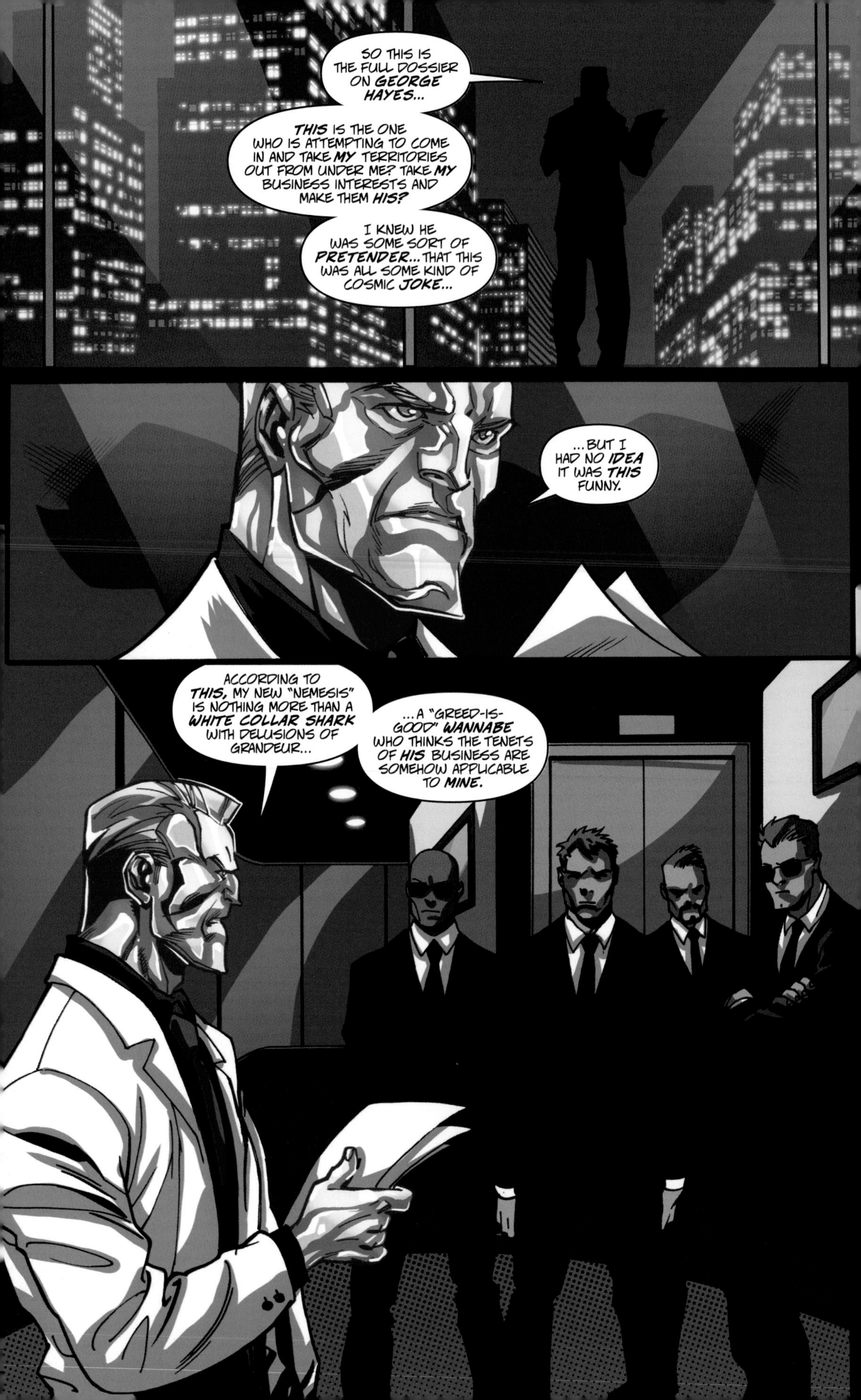
SO THIS IS THE FULL DOSSIER ON GEORGE HAYES...
THIS IS THE ONE WHO IS ATTEMPTING TO COME IN AND TAKE MY TERRITORIES OUT FROM UNDER ME? TAKE MY BUSINESS INTERESTS AND MAKE THEM HIS?
I KNEW HE WAS SOME SORT OF PRETENDER... THAT THIS WAS ALL SOME KIND OF COSMIC JOKE...
...BUT I HAD NO IDEA IT WAS THIS FUNNY.
ACCORDING TO THIS, MY NEW "NEMESIS" IS NOTHING MORE THAN A WHITE COLLAR SHARK WITH DELUSIONS OF GRANDEUR...
...A "GREED-IS-GOOD" WANNABE WHO THINKS THE TENETS OF HIS BUSINESS ARE SOMEHOW APPLICABLE TO MINE.

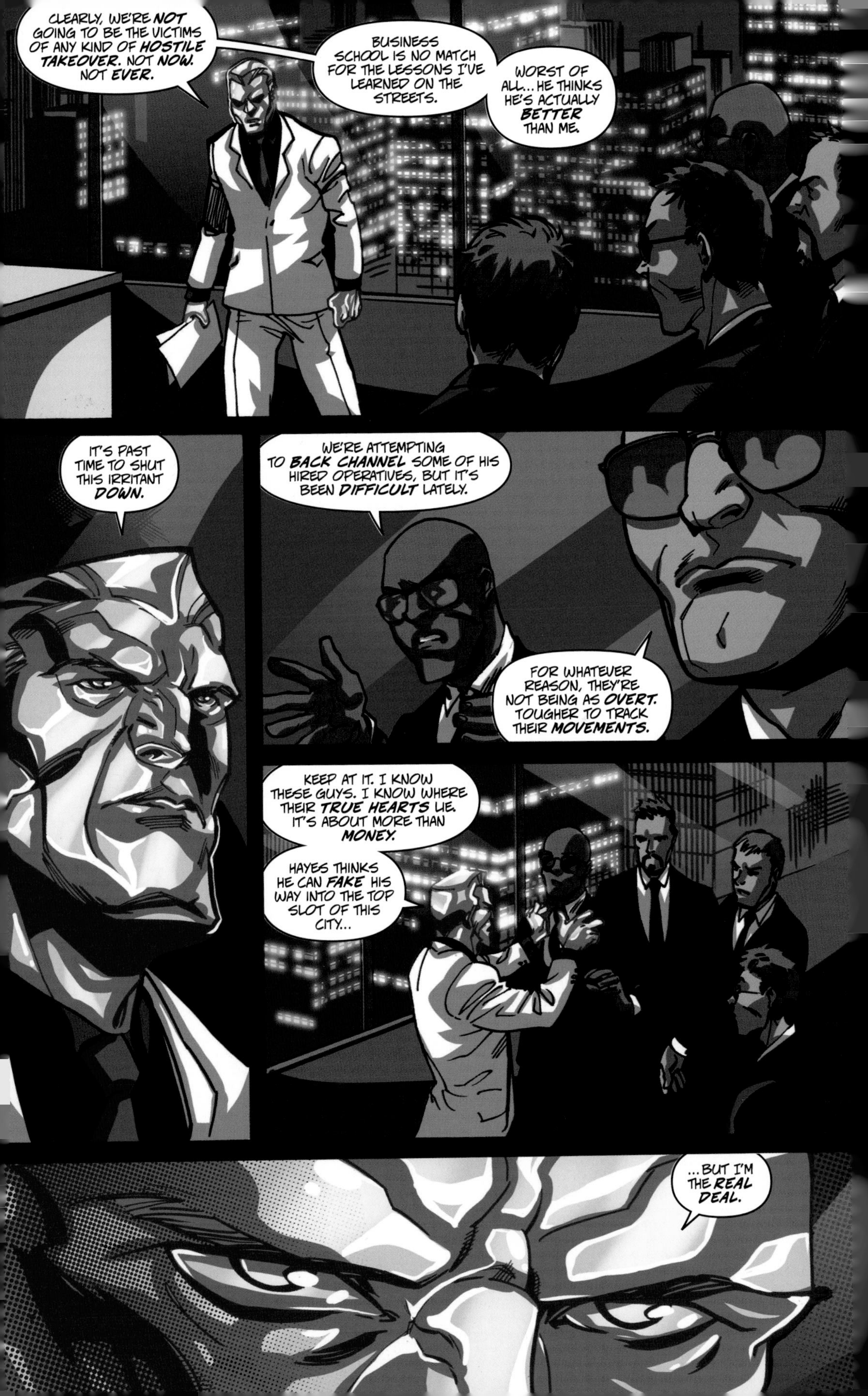
CLEARLY, WE'RE NOT GOING TO BE THE VICTIMS OF ANY KIND OF HOSTILE TAKEOVER. NOT NOW. NOT EVER.
BUSINESS SCHOOL IS NO MATCH FOR THE LESSONS I'VE LEARNED ON THE STREETS.
WORST OF ALL... HE THINKS HE'S ACTUALLY BETTER THAN ME.
IT'S PAST TIME TO SHUT THIS IRRITANT DOWN.
WE'RE ATTEMPTING TO BACK CHANNEL SOME OF HIS HIRED OPERATIVES, BUT IT'S BEEN DIFFICULT LATELY.
FOR WHATEVER REASON, THEY'RE NOT BEING AS OVERT. TOUGHER TO TRACK THEIR MOVEMENTS.
KEEP AT IT. I KNOW THESE GUYS. I KNOW WHERE THEIR TRUE HEARTS LIE. IT'S ABOUT MORE THAN MONEY.
HAYES THINKS HE CAN FAKE HIS WAY INTO THE TOP SLOT OF THIS CITY...
...BUT I'M THE REAL DEAL.

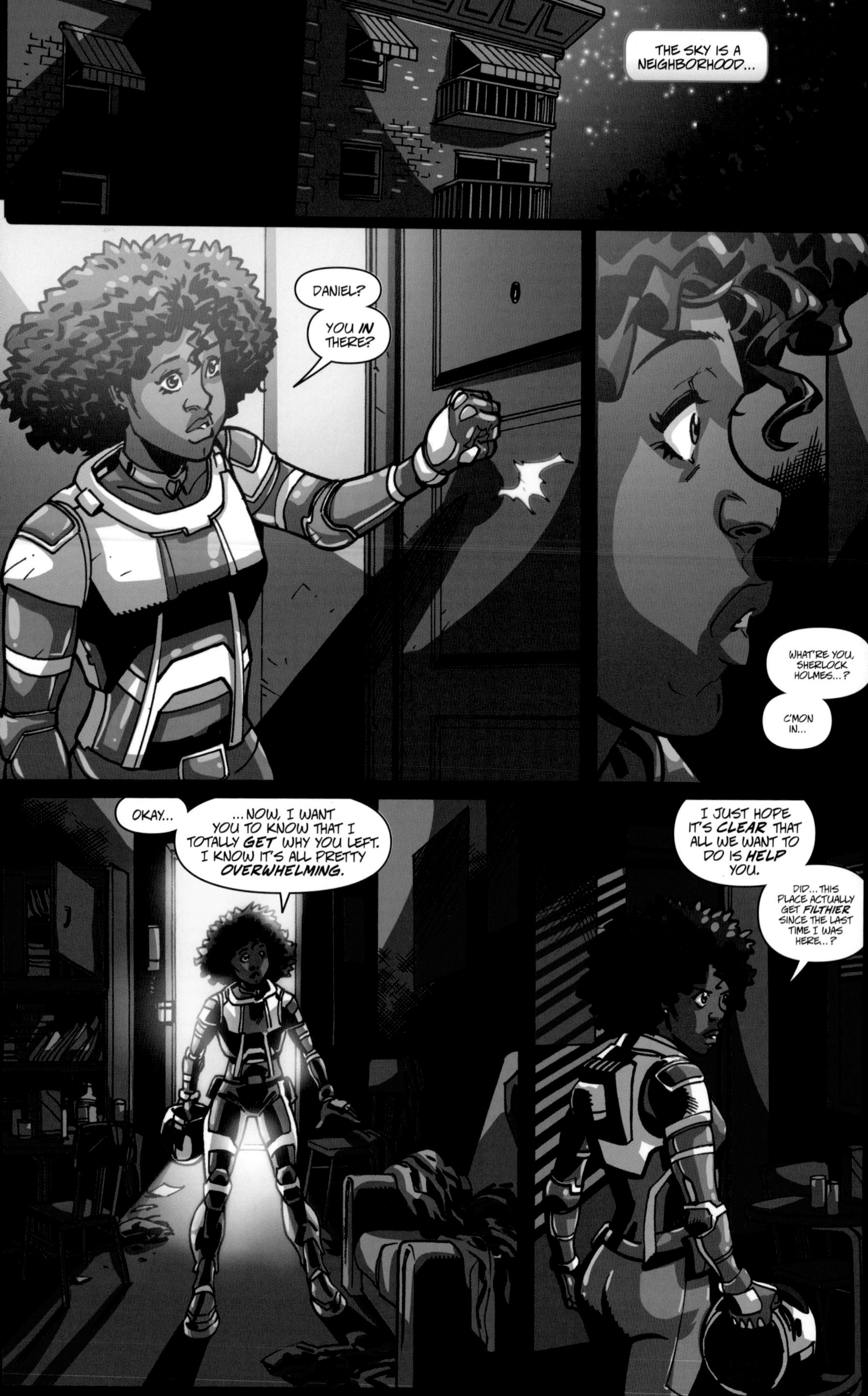
THE SKY IS A NEIGHBORHOOD...
DANIEL?
YOU IN THERE?
WHAT'RE YOU, SHERLOCK HOLMES...?
C'MON IN...
OKAY...
...NOW, I WANT YOU TO KNOW THAT I TOTALLY GET WHY YOU LEFT. I KNOW IT'S ALL PRETTY OVERWHELMING.
I JUST HOPE IT'S CLEAR THAT ALL WE WANT TO DO IS HELP YOU.
DID... THIS PLACE ACTUALLY GET FILTHIER SINCE THE LAST TIME I WAS HERE...?

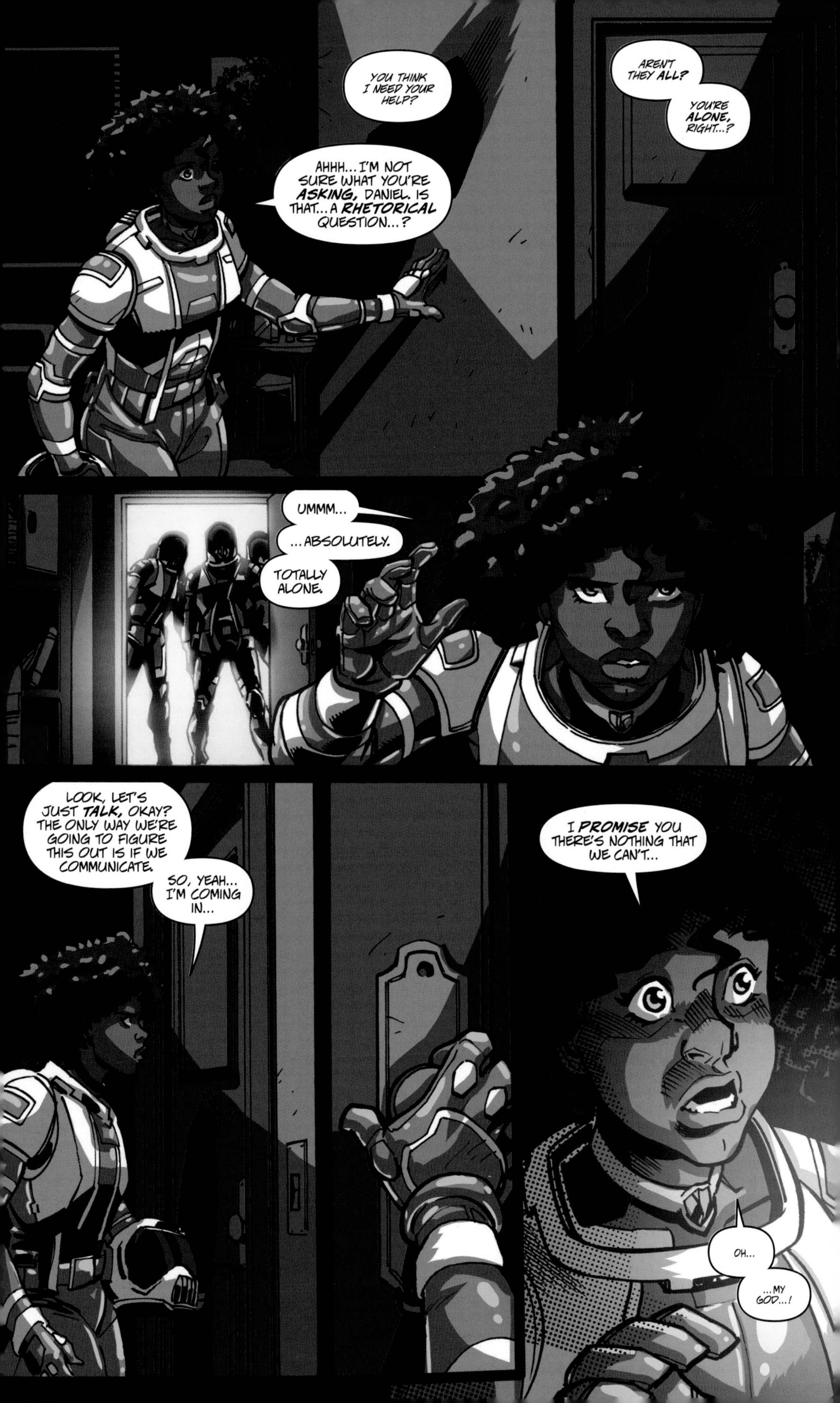
YOU THINK I NEED YOUR HELP?
AHHH... I'M NOT SURE WHAT YOU'RE ASKING, DANIEL. IS THAT... A RHETORICAL QUESTION...?
AREN'T THEY ALL?
YOU'RE ALONE, RIGHT...?
UMMM...
...ABSOLUTELY.
TOTALLY ALONE.
LOOK, LET'S JUST TALK, OKAY? THE ONLY WAY WE'RE GOING TO FIGURE THIS OUT IS IF WE COMMUNICATE.
SO, YEAH... I'M COMING IN...
I PROMISE YOU THERE'S NOTHING THAT WE CAN'T...
OH...
...MY GOD...!

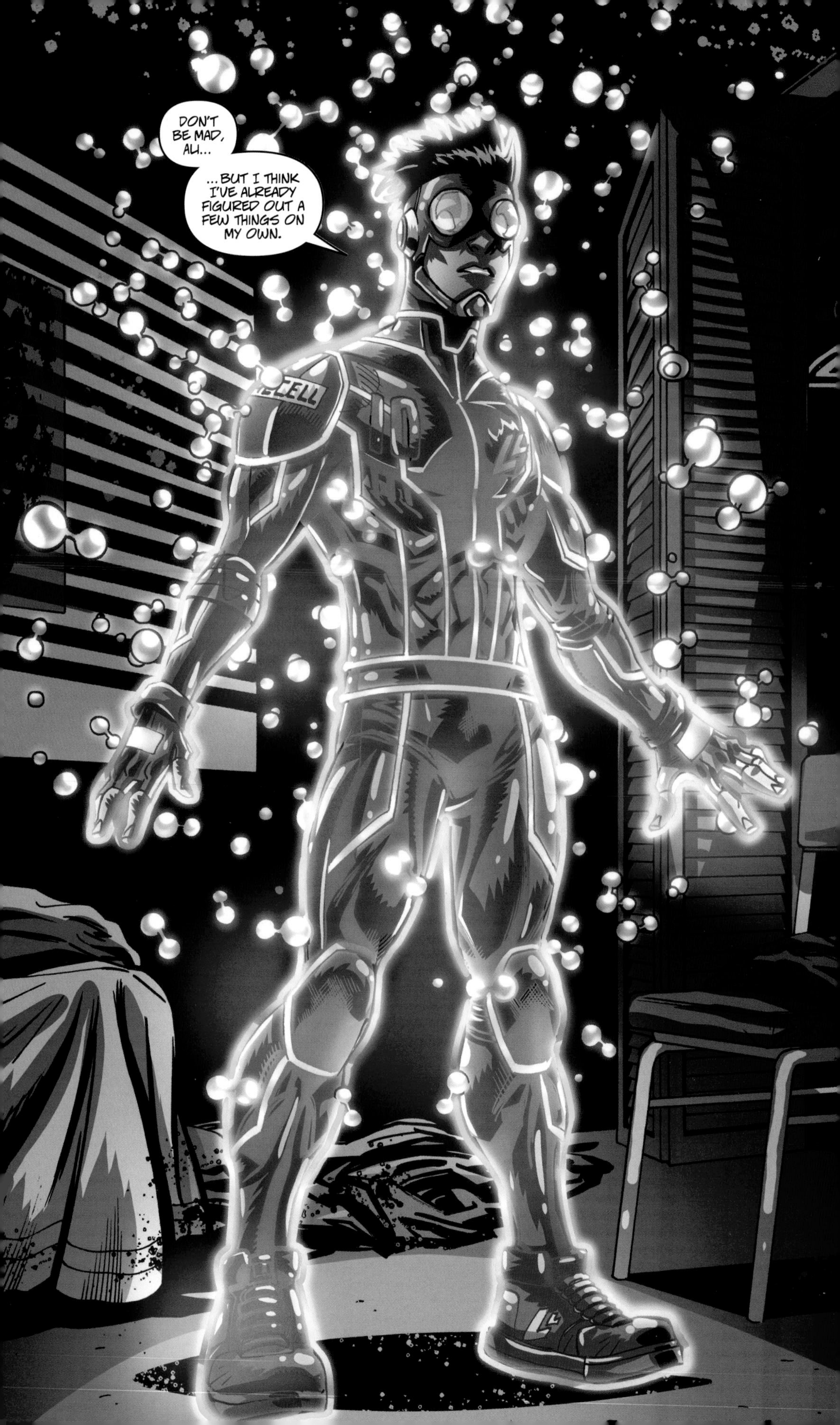
DON'T BE MAD, ALI...
...BUT I THINK I'VE ALREADY FIGURED OUT A FEW THINGS ON MY OWN.

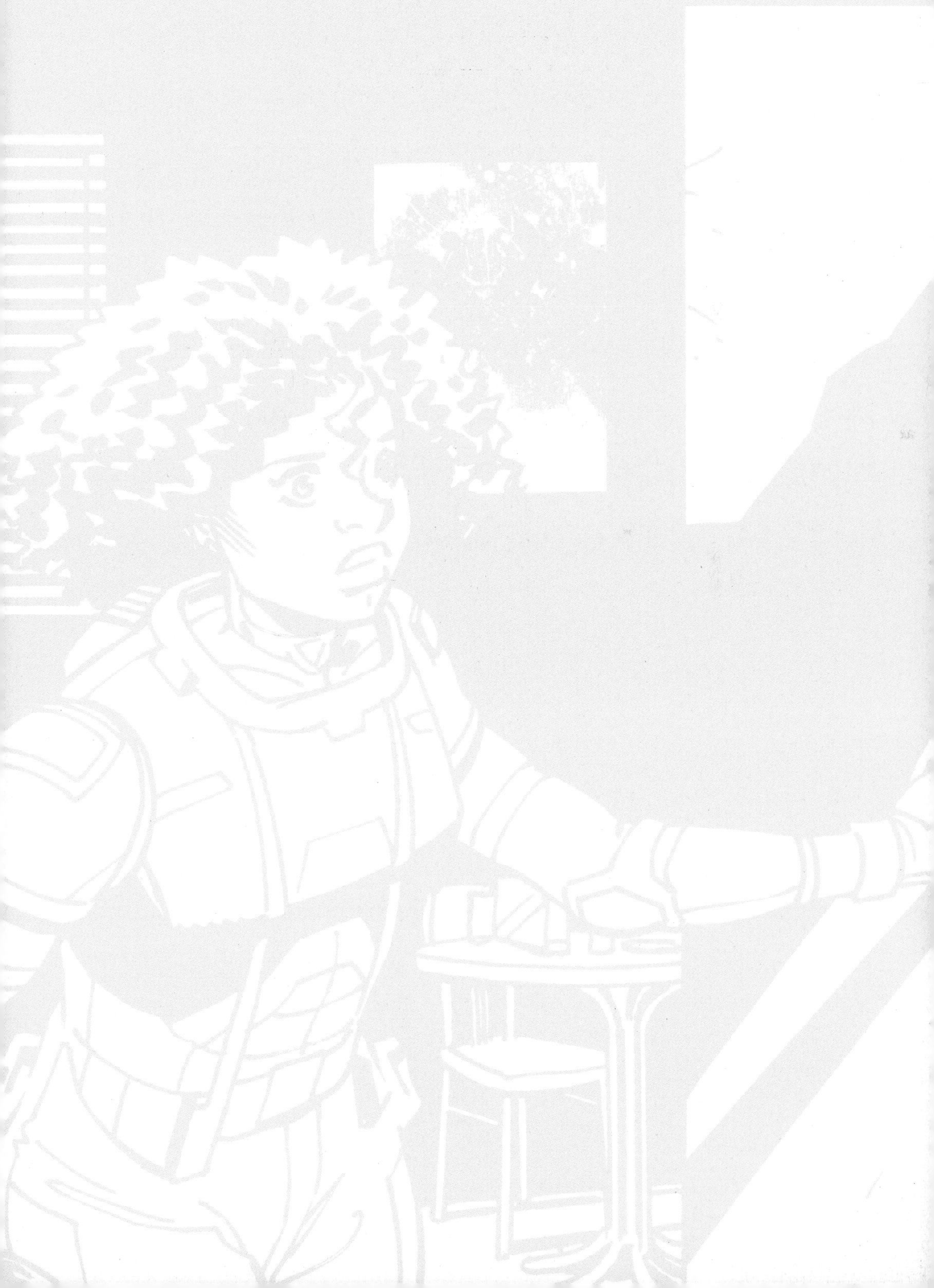

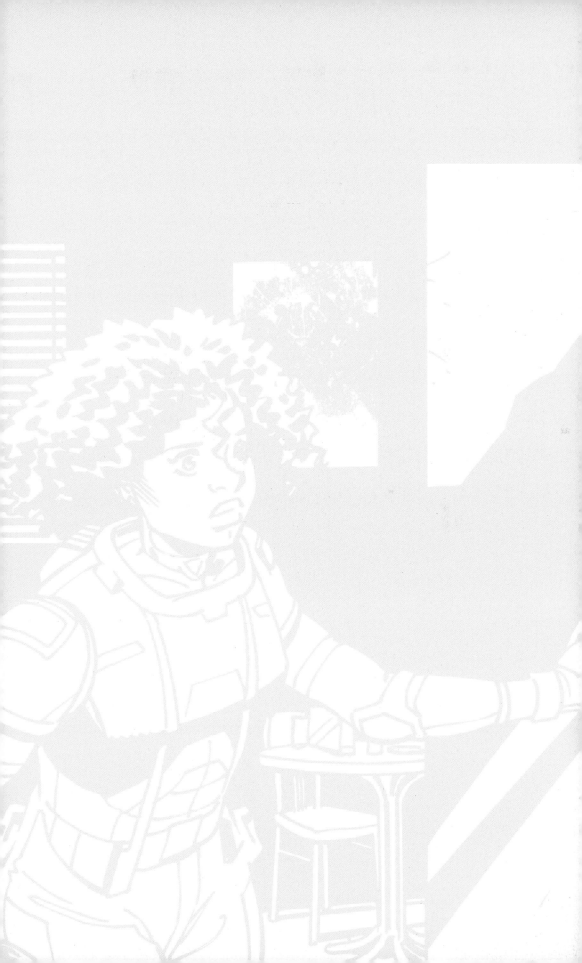

CHAPTER FOUR

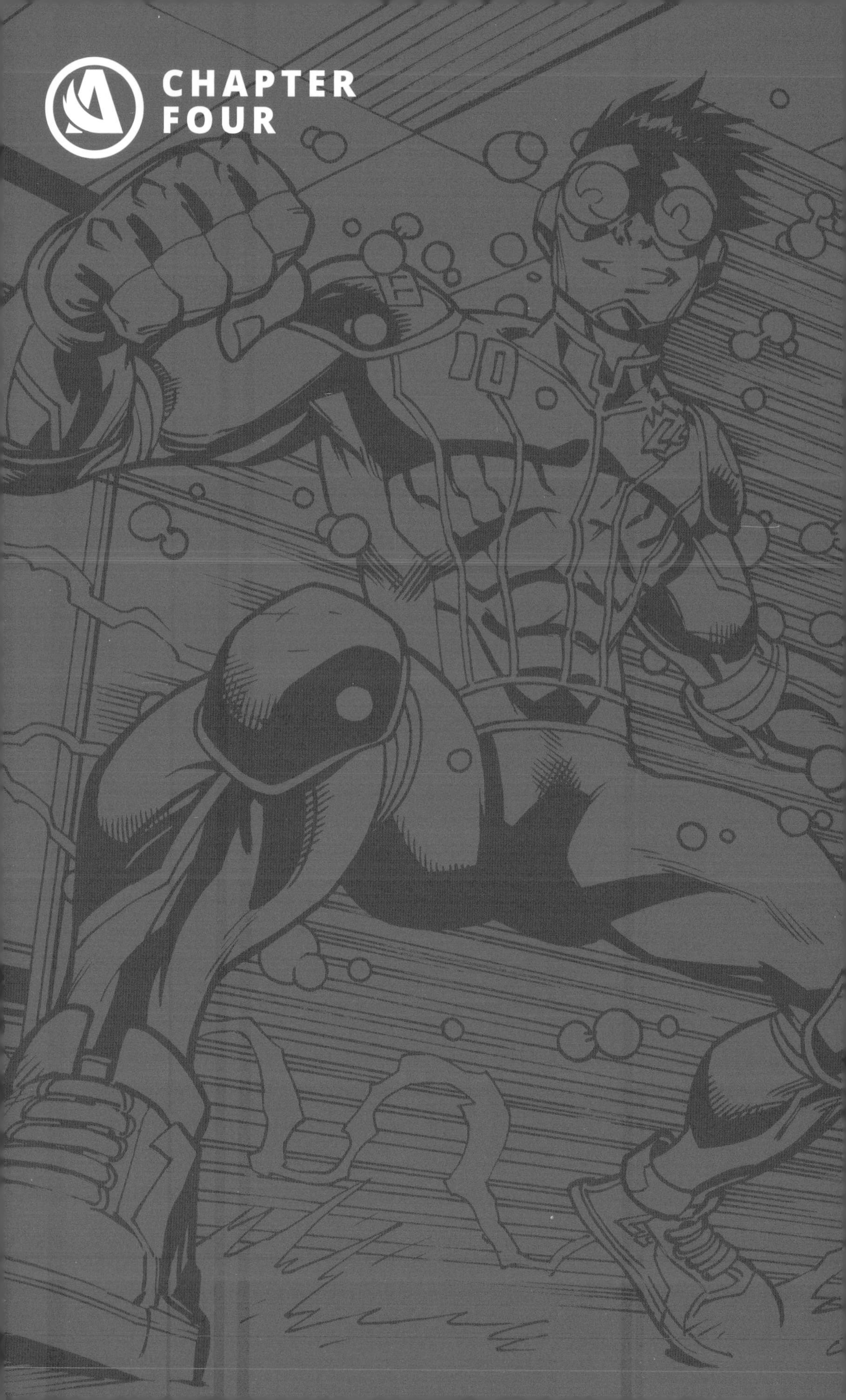

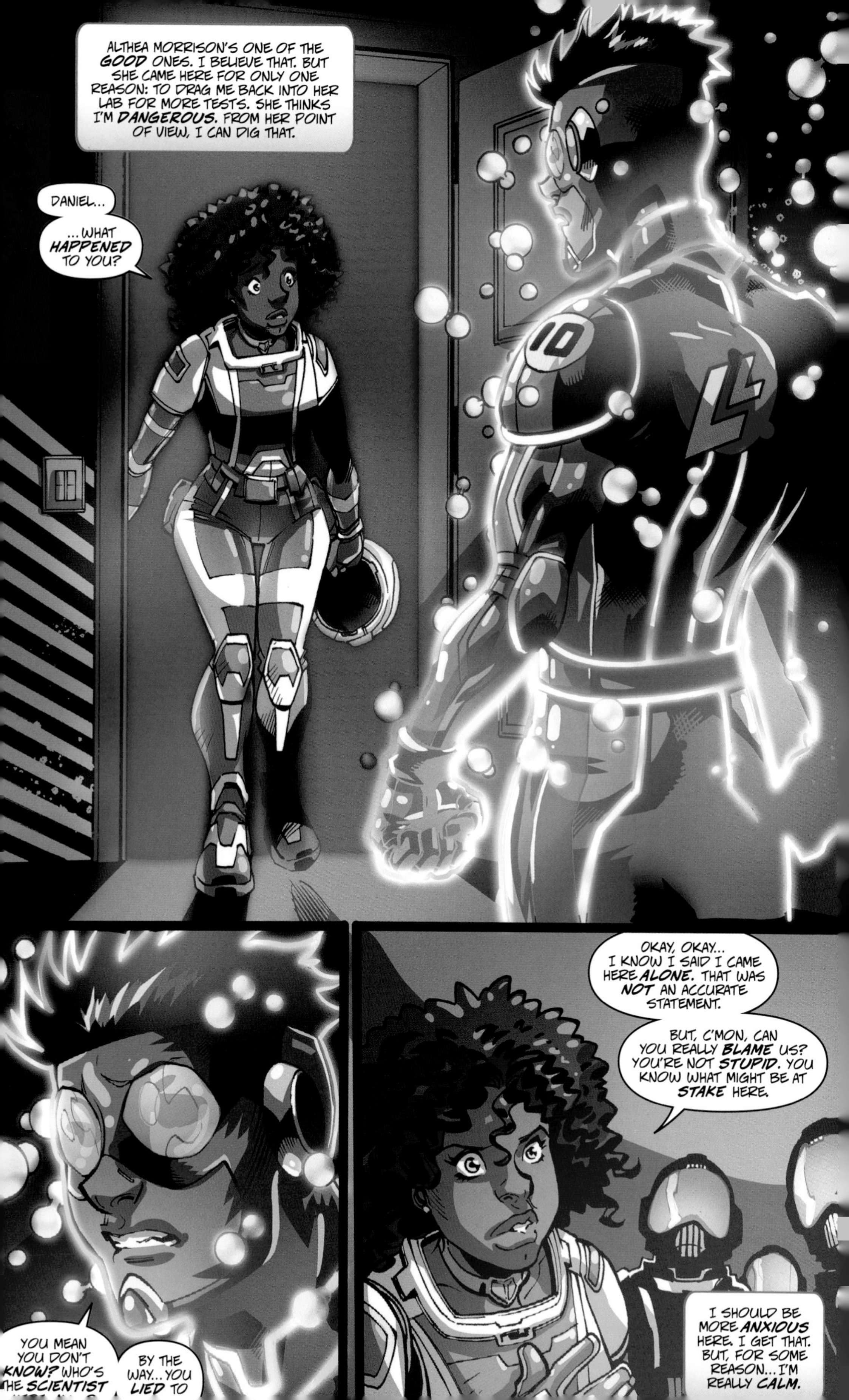
ALTHEA MORRISON'S ONE OF THE GOOD ONES. I BELIEVE THAT. BUT SHE CAME HERE FOR ONLY ONE REASON: TO DRAG ME BACK INTO HER LAB FOR MORE TESTS. SHE THINKS I'M DANGEROUS. FROM HER POINT OF VIEW, I CAN DIG THAT.
DANIEL...
...WHAT HAPPENED TO YOU?
YOU MEAN YOU DON'T KNOW? WHO'S HE SCIENTIST
BY THE WAY... YOU LIED TO
OKAY, OKAY... I KNOW I SAID I CAME HERE ALONE. THAT WAS NOT AN ACCURATE STATEMENT.
BUT, C'MON, CAN YOU REALLY BLAME US? YOU'RE NOT STUPID. YOU KNOW WHAT MIGHT BE AT STAKE HERE.
I SHOULD BE MORE ANXIOUS HERE. I GET THAT. BUT, FOR SOME REASON... I'M REALLY CALM.

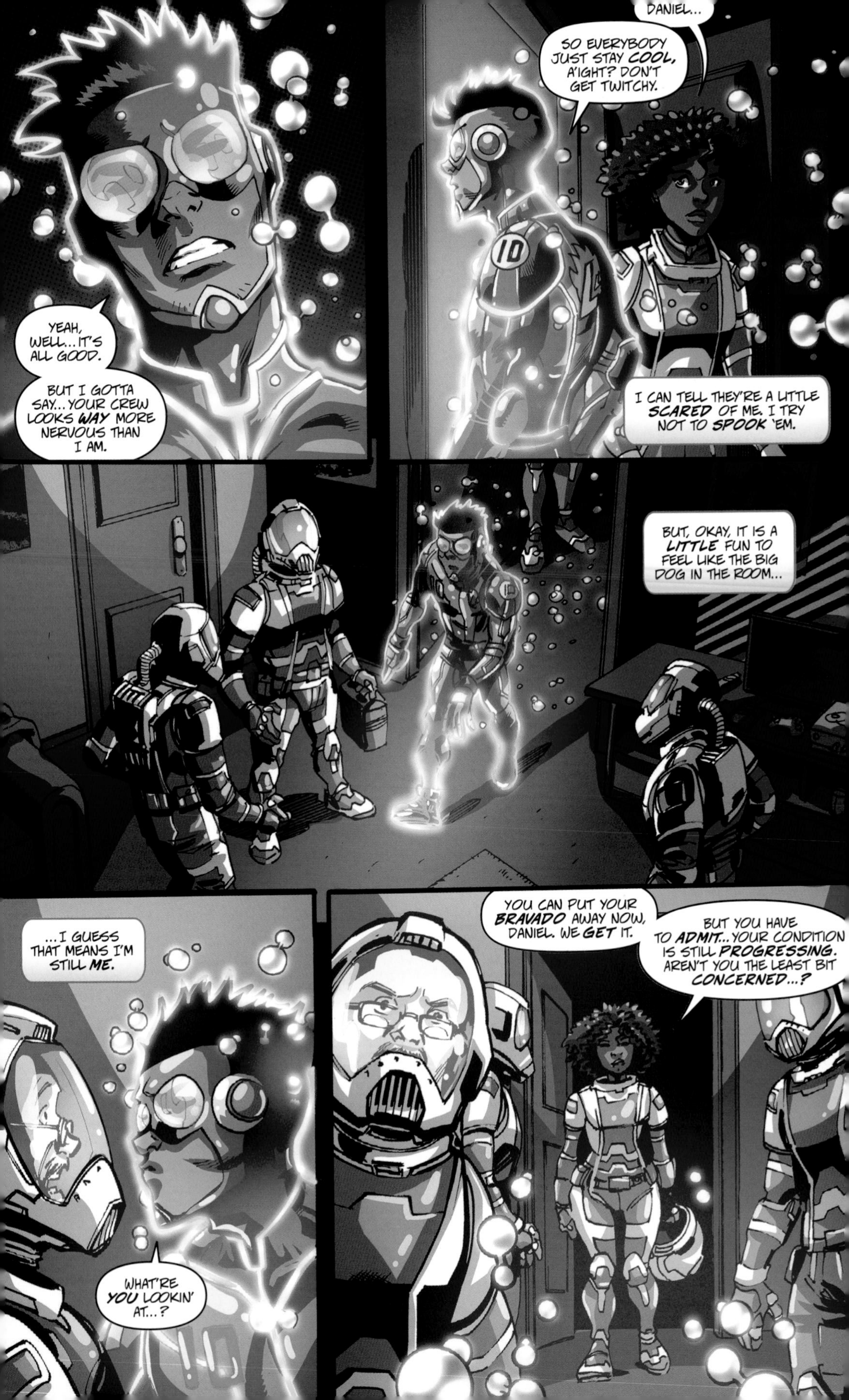
YEAH, WELL... IT'S ALL GOOD.
BUT I GOTTA SAY... YOUR CREW LOOKS WAY MORE NERVOUS THAN I AM.
DANIEL...
SO EVERYBODY JUST STAY COOL, A'IGHT? DON'T GET TWITCHY.
I CAN TELL THEY'RE A LITTLE SCARED OF ME. I TRY NOT TO SPOOK 'EM.
BUT, OKAY, IT IS A LITTLE FUN TO FEEL LIKE THE BIG DOG IN THE ROOM...
...I GUESS THAT MEANS I'M STILL ME.
WHAT'RE YOU LOOKIN' AT...?
YOU CAN PUT YOUR BRAVADO AWAY NOW, DANIEL. WE GET IT.
BUT YOU HAVE TO ADMIT... YOUR CONDITION IS STILL PROGRESSING. AREN'T YOU THE LEAST BIT CONCERNED...?

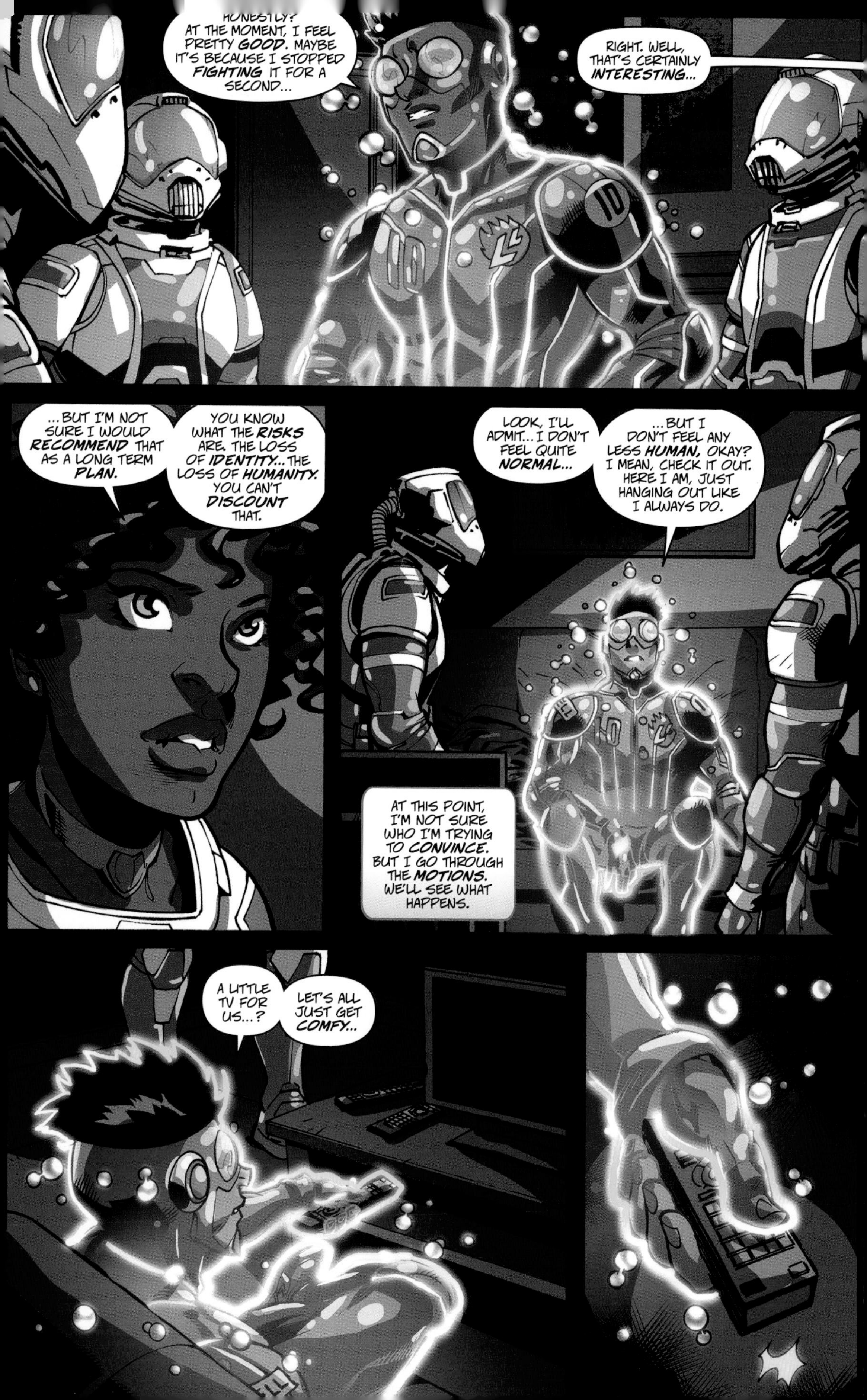
HONESTLY? AT THE MOMENT, I FEEL PRETTY GOOD. MAYBE IT'S BECAUSE I STOPPED FIGHTING IT FOR A SECOND...
RIGHT. WELL, THAT'S CERTAINLY INTERESTING...
...BUT I'M NOT SURE I WOULD RECOMMEND THAT AS A LONG TERM PLAN.
YOU KNOW WHAT THE RISKS ARE. THE LOSS OF IDENTITY... THE LOSS OF HUMANITY. YOU CAN'T DISCOUNT THAT.
LOOK, I'LL ADMIT... I DON'T FEEL QUITE NORMAL...
...BUT I DON'T FEEL ANY LESS HUMAN, OKAY? I MEAN, CHECK IT OUT. HERE I AM, JUST HANGING OUT LIKE I ALWAYS DO.
AT THIS POINT, I'M NOT SURE WHO I'M TRYING TO CONVINCE. BUT I GO THROUGH THE MOTIONS. WE'LL SEE WHAT HAPPENS.
A LITTLE TV FOR US...?
LET'S ALL JUST GET COMFY...

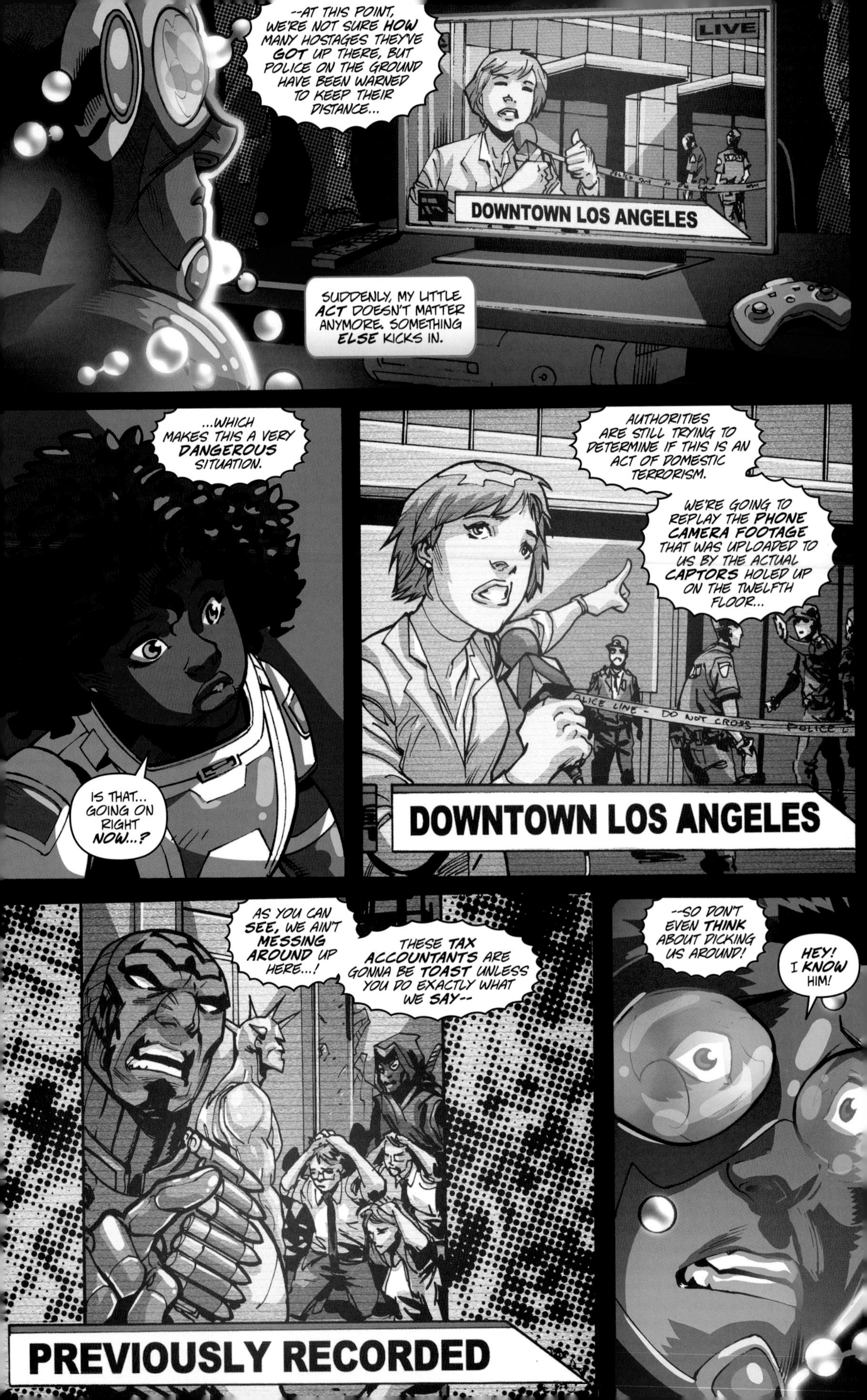
--AT THIS POINT, WE'RE NOT SURE HOW MANY HOSTAGES THEY'VE GOT UP THERE, BUT POLICE ON THE GROUND HAVE BEEN WARNED TO KEEP THEIR DISTANCE...
LIVE
DOWNTOWN LOS ANGELES
SUDDENLY, MY LITTLE ACT DOESN'T MATTER ANYMORE. SOMETHING ELSE KICKS IN.
...WHICH MAKES THIS A VERY DANGEROUS SITUATION.
IS THAT... GOING ON RIGHT NOW...?
AUTHORITIES ARE STILL TRYING TO DETERMINE IF THIS IS AN ACT OF DOMESTIC TERRORISM.
WE'RE GOING TO REPLAY THE PHONE CAMERA FOOTAGE THAT WAS UPLOADED TO US BY THE ACTUAL CAPTORS HOLED UP ON THE TWELFTH FLOOR...
POLICE LINE - DO NOT CROSS
DOWNTOWN LOS ANGELES
AS YOU CAN SEE, WE AIN'T MESSING AROUND UP HERE...!
THESE TAX ACCOUNTANTS ARE GONNA BE TOAST UNLESS YOU DO EXACTLY WHAT WE SAY--
PREVIOUSLY RECORDED
--SO DON'T EVEN THINK ABOUT DICKING US AROUND!
HEY! I KNOW HIM!

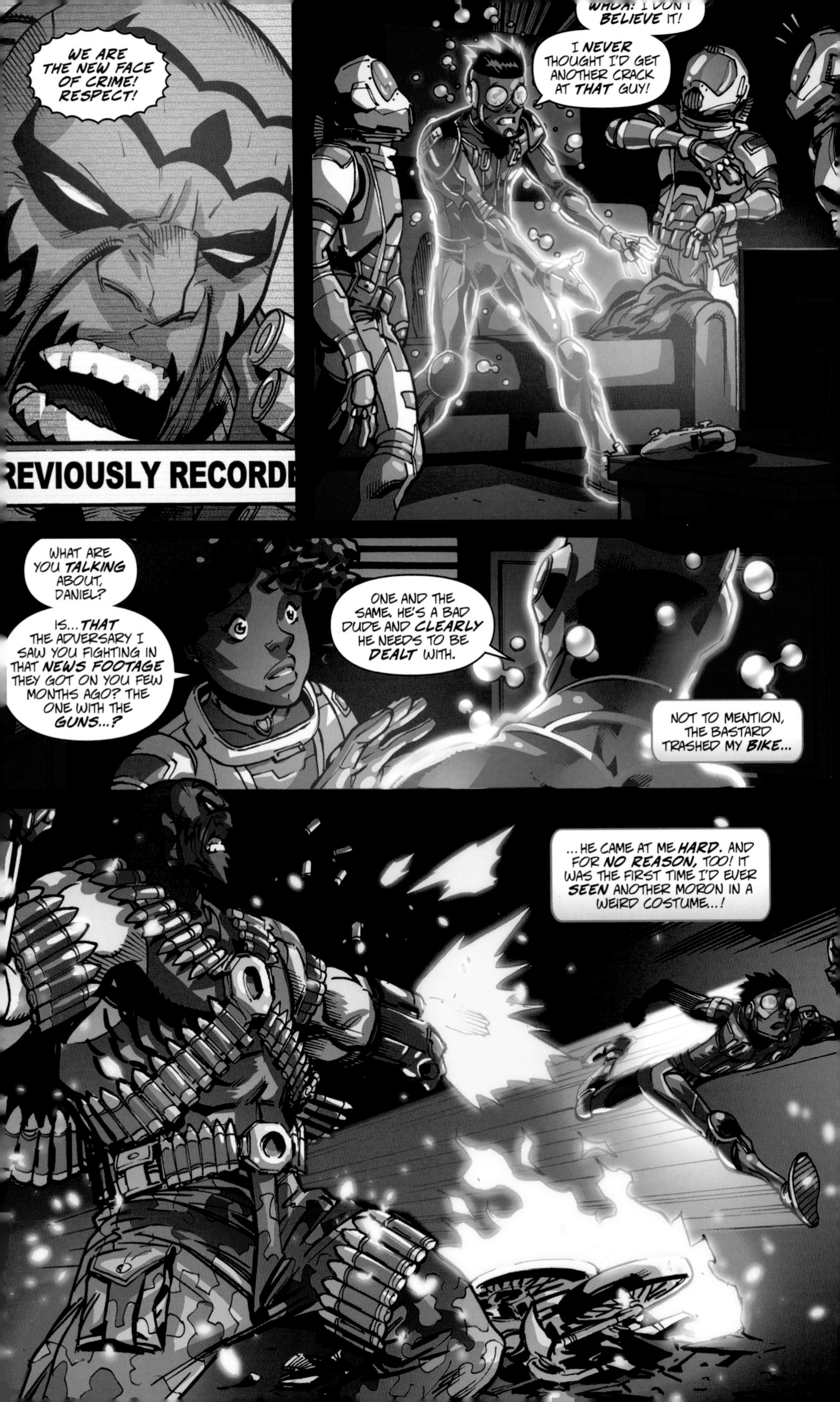
WE ARE THE NEW FACE OF CRIME! RESPECT!
REVIOUSLY RECORDE
WHOA! I DON'T BELIEVE IT!
I NEVER THOUGHT I'D GET ANOTHER CRACK AT THAT GUY!
WHAT ARE YOU TALKING ABOUT, DANIEL?
IS...THAT THE ADVERSARY I SAW YOU FIGHTING IN THAT NEWS FOOTAGE THEY GOT ON YOU FEW MONTHS AGO? THE ONE WITH THE GUNS...?
ONE AND THE SAME. HE'S A BAD DUDE AND CLEARLY HE NEEDS TO BE DEALT WITH.
NOT TO MENTION, THE BASTARD TRASHED MY BIKE...
...HE CAME AT ME HARD. AND FOR NO REASON, TOO! IT WAS THE FIRST TIME I'D EVER SEEN ANOTHER MORON IN A WEIRD COSTUME...!

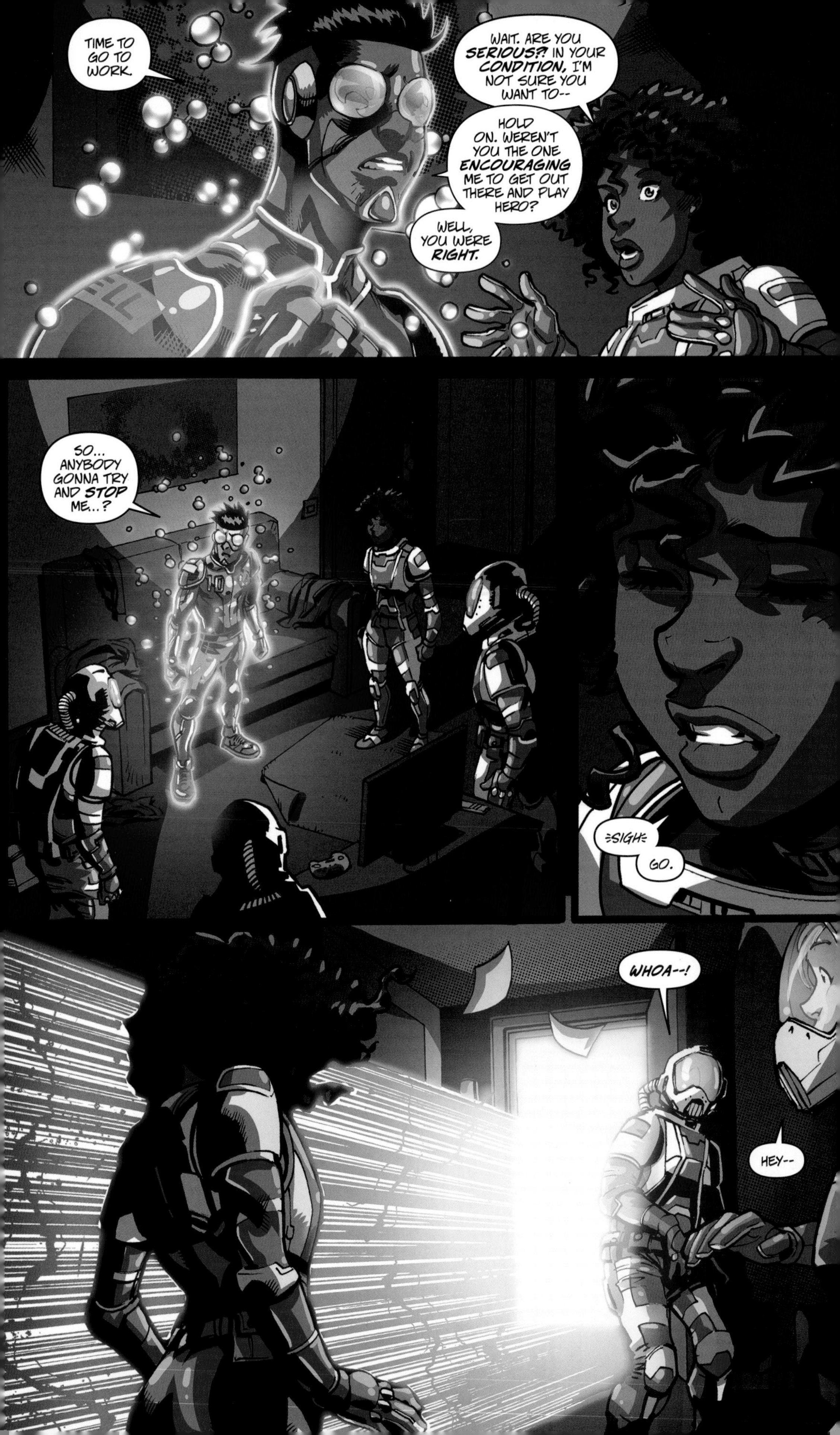
TIME TO GO TO WORK.
WAIT. ARE YOU SERIOUS?! IN YOUR CONDITION, I'M NOT SURE YOU WANT TO--
HOLD ON. WEREN'T YOU THE ONE ENCOURAGING ME TO GET OUT THERE AND PLAY HERO?
WELL, YOU WERE RIGHT.
SO... ANYBODY GONNA TRY AND STOP ME...?
≈SIGH≈
GO.
WHOA--!
HEY--

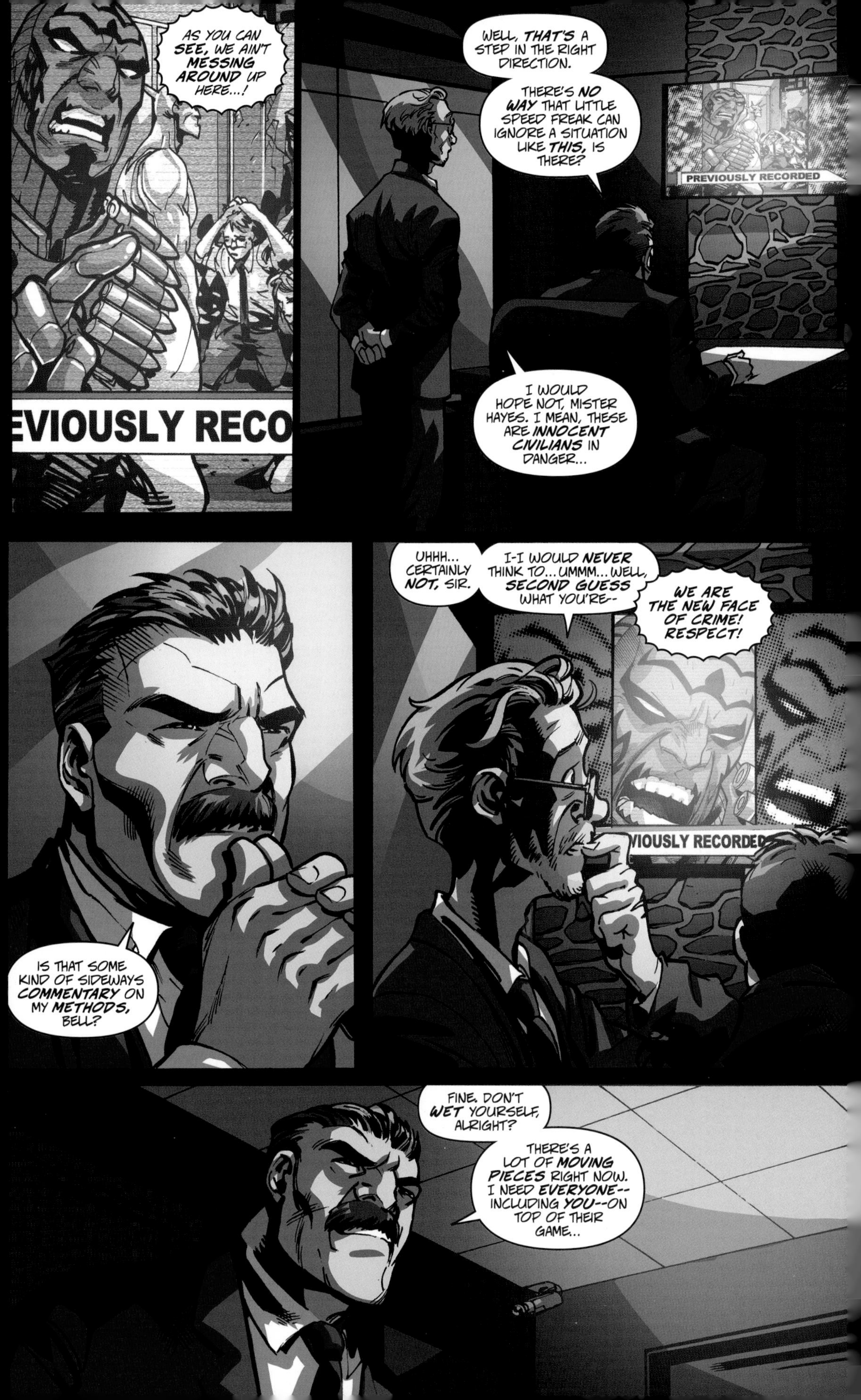
AS YOU CAN SEE, WE AIN'T MESSING AROUND UP HERE...!
EVIOUSLY RECO
WELL, THAT'S A STEP IN THE RIGHT DIRECTION.
THERE'S NO WAY THAT LITTLE SPEED FREAK CAN IGNORE A SITUATION LIKE THIS, IS THERE?
PREVIOUSLY RECORDED
I WOULD HOPE NOT, MISTER HAYES. I MEAN, THESE ARE INNOCENT CIVILIANS IN DANGER...
IS THAT SOME KIND OF SIDEWAYS COMMENTARY ON MY METHODS, BELL?
UHHH... CERTAINLY NOT, SIR.
I-I WOULD NEVER THINK TO... UMMM... WELL, SECOND GUESS WHAT YOU'RE--
WE ARE THE NEW FACE OF CRIME! RESPECT!
VIOUSLY RECORDED
FINE. DON'T WET YOURSELF, ALRIGHT?
THERE'S A LOT OF MOVING PIECES RIGHT NOW. I NEED EVERYONE--INCLUDING YOU--ON TOP OF THEIR GAME...

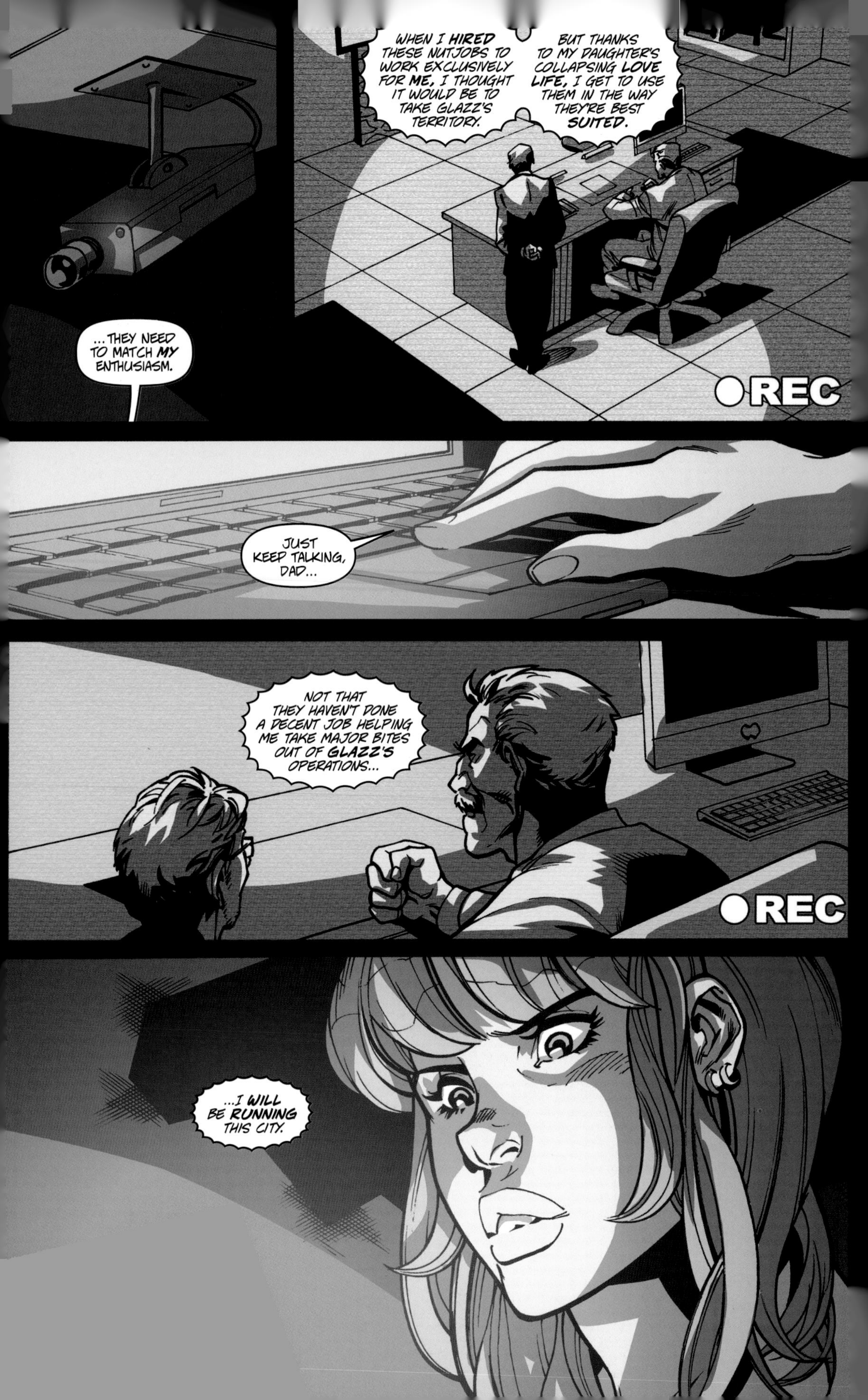
WHEN I HIRED THESE NUTJOBS TO WORK EXCLUSIVELY FOR ME, I THOUGHT IT WOULD BE TO TAKE GLAZZ'S TERRITORY.
BUT THANKS TO MY DAUGHTER'S COLLAPSING LOVE LIFE, I GET TO USE THEM IN THE WAY THEY'RE BEST SUITED.
...THEY NEED TO MATCH MY ENTHUSIASM.
REC
JUST KEEP TALKING, DAD...
NOT THAT THEY HAVEN'T DONE A DECENT JOB HELPING ME TAKE MAJOR BITES OUT OF GLAZZ'S OPERATIONS...
REC
...I WILL BE RUNNING THIS CITY.

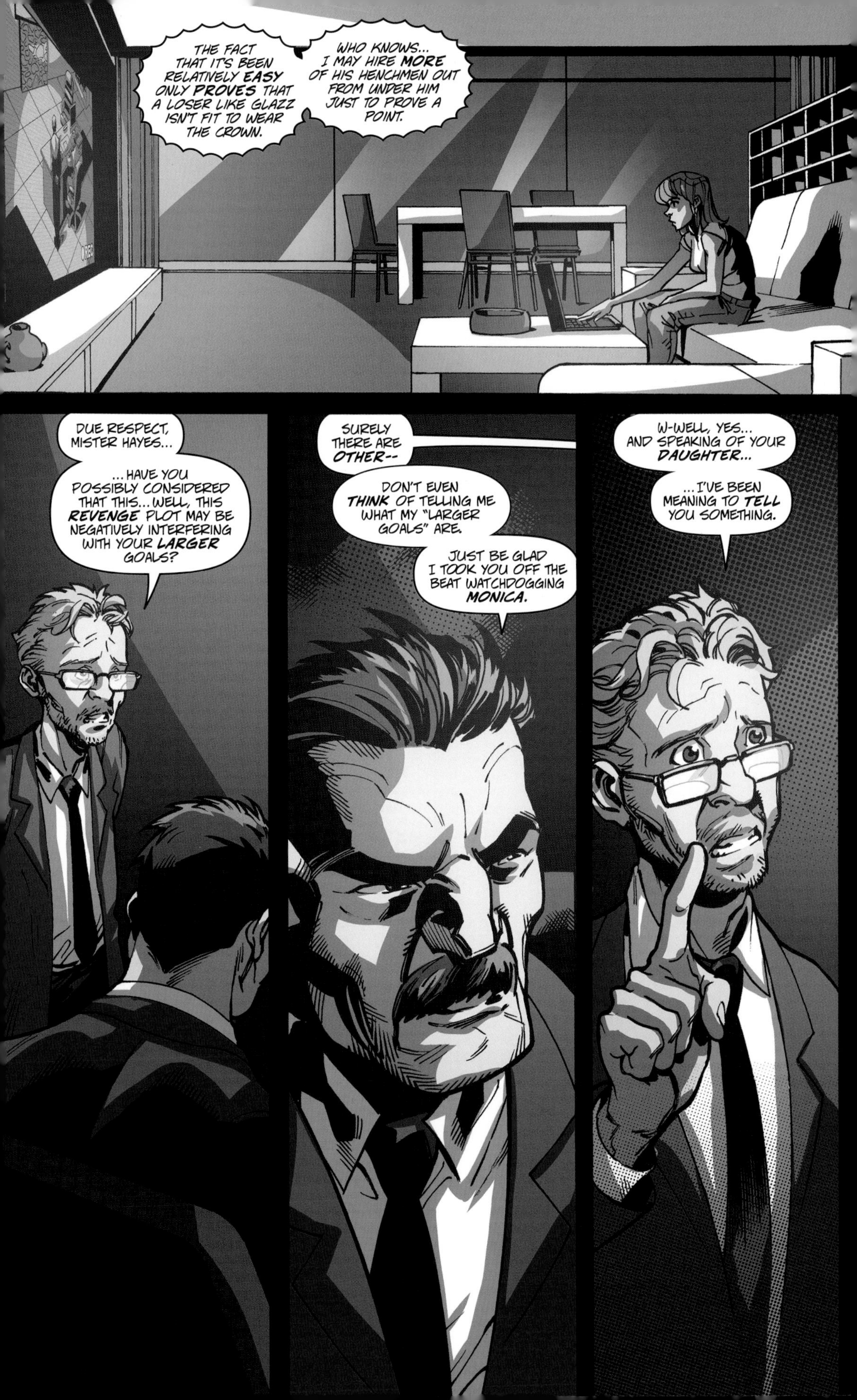
THE FACT THAT IT'S BEEN RELATIVELY EASY ONLY PROVES THAT A LOSER LIKE GLAZZ ISN'T FIT TO WEAR THE CROWN.
WHO KNOWS... I MAY HIRE MORE OF HIS HENCHMEN OUT FROM UNDER HIM JUST TO PROVE A POINT.
DUE RESPECT, MISTER HAYES...
...HAVE YOU POSSIBLY CONSIDERED THAT THIS...WELL, THIS REVENGE PLOT MAY BE NEGATIVELY INTERFERING WITH YOUR LARGER GOALS?
SURELY THERE ARE OTHER--
DON'T EVEN THINK OF TELLING ME WHAT MY "LARGER GOALS" ARE.
JUST BE GLAD I TOOK YOU OFF THE BEAT WATCHDOGGING MONICA.
W-WELL, YES... AND SPEAKING OF YOUR DAUGHTER...
...I'VE BEEN MEANING TO TELL YOU SOMETHING.

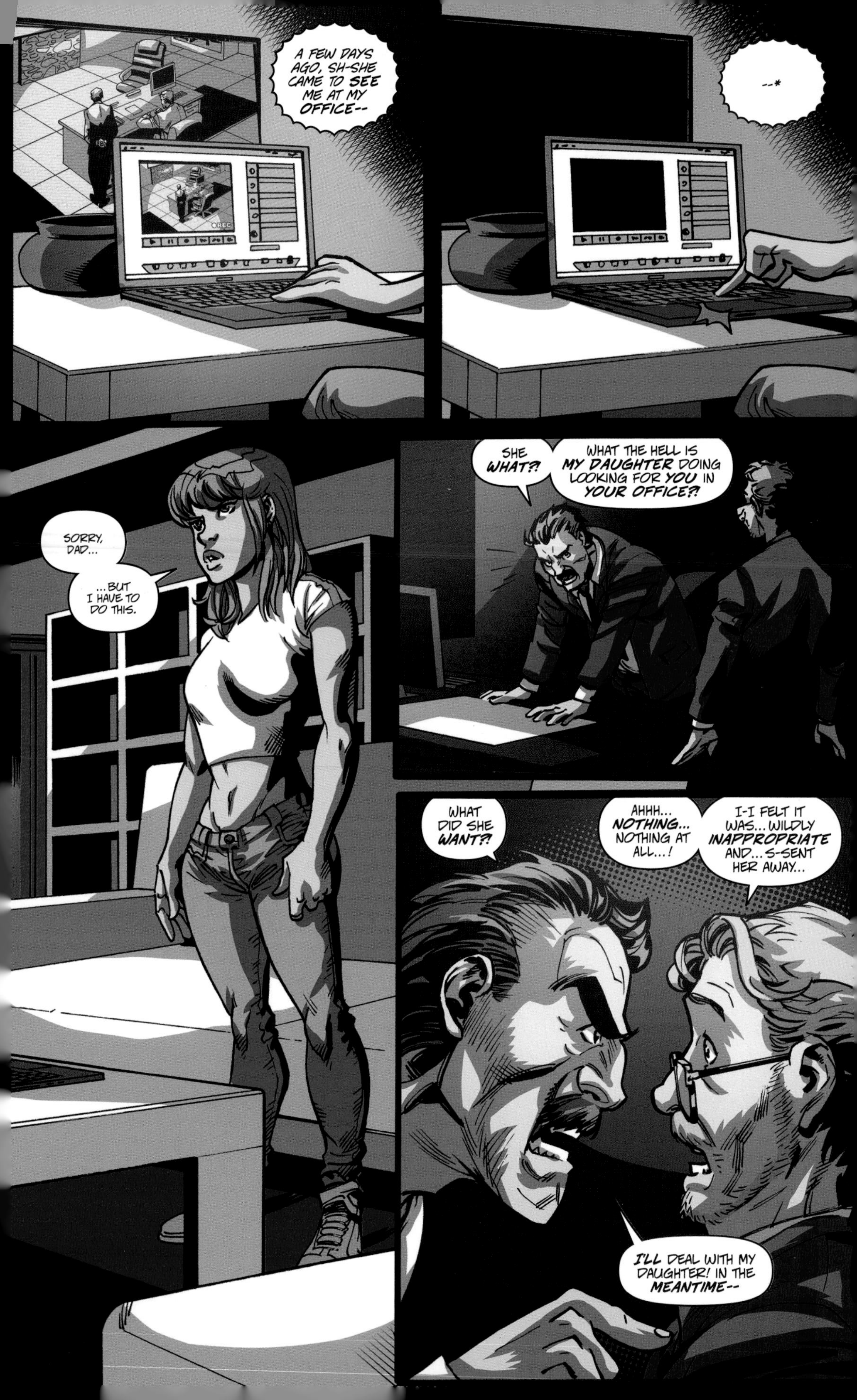
A FEW DAYS AGO, SH-SHE CAME TO SEE ME AT MY OFFICE--
--*
SORRY, DAD...
...BUT I HAVE TO DO THIS.
SHE WHAT?!
WHAT THE HELL IS MY DAUGHTER DOING LOOKING FOR YOU IN YOUR OFFICE?!
WHAT DID SHE WANT?!
AHHH... NOTHING... NOTHING AT ALL...!
I-I FELT IT WAS... WILDLY INAPPROPRIATE AND... S-SENT HER AWAY...
I'LL DEAL WITH MY DAUGHTER! IN THE MEANTIME--

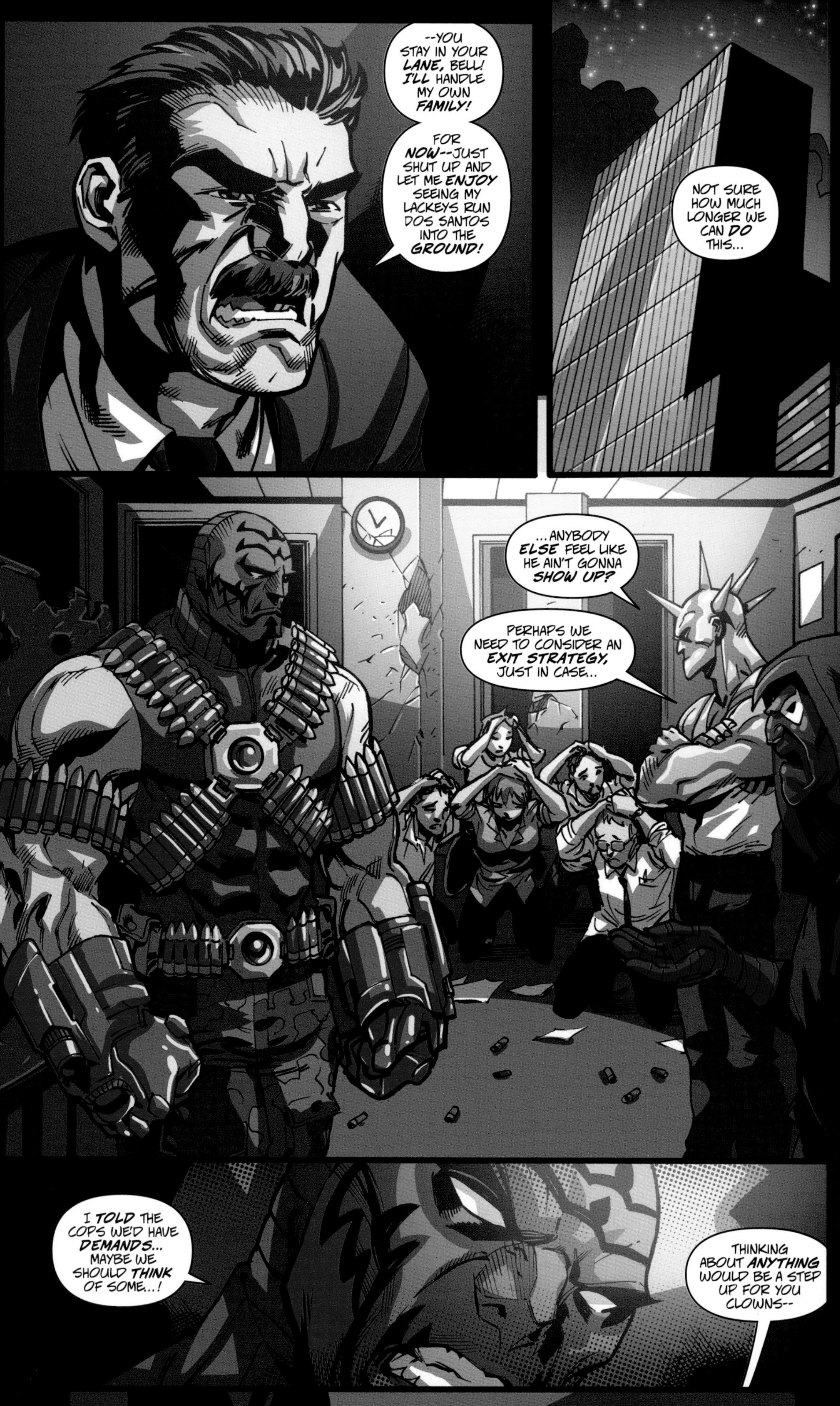
--YOU STAY IN YOUR LANE, BELL! I'LL HANDLE MY OWN FAMILY!
FOR NOW--JUST SHUT UP AND LET ME ENJOY SEEING MY LACKEYS RUN DOS SANTOS INTO THE GROUND!
NOT SURE HOW MUCH LONGER WE CAN DO THIS...
...ANYBODY ELSE FEEL LIKE HE AIN'T GONNA SHOW UP?
PERHAPS WE NEED TO CONSIDER AN EXIT STRATEGY, JUST IN CASE...
I TOLD THE COPS WE'D HAVE DEMANDS... MAYBE WE SHOULD THINK OF SOME...!
THINKING ABOUT ANYTHING WOULD BE A STEP UP FOR YOU CLOWNS--

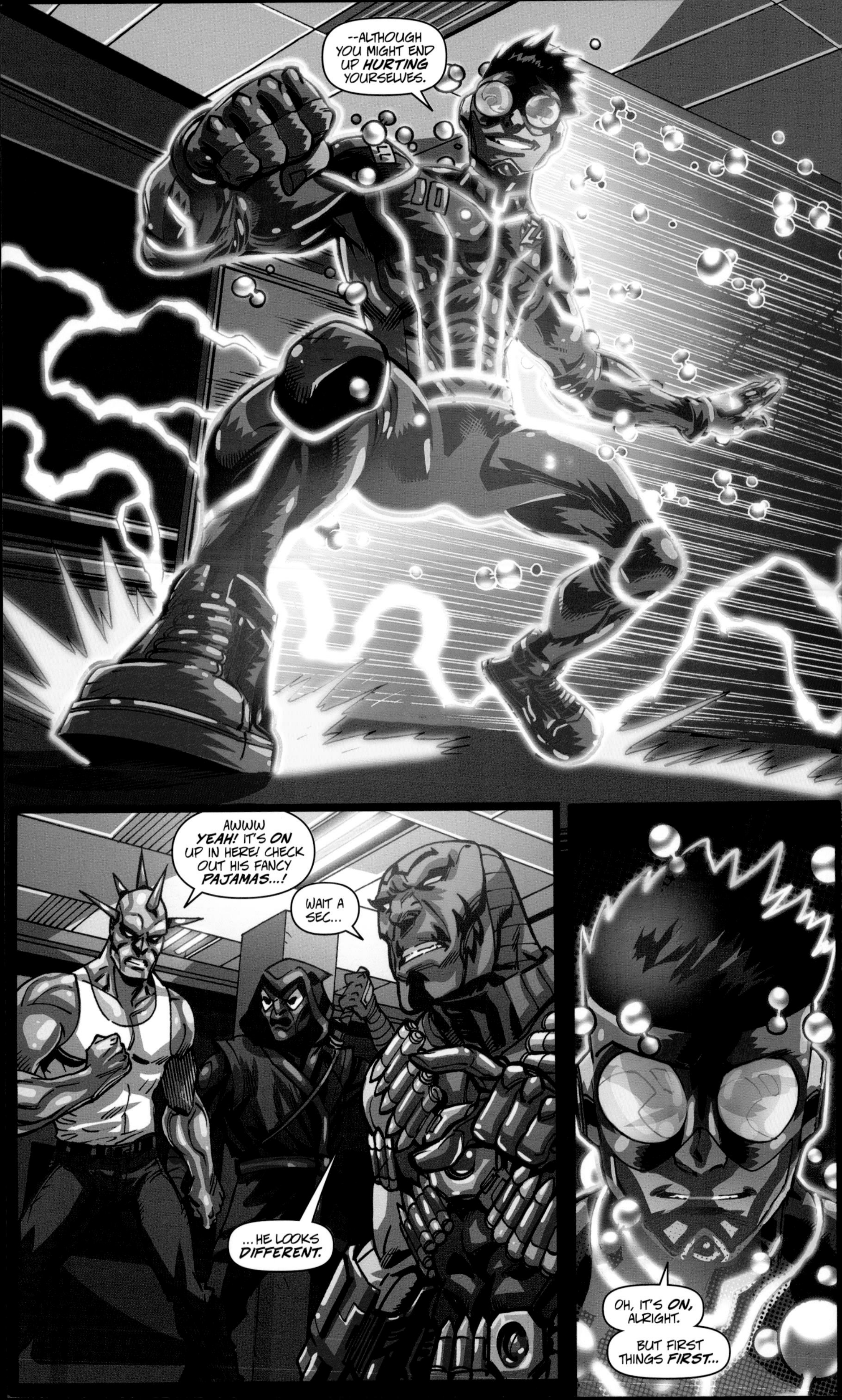
--ALTHOUGH YOU MIGHT END UP **HURTING** YOURSELVES.
AWWW **YEAH!** IT'S **ON** UP IN HERE! CHECK OUT HIS FANCY **PAJAMAS**...!
WAIT A SEC...
...HE LOOKS **DIFFERENT**.
OH, IT'S **ON**, ALRIGHT.
BUT FIRST THINGS **FIRST**...

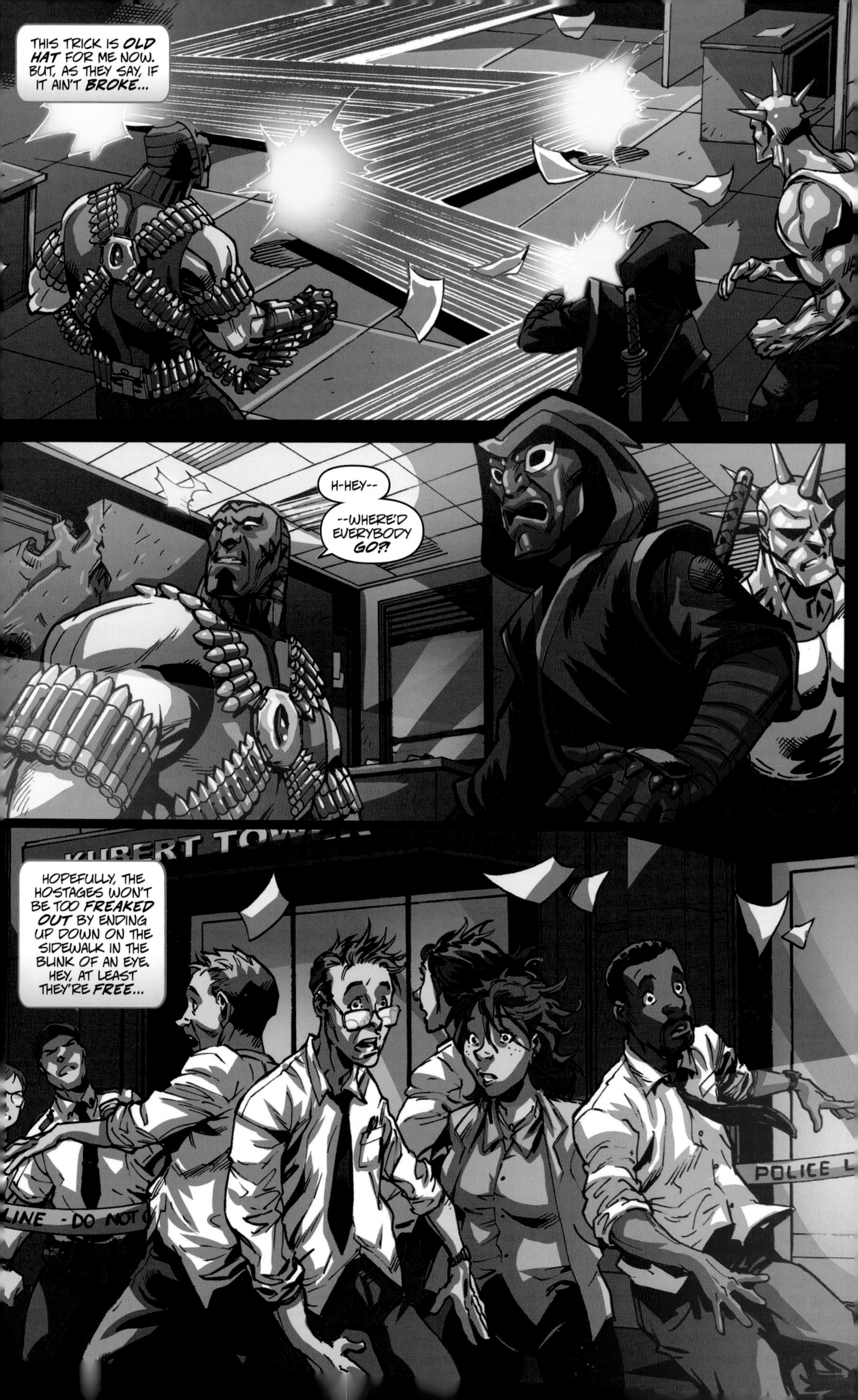
THIS TRICK IS OLD HAT FOR ME NOW. BUT, AS THEY SAY, IF IT AIN'T BROKE...
H-HEY--
--WHERE'D EVERYBODY GO?!
KUBERT TOW
HOPEFULLY, THE HOSTAGES WON'T BE TOO FREAKED OUT BY ENDING UP DOWN ON THE SIDEWALK IN THE BLINK OF AN EYE. HEY, AT LEAST THEY'RE FREE...
POLICE L
LINE - DO NOT

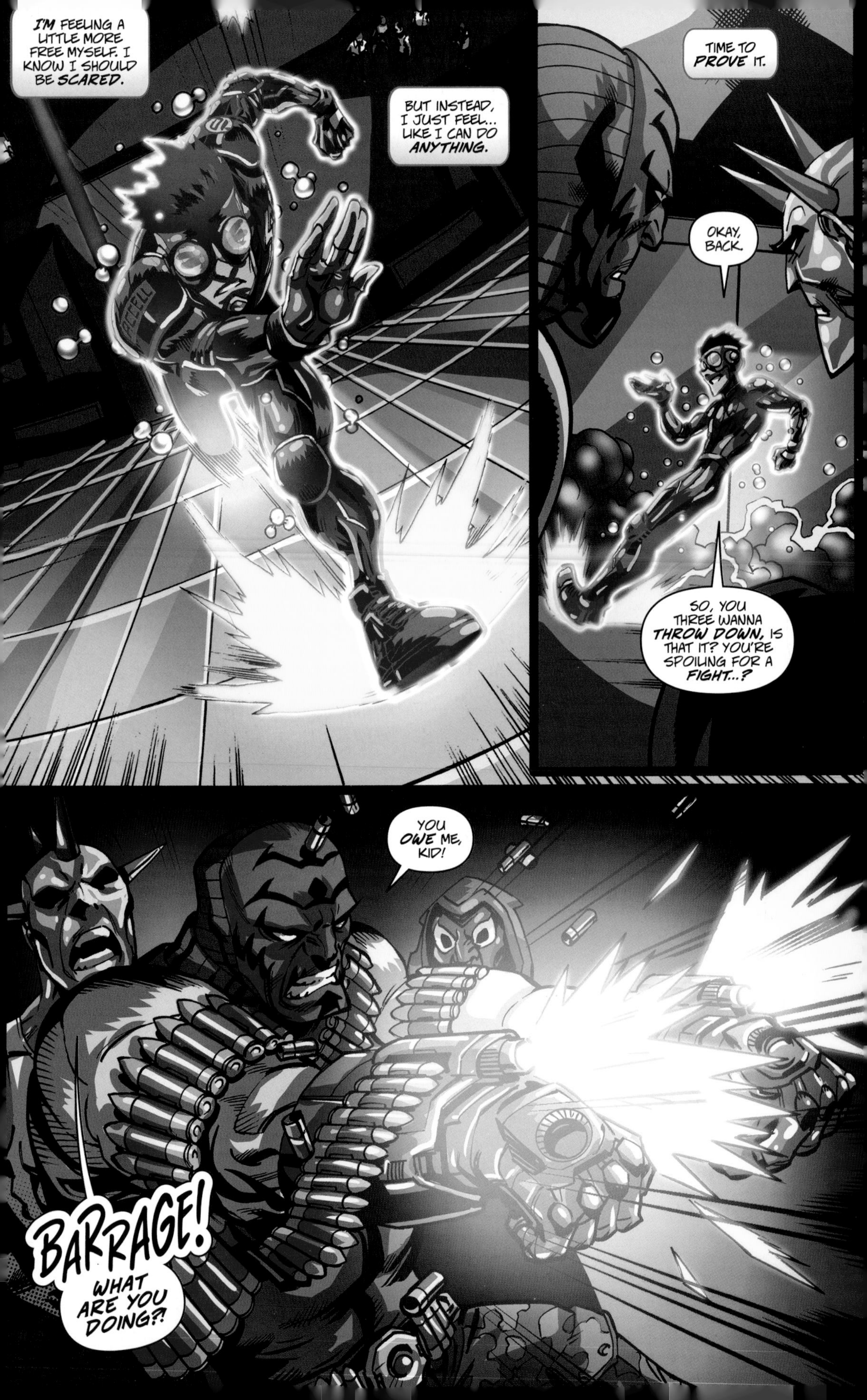

I'M FEELING A LITTLE MORE FREE MYSELF. I KNOW I SHOULD BE SCARED.
BUT INSTEAD, I JUST FEEL... LIKE I CAN DO ANYTHING.
TIME TO PROVE IT.
OKAY, BACK.
SO, YOU THREE WANNA THROW DOWN, IS THAT IT? YOU'RE SPOILING FOR A FIGHT...?
YOU OWE ME, KID!
BARRAGE! WHAT ARE YOU DOING?!

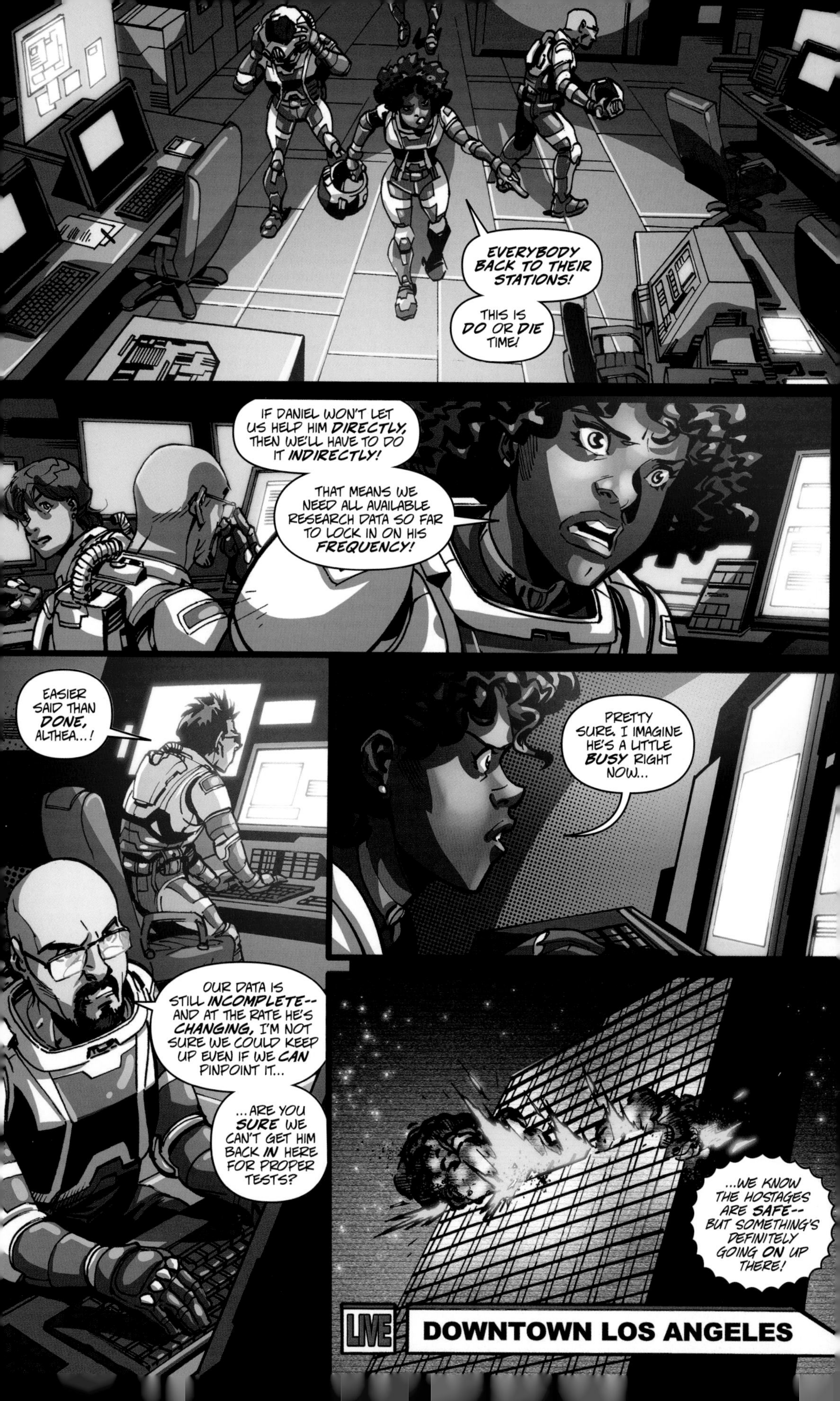
EVERYBODY BACK TO THEIR STATIONS!
THIS IS DO OR DIE TIME!
IF DANIEL WON'T LET US HELP HIM DIRECTLY, THEN WE'LL HAVE TO DO IT INDIRECTLY!
THAT MEANS WE NEED ALL AVAILABLE RESEARCH DATA SO FAR TO LOCK IN ON HIS FREQUENCY!
EASIER SAID THAN DONE, ALTHEA...!
OUR DATA IS STILL INCOMPLETE-- AND AT THE RATE HE'S CHANGING, I'M NOT SURE WE COULD KEEP UP EVEN IF WE CAN PINPOINT IT...
...ARE YOU SURE WE CAN'T GET HIM BACK IN HERE FOR PROPER TESTS?
PRETTY SURE. I IMAGINE HE'S A LITTLE BUSY RIGHT NOW...
...WE KNOW THE HOSTAGES ARE SAFE-- BUT SOMETHING'S DEFINITELY GOING ON UP THERE!
LIVE
DOWNTOWN LOS ANGELES

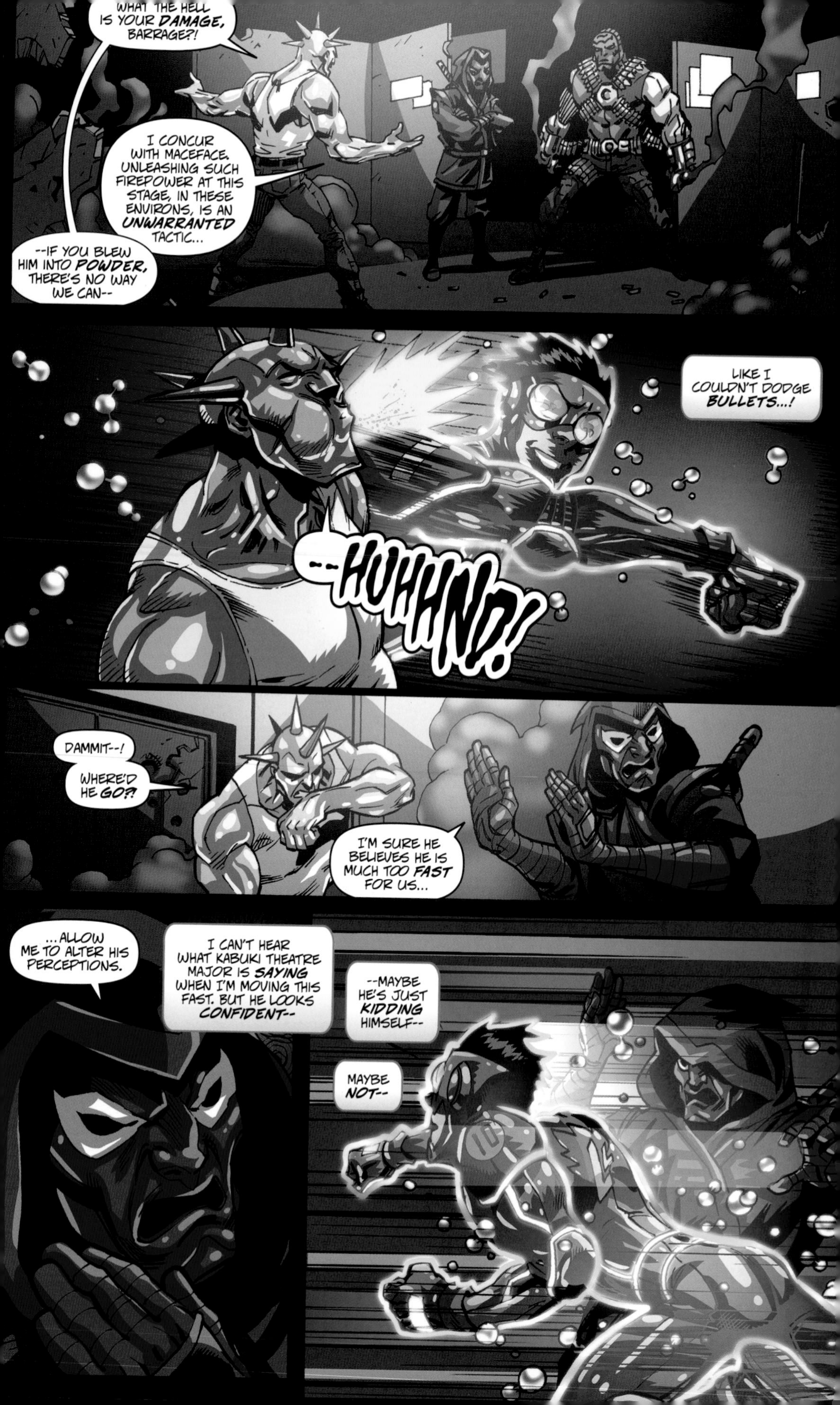
WHAT THE HELL IS YOUR DAMAGE, BARRAGE?!
I CONCUR WITH MACEFACE. UNLEASHING SUCH FIREPOWER AT THIS STAGE, IN THESE ENVIRONS, IS AN UNWARRANTED TACTIC...
--IF YOU BLEW HIM INTO POWDER, THERE'S NO WAY WE CAN--
LIKE I COULDN'T DODGE BULLETS...!
--HUHHND?!
DAMMIT--!
WHERE'D HE GO?!
I'M SURE HE BELIEVES HE IS MUCH TOO FAST FOR US...
...ALLOW ME TO ALTER HIS PERCEPTIONS.
I CAN'T HEAR WHAT KABUKI THEATRE MAJOR IS SAYING WHEN I'M MOVING THIS FAST. BUT HE LOOKS CONFIDENT--
--MAYBE HE'S JUST KIDDING HIMSELF--
MAYBE NOT--

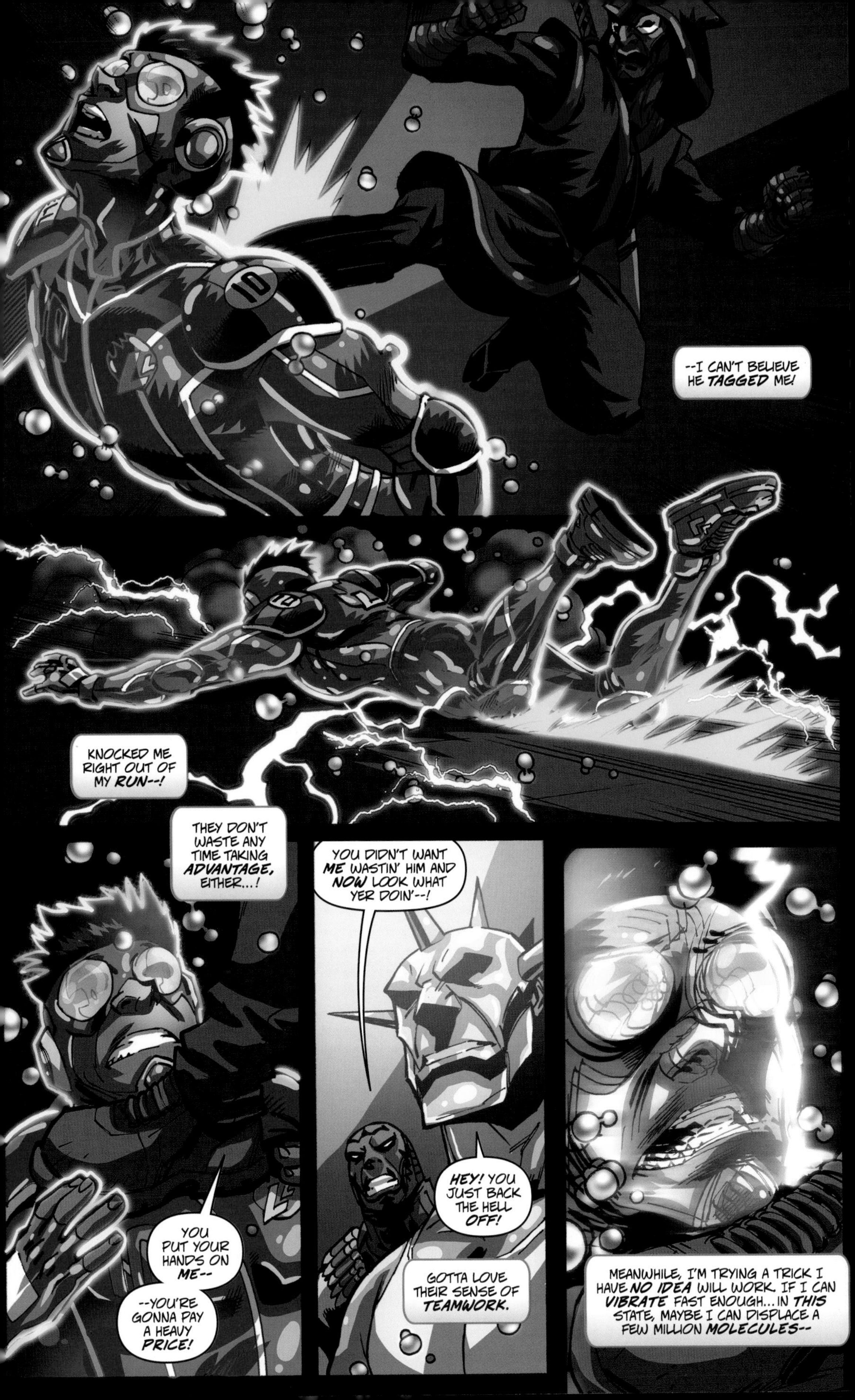
--I CAN'T BELIEVE HE TAGGED ME!
KNOCKED ME RIGHT OUT OF MY RUN--!
THEY DON'T WASTE ANY TIME TAKING ADVANTAGE, EITHER...!
YOU PUT YOUR HANDS ON ME--
--YOU'RE GONNA PAY A HEAVY PRICE!
YOU DIDN'T WANT ME WASTIN' HIM AND NOW LOOK WHAT YER DOIN'--!
HEY! YOU JUST BACK THE HELL OFF!
GOTTA LOVE THEIR SENSE OF TEAMWORK.
MEANWHILE, I'M TRYING A TRICK I HAVE NO IDEA WILL WORK. IF I CAN VIBRATE FAST ENOUGH... IN THIS STATE, MAYBE I CAN DISPLACE A FEW MILLION MOLECULES--

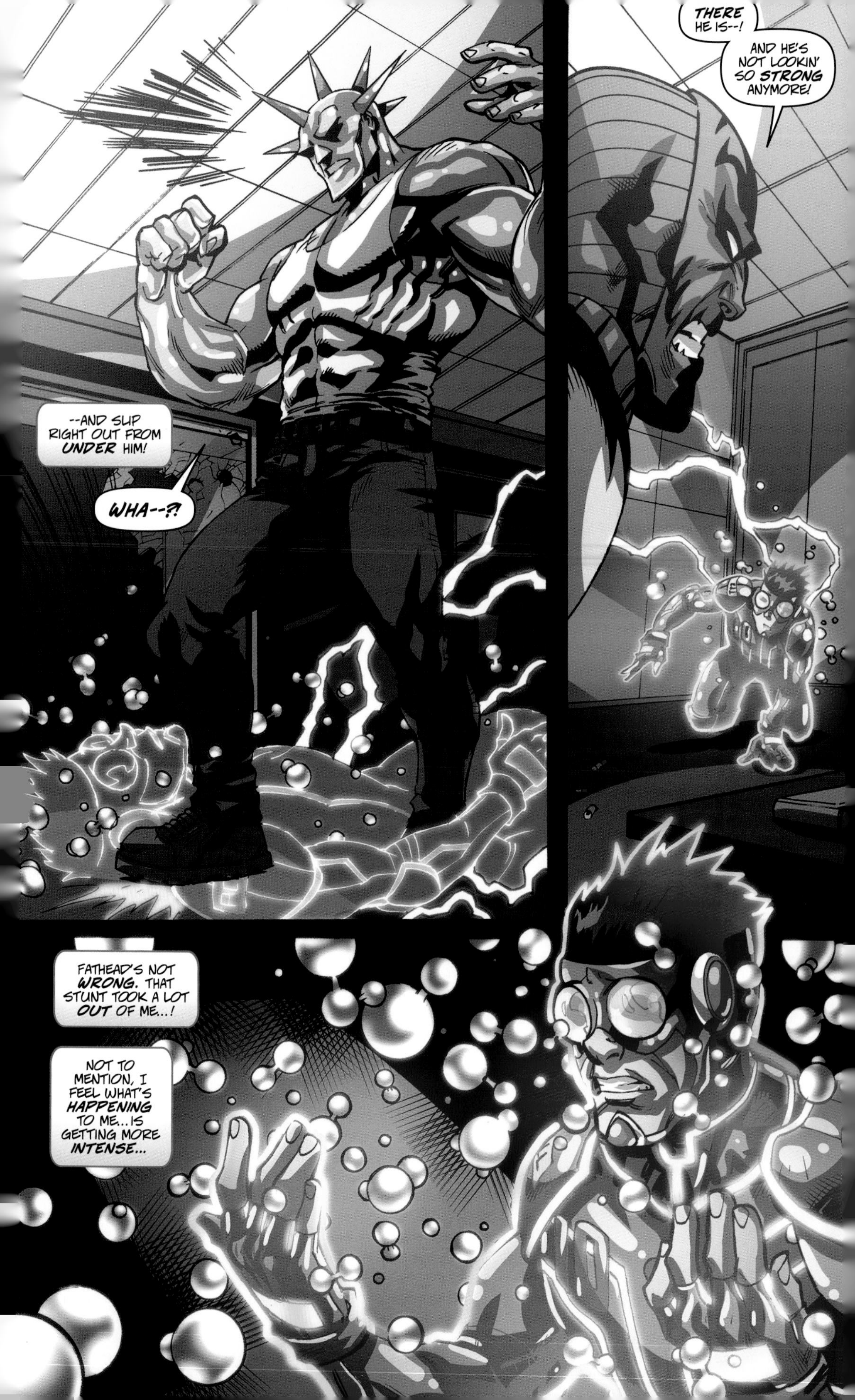
--AND SLIP RIGHT OUT FROM UNDER HIM!
WHA--?!
THERE HE IS--!
AND HE'S NOT LOOKIN' SO STRONG ANYMORE!
FATHEAD'S NOT WRONG. THAT STUNT TOOK A LOT OUT OF ME...!
NOT TO MENTION, I FEEL WHAT'S HAPPENING TO ME...IS GETTING MORE INTENSE...

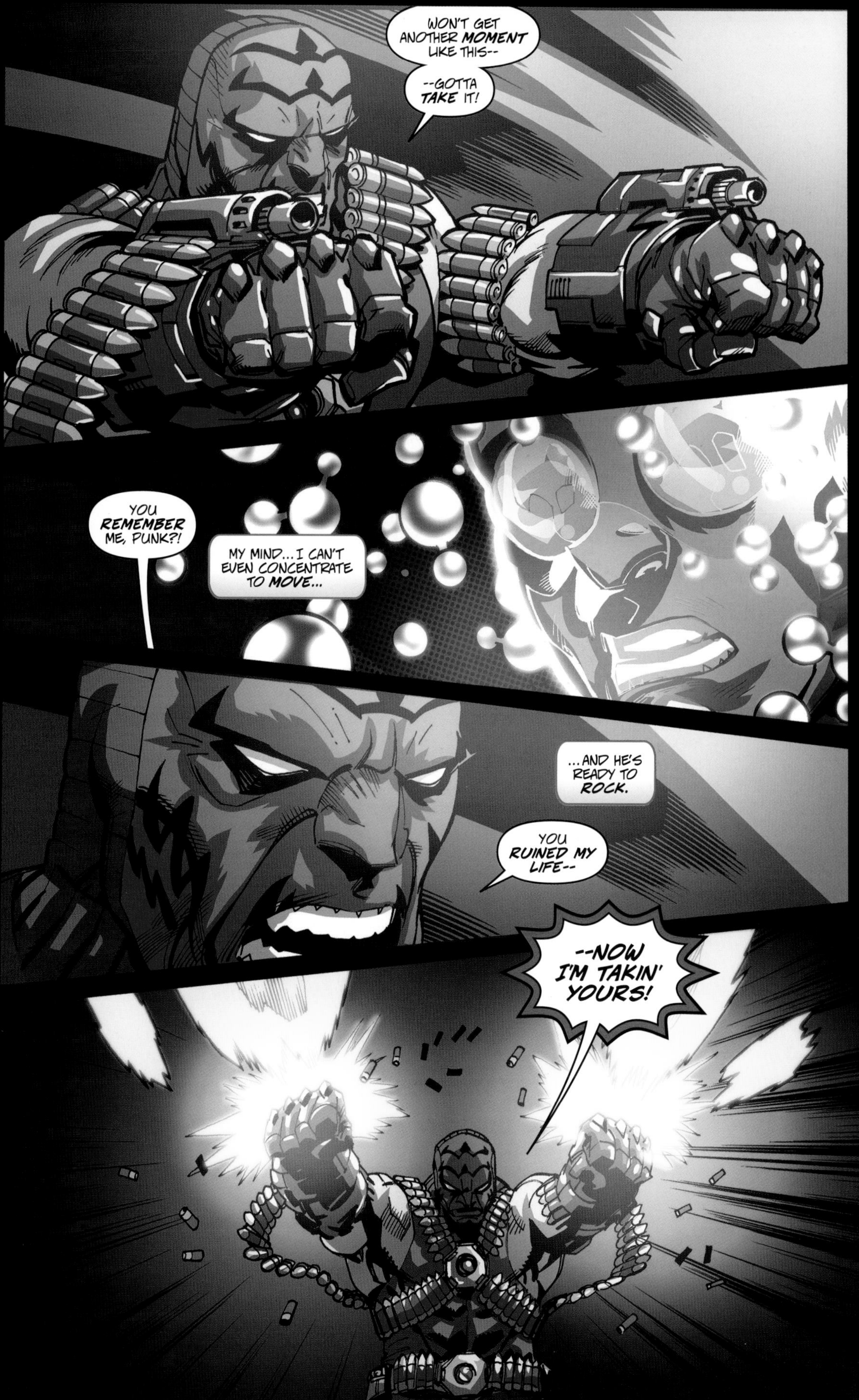
WON'T GET ANOTHER MOMENT LIKE THIS--
--GOTTA TAKE IT!
YOU REMEMBER ME, PUNK?!
MY MIND... I CAN'T EVEN CONCENTRATE TO MOVE...
...AND HE'S READY TO ROCK.
YOU RUINED MY LIFE--
--NOW I'M TAKIN' YOURS!

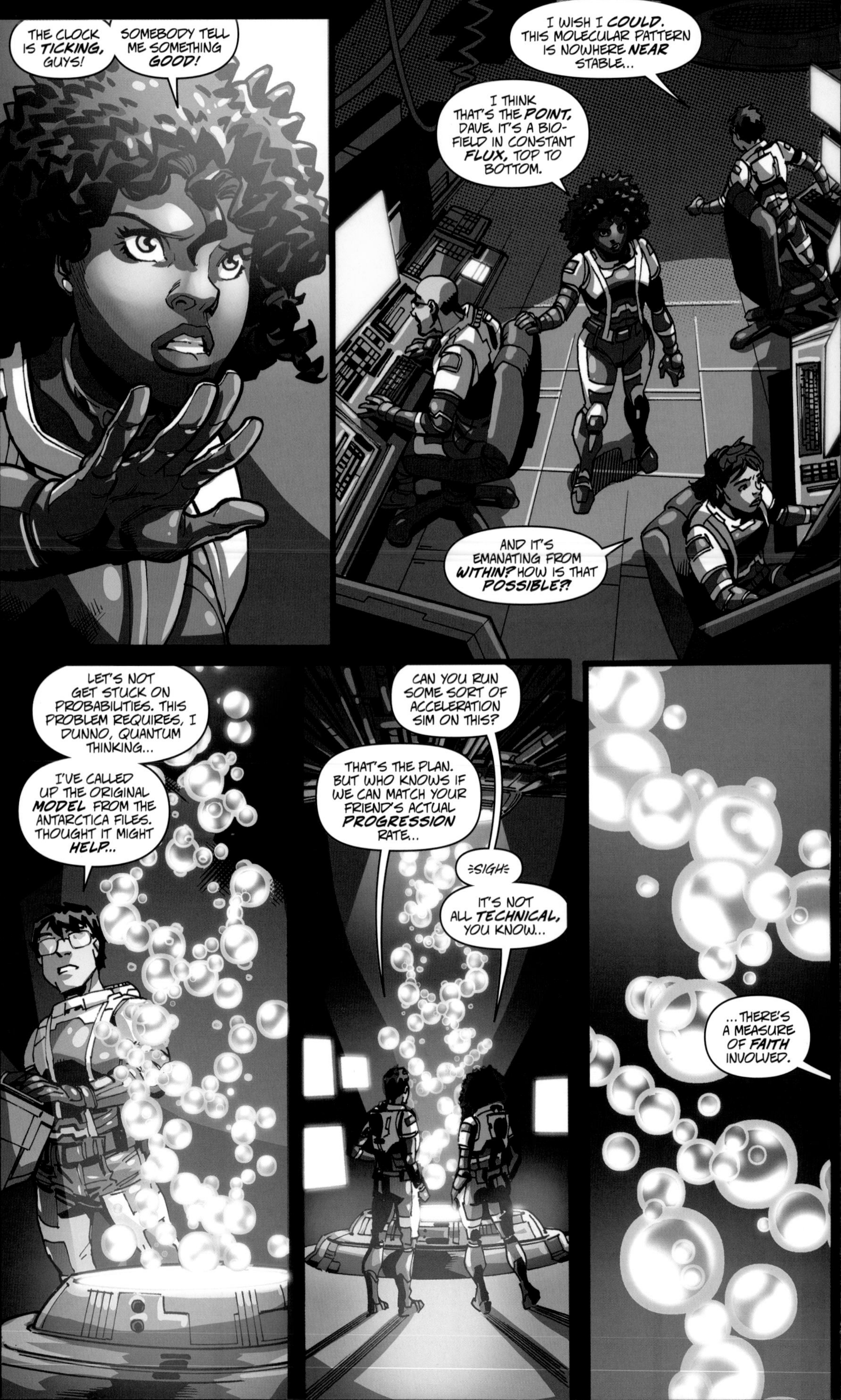
THE CLOCK IS TICKING, GUYS!
SOMEBODY TELL ME SOMETHING GOOD!
I WISH I COULD. THIS MOLECULAR PATTERN IS NOWHERE NEAR STABLE...
I THINK THAT'S THE POINT, DAVE. IT'S A BIO-FIELD IN CONSTANT FLUX, TOP TO BOTTOM.
AND IT'S EMANATING FROM WITHIN? HOW IS THAT POSSIBLE?!
LET'S NOT GET STUCK ON PROBABILITIES. THIS PROBLEM REQUIRES, I DUNNO, QUANTUM THINKING...
I'VE CALLED UP THE ORIGINAL MODEL FROM THE ANTARCTICA FILES. THOUGHT IT MIGHT HELP...
CAN YOU RUN SOME SORT OF ACCELERATION SIM ON THIS?
THAT'S THE PLAN. BUT WHO KNOWS IF WE CAN MATCH YOUR FRIEND'S ACTUAL PROGRESSION RATE...
SIGH
IT'S NOT ALL TECHNICAL, YOU KNOW...
...THERE'S A MEASURE OF FAITH INVOLVED.

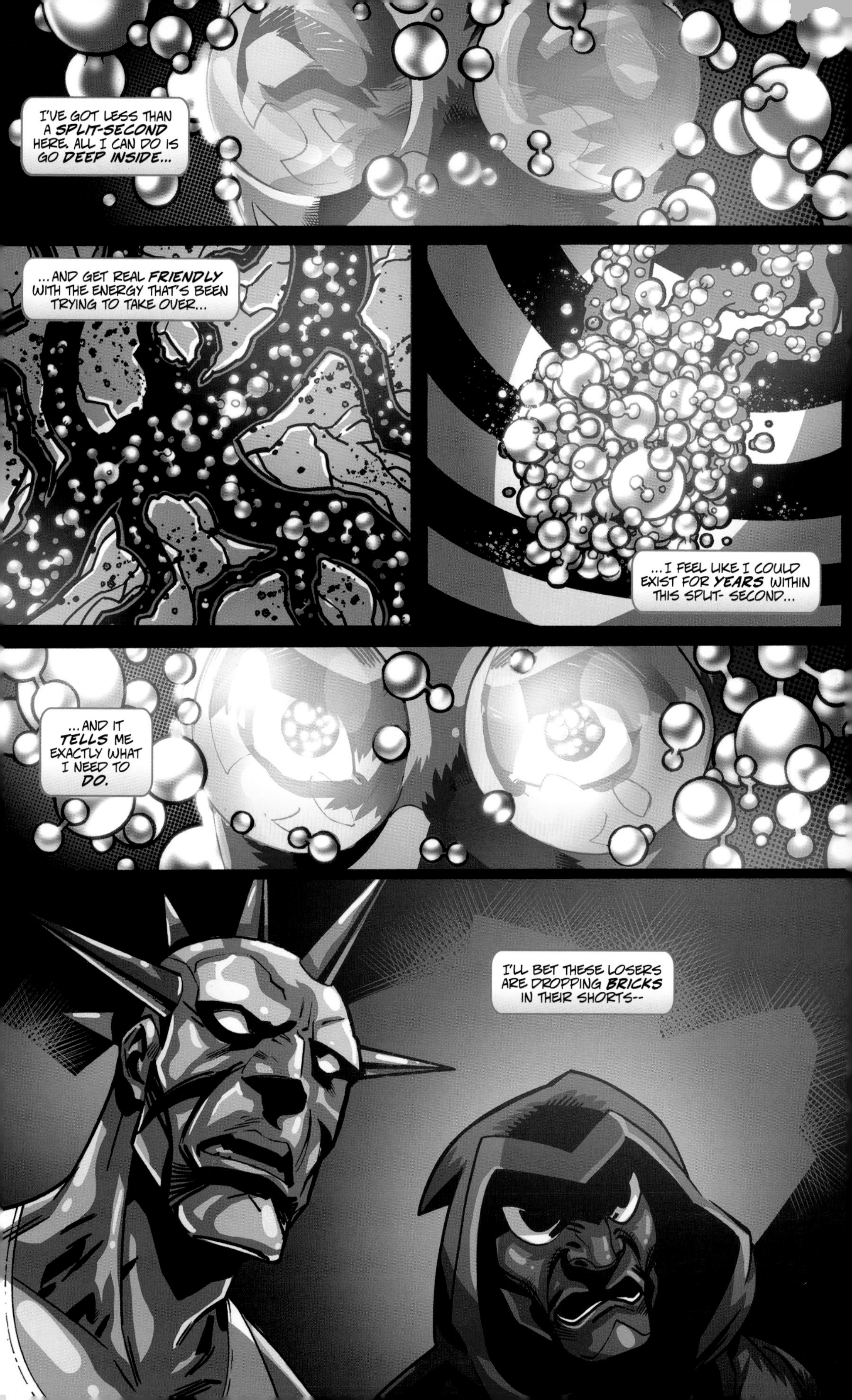
I'VE GOT LESS THAN A SPLIT-SECOND HERE. ALL I CAN DO IS GO DEEP INSIDE...
...AND GET REAL FRIENDLY WITH THE ENERGY THAT'S BEEN TRYING TO TAKE OVER...
...I FEEL LIKE I COULD EXIST FOR YEARS WITHIN THIS SPLIT- SECOND...
...AND IT TELLS ME EXACTLY WHAT I NEED TO DO.
I'LL BET THESE LOSERS ARE DROPPING BRICKS IN THEIR SHORTS--

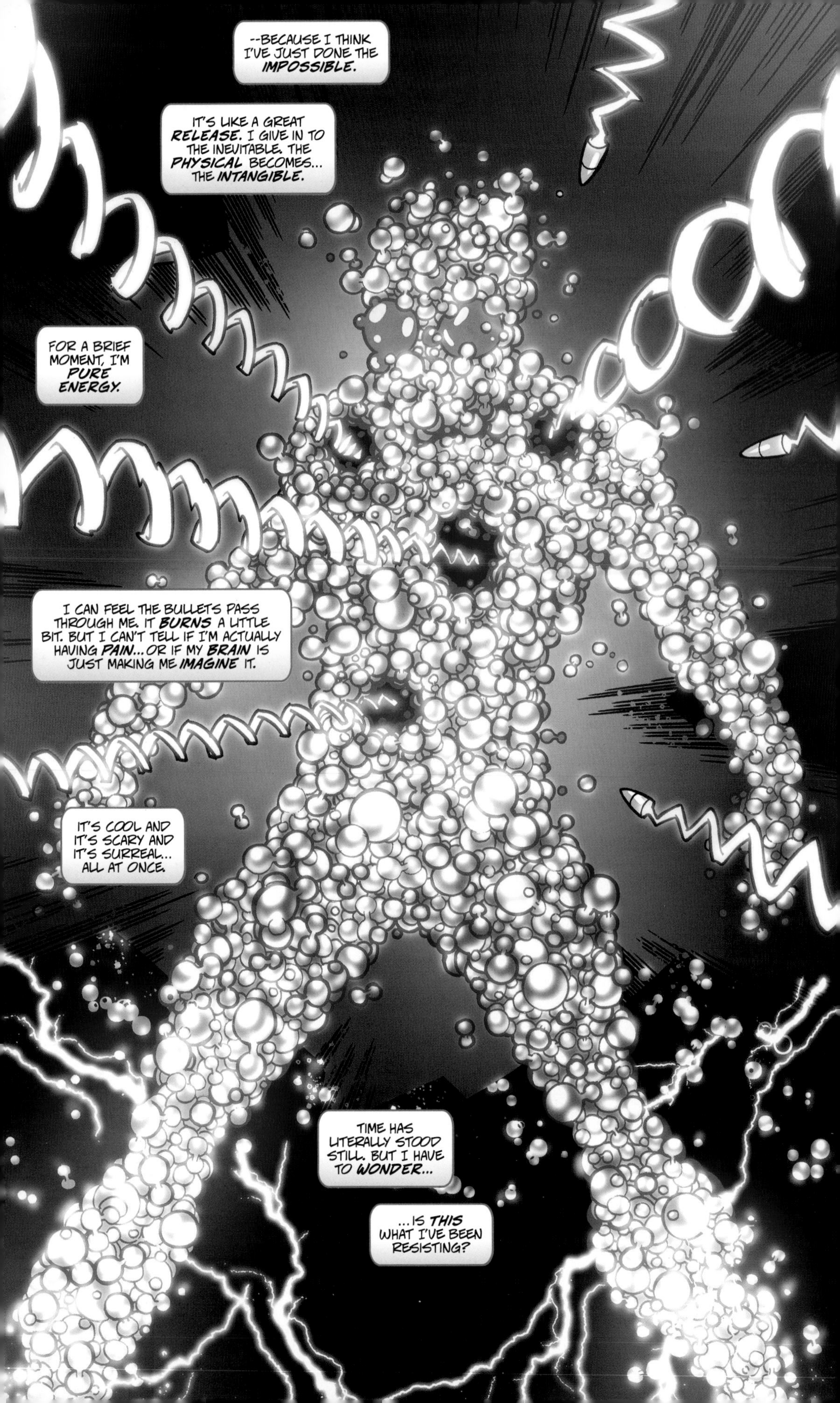
--BECAUSE I THINK I'VE JUST DONE THE *IMPOSSIBLE*.
IT'S LIKE A GREAT *RELEASE*. I GIVE IN TO THE INEVITABLE. THE *PHYSICAL* BECOMES... THE *INTANGIBLE*.
FOR A BRIEF MOMENT, I'M *PURE ENERGY*.
I CAN FEEL THE BULLETS PASS THROUGH ME. IT *BURNS* A LITTLE BIT. BUT I CAN'T TELL IF I'M ACTUALLY HAVING *PAIN*...OR IF MY *BRAIN* IS JUST MAKING ME *IMAGINE* IT.
IT'S COOL AND IT'S SCARY AND IT'S SURREAL... ALL AT ONCE.
TIME HAS LITERALLY STOOD STILL. BUT I HAVE TO *WONDER*...
...IS *THIS* WHAT I'VE BEEN RESISTING?

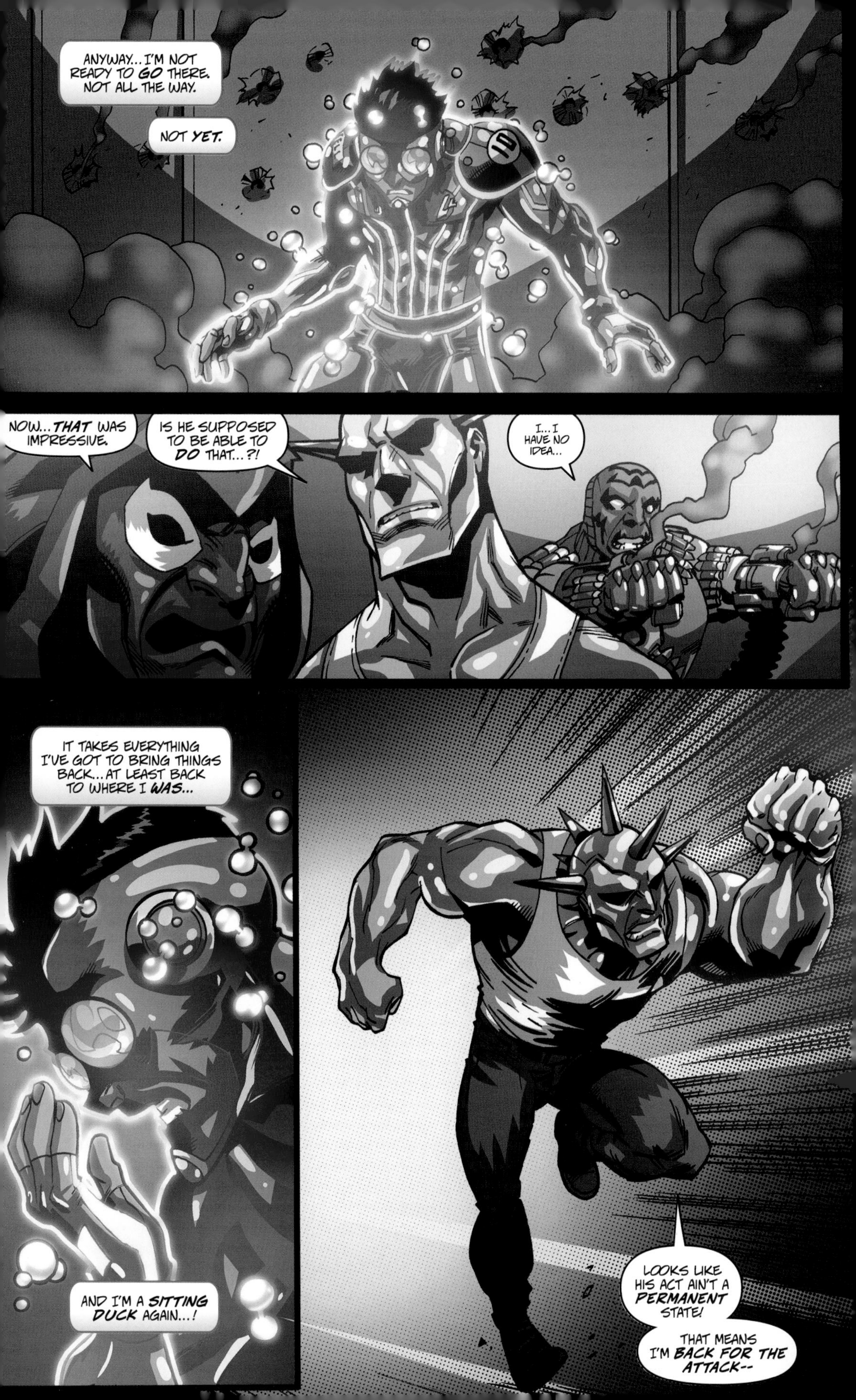
ANYWAY... I'M NOT READY TO GO THERE. NOT ALL THE WAY.
NOT YET.
NOW... THAT WAS IMPRESSIVE.
IS HE SUPPOSED TO BE ABLE TO DO THAT...?!
I... I HAVE NO IDEA...
IT TAKES EVERYTHING I'VE GOT TO BRING THINGS BACK... AT LEAST BACK TO WHERE I WAS...
AND I'M A SITTING DUCK AGAIN...!
LOOKS LIKE HIS ACT AIN'T A PERMANENT STATE!
THAT MEANS I'M BACK FOR THE ATTACK--

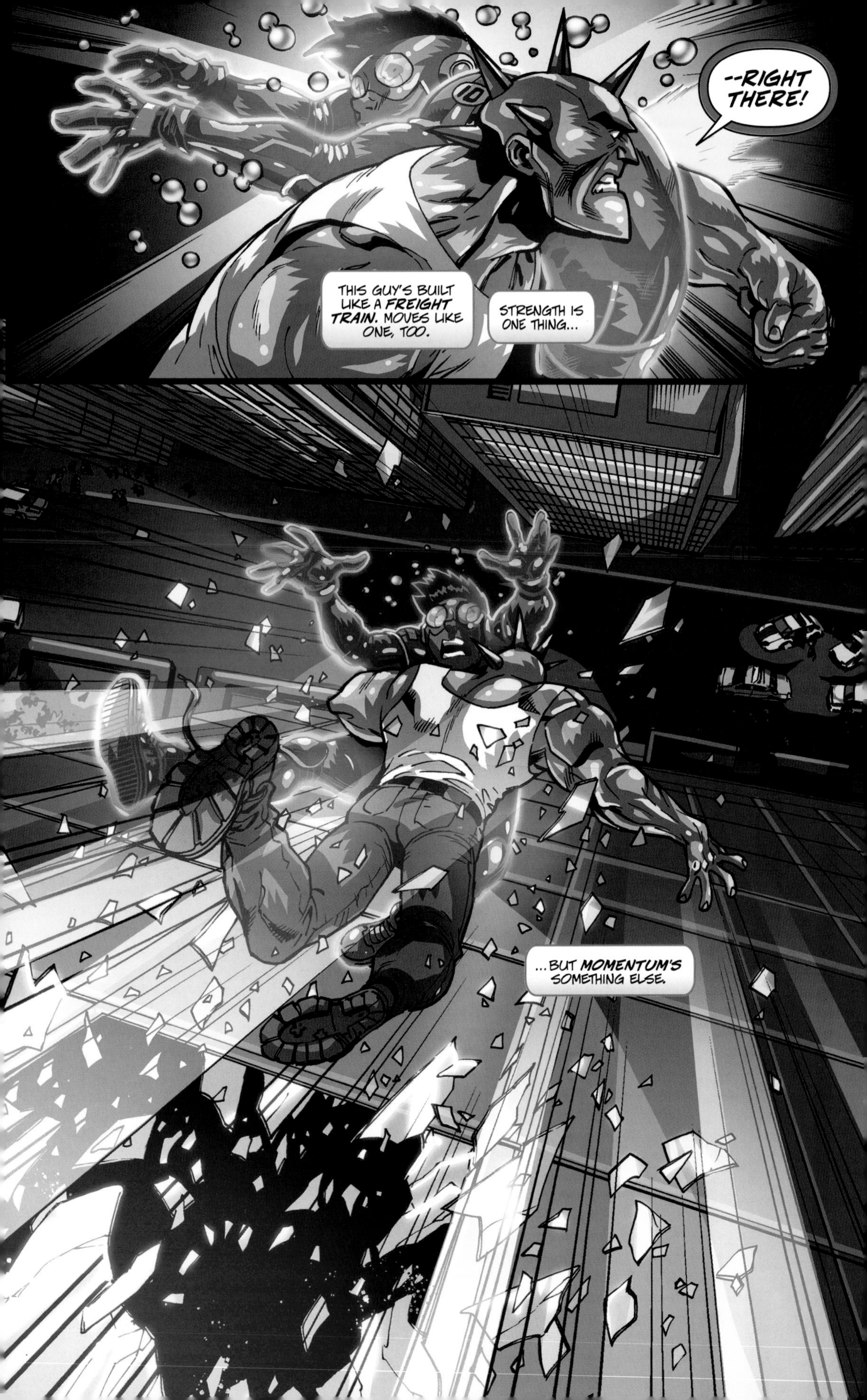
--RIGHT THERE!
THIS GUY'S BUILT LIKE A FREIGHT TRAIN. MOVES LIKE ONE, TOO.
STRENGTH IS ONE THING...
...BUT MOMENTUM'S SOMETHING ELSE.

CHAPTER FIVE

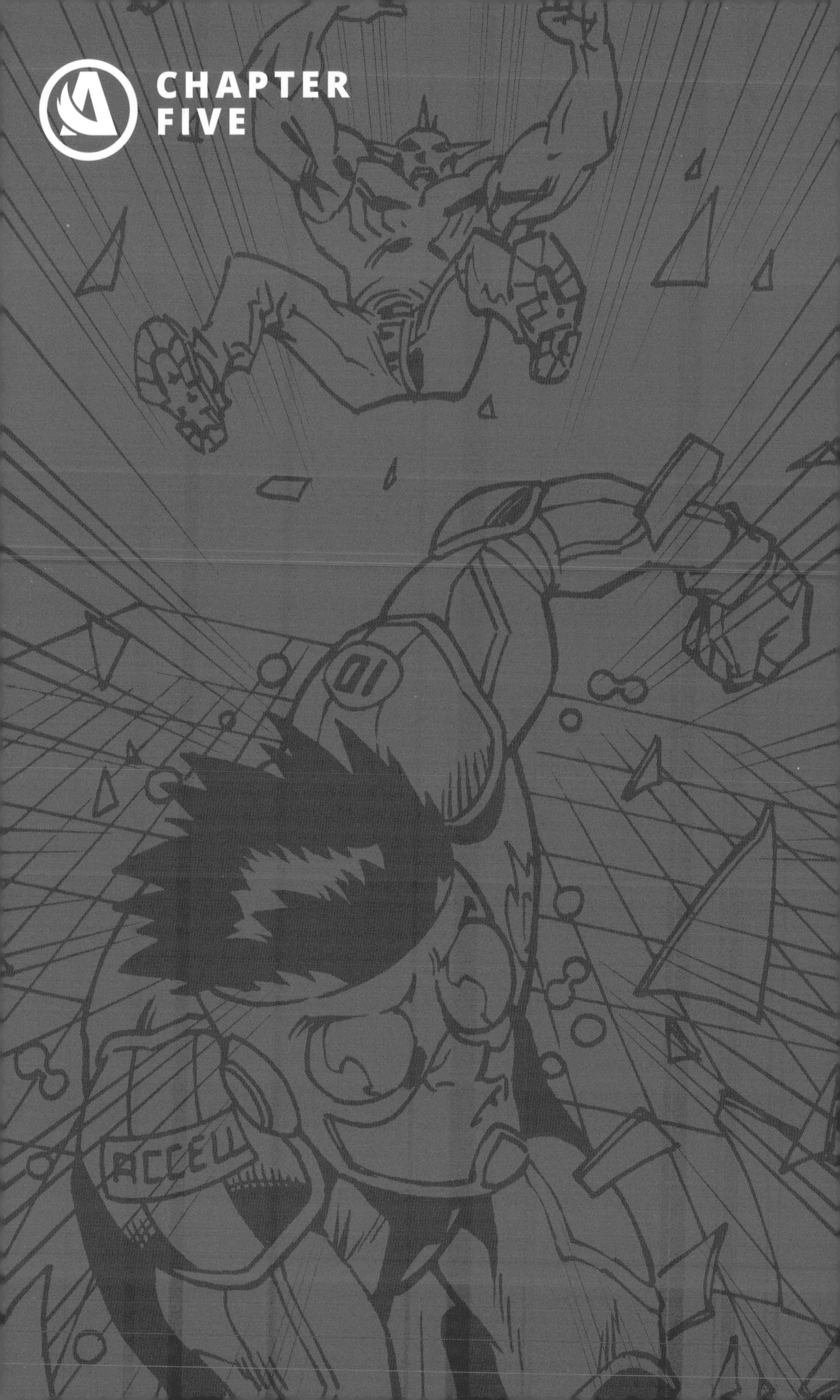
ACCEL

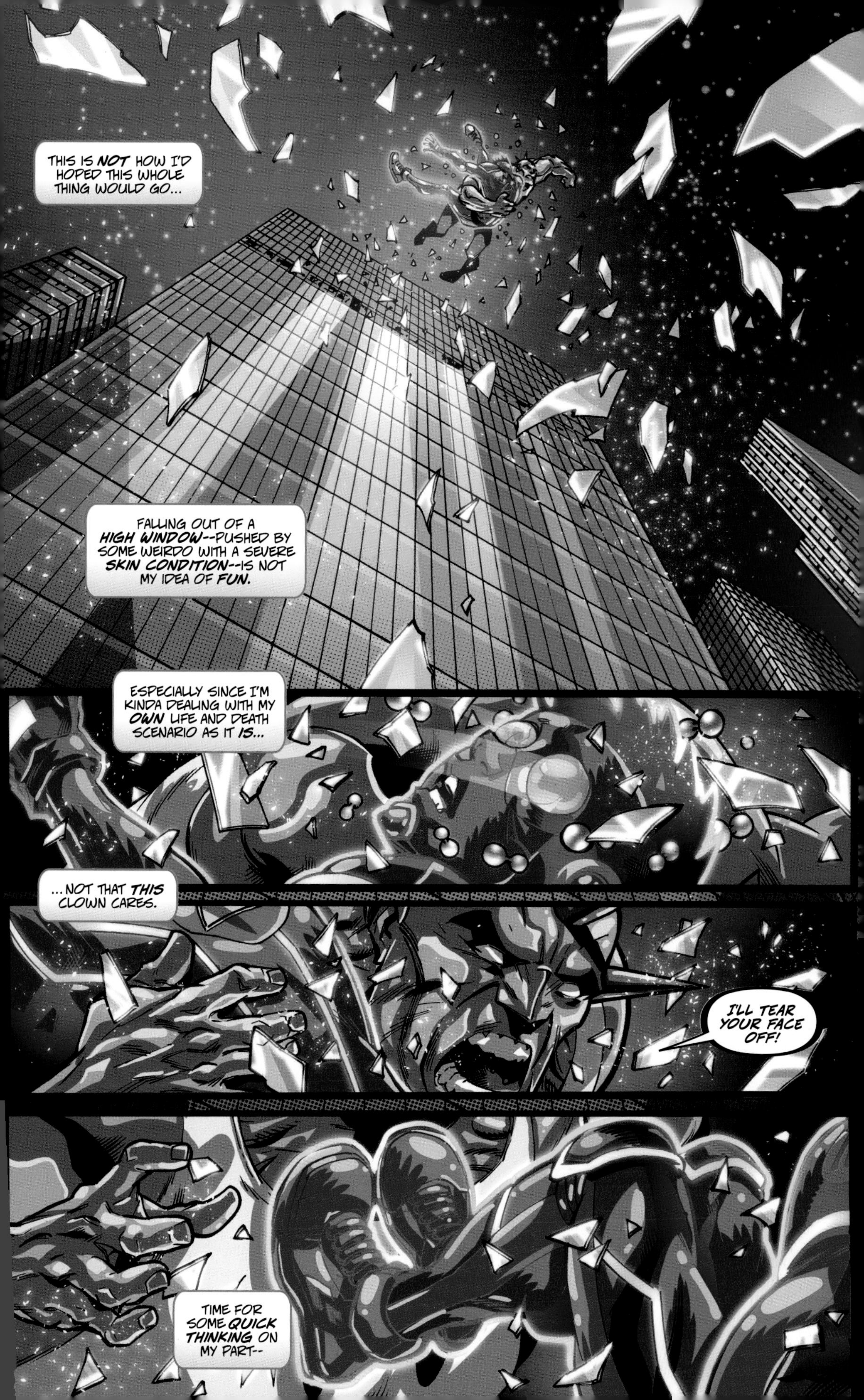
THIS IS NOT HOW I'D HOPED THIS WHOLE THING WOULD GO...
FALLING OUT OF A HIGH WINDOW--PUSHED BY SOME WEIRDO WITH A SEVERE SKIN CONDITION--IS NOT MY IDEA OF FUN.
ESPECIALLY SINCE I'M KINDA DEALING WITH MY OWN LIFE AND DEATH SCENARIO AS IT IS...
...NOT THAT THIS CLOWN CARES.
I'LL TEAR YOUR FACE OFF!
TIME FOR SOME QUICK THINKING ON MY PART--

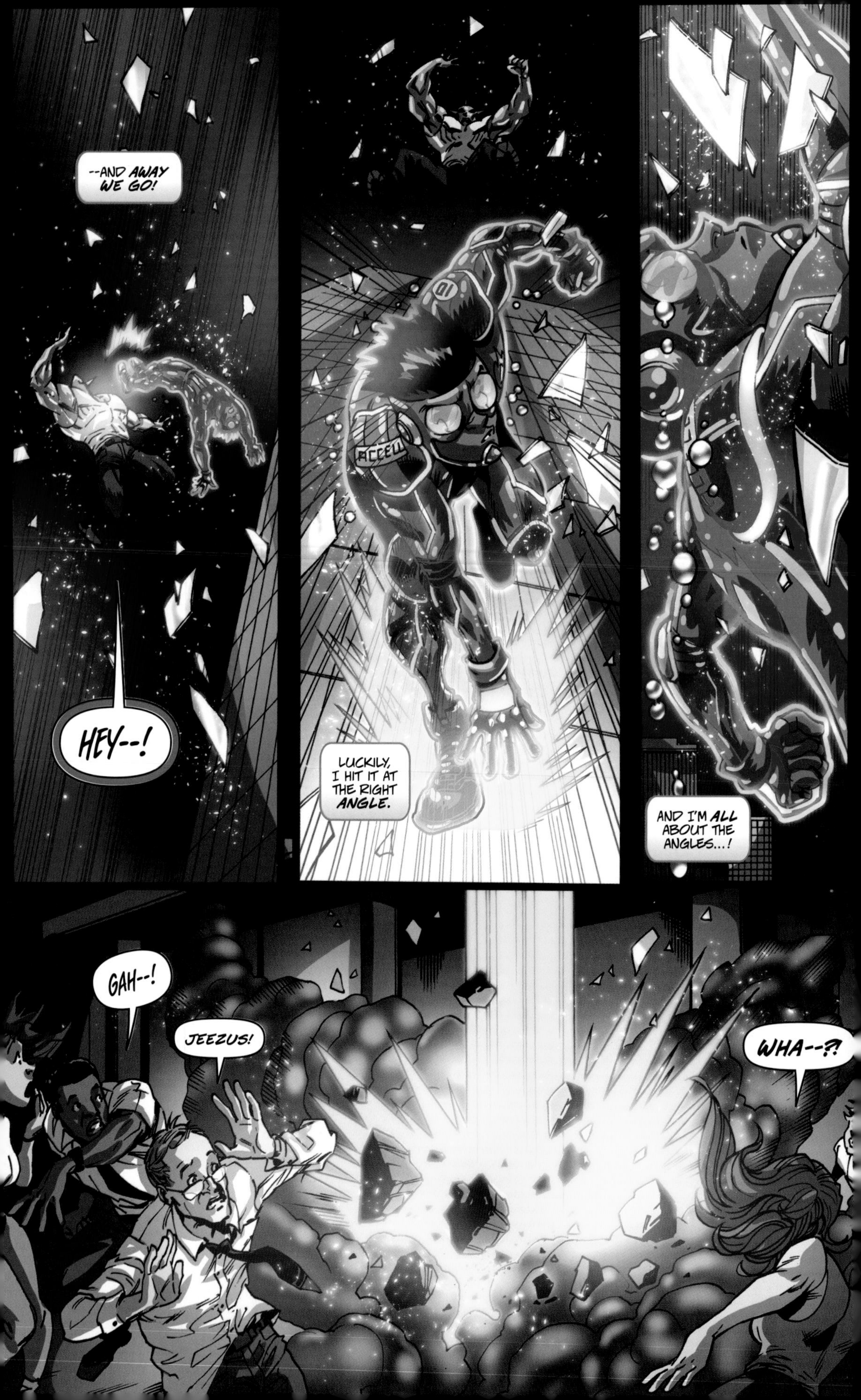
--AND AWAY WE GO!
HEY--!
LUCKILY, I HIT IT AT THE RIGHT ANGLE.
AND I'M ALL ABOUT THE ANGLES...!
GAH--!
JEEZUS!
WHA--?!

ONE DOWN. TWO TO GO.
MAYBE EVEN JUST ONE AND A HALF..
DID YOU SEE THAT?!
WHO THE HELL DOES MACEFACE THINK HE IS?!
WHAT'S YOUR ISSUE...?
I GOT HISTORY WITH THIS SPEEDSTER. HE'S THE REASON I'M IN THIS FIX!
HOW MANY TIMES DID I SAY I WANTED A PIECE OF HIM--
ACCELL

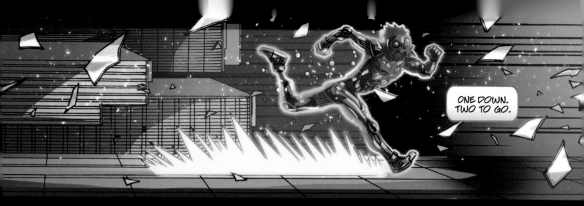

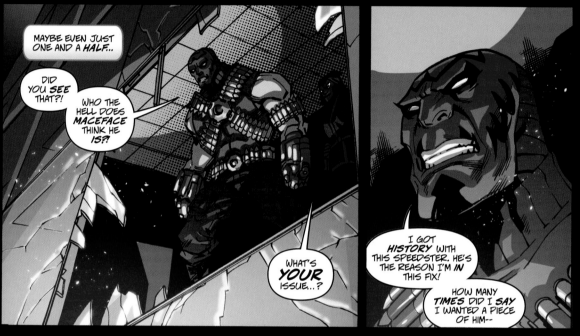

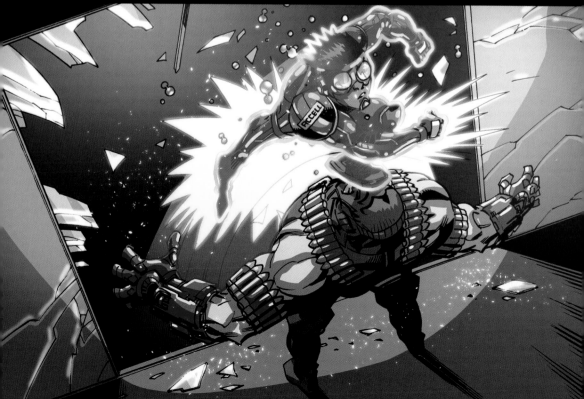

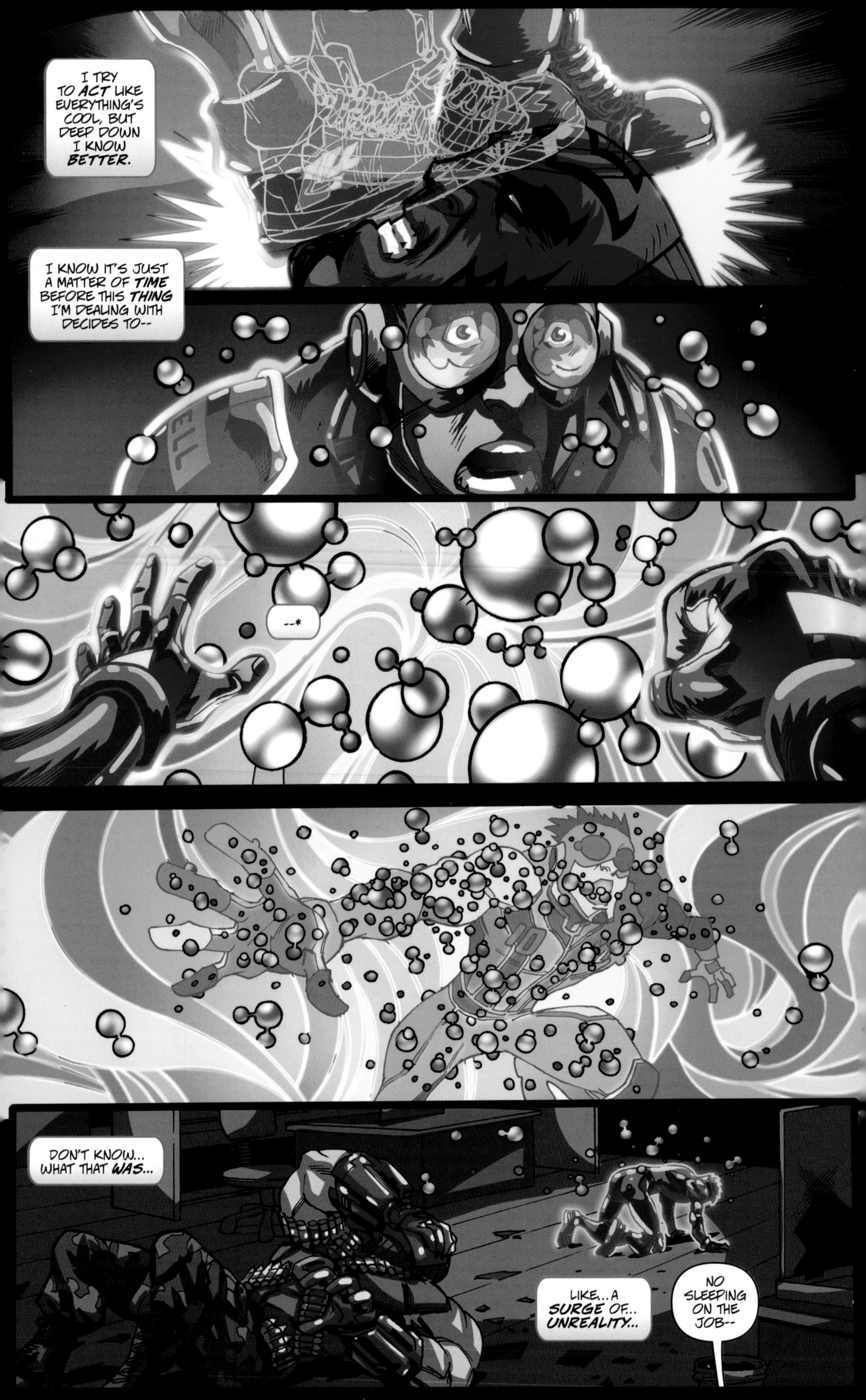
I TRY TO ACT LIKE EVERYTHING'S COOL, BUT DEEP DOWN I KNOW BETTER.
I KNOW IT'S JUST A MATTER OF TIME BEFORE THIS THING I'M DEALING WITH DECIDES TO--
--*
DON'T KNOW... WHAT THAT WAS...
LIKE... A SURGE OF.. UNREALITY...
NO SLEEPING ON THE JOB--

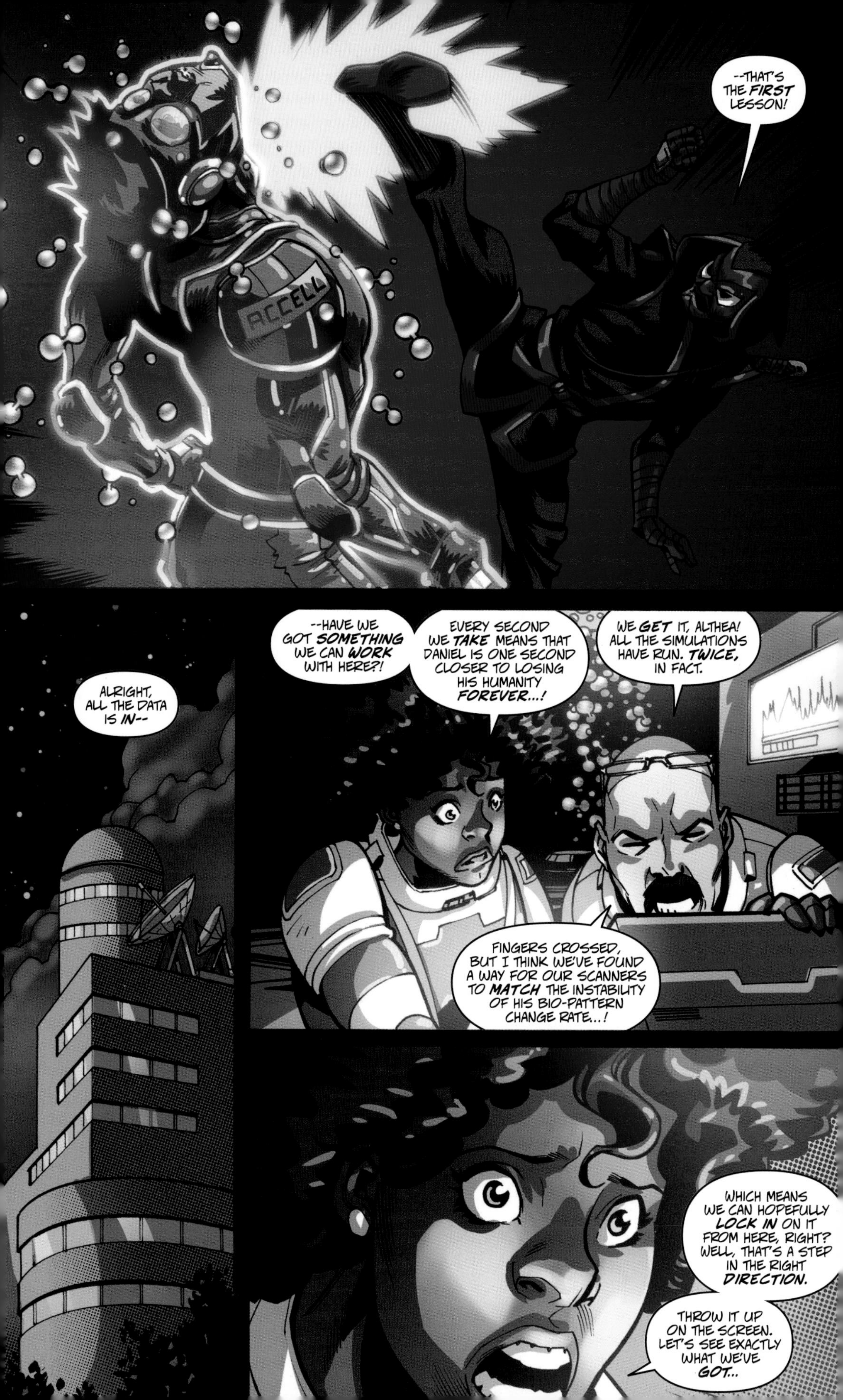
ACCELL
--THAT'S THE FIRST LESSON!
ALRIGHT, ALL THE DATA IS IN--
--HAVE WE GOT SOMETHING WE CAN WORK WITH HERE?!
EVERY SECOND WE TAKE MEANS THAT DANIEL IS ONE SECOND CLOSER TO LOSING HIS HUMANITY FOREVER...!
WE GET IT, ALTHEA! ALL THE SIMULATIONS HAVE RUN. TWICE, IN FACT.
FINGERS CROSSED, BUT I THINK WE'VE FOUND A WAY FOR OUR SCANNERS TO MATCH THE INSTABILITY OF HIS BIO-PATTERN CHANGE RATE...!
WHICH MEANS WE CAN HOPEFULLY LOCK IN ON IT FROM HERE, RIGHT? WELL, THAT'S A STEP IN THE RIGHT DIRECTION.
THROW IT UP ON THE SCREEN. LET'S SEE EXACTLY WHAT WE'VE GOT...

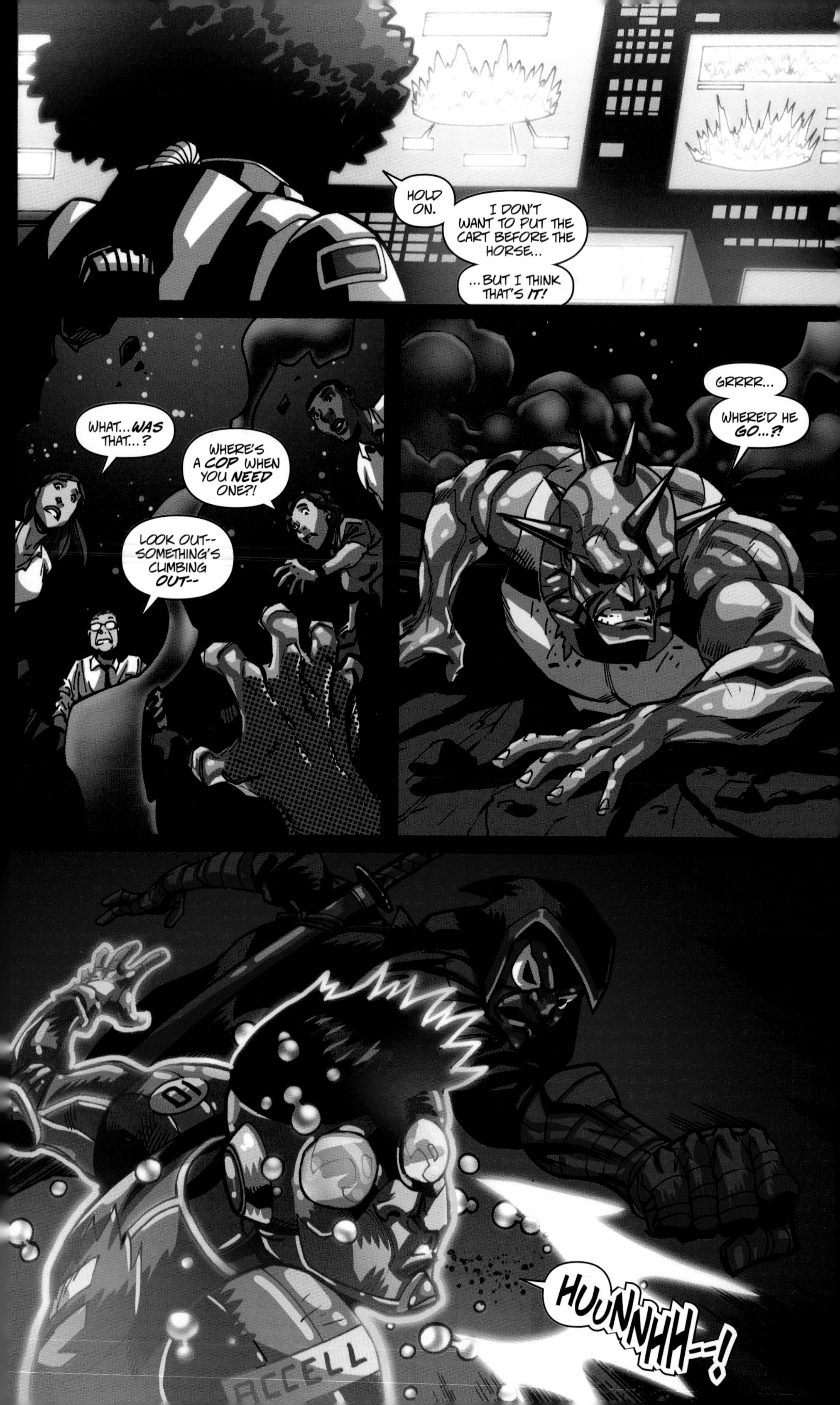
HOLD ON.
I DON'T WANT TO PUT THE CART BEFORE THE HORSE...
...BUT I THINK THAT'S IT!
WHAT...WAS THAT...?
WHERE'S A COP WHEN YOU NEED ONE?!
LOOK OUT-- SOMETHING'S CLIMBING OUT--
GRRRR...
WHERE'D HE GO...?!
HUUNNHH--!
ACCELL

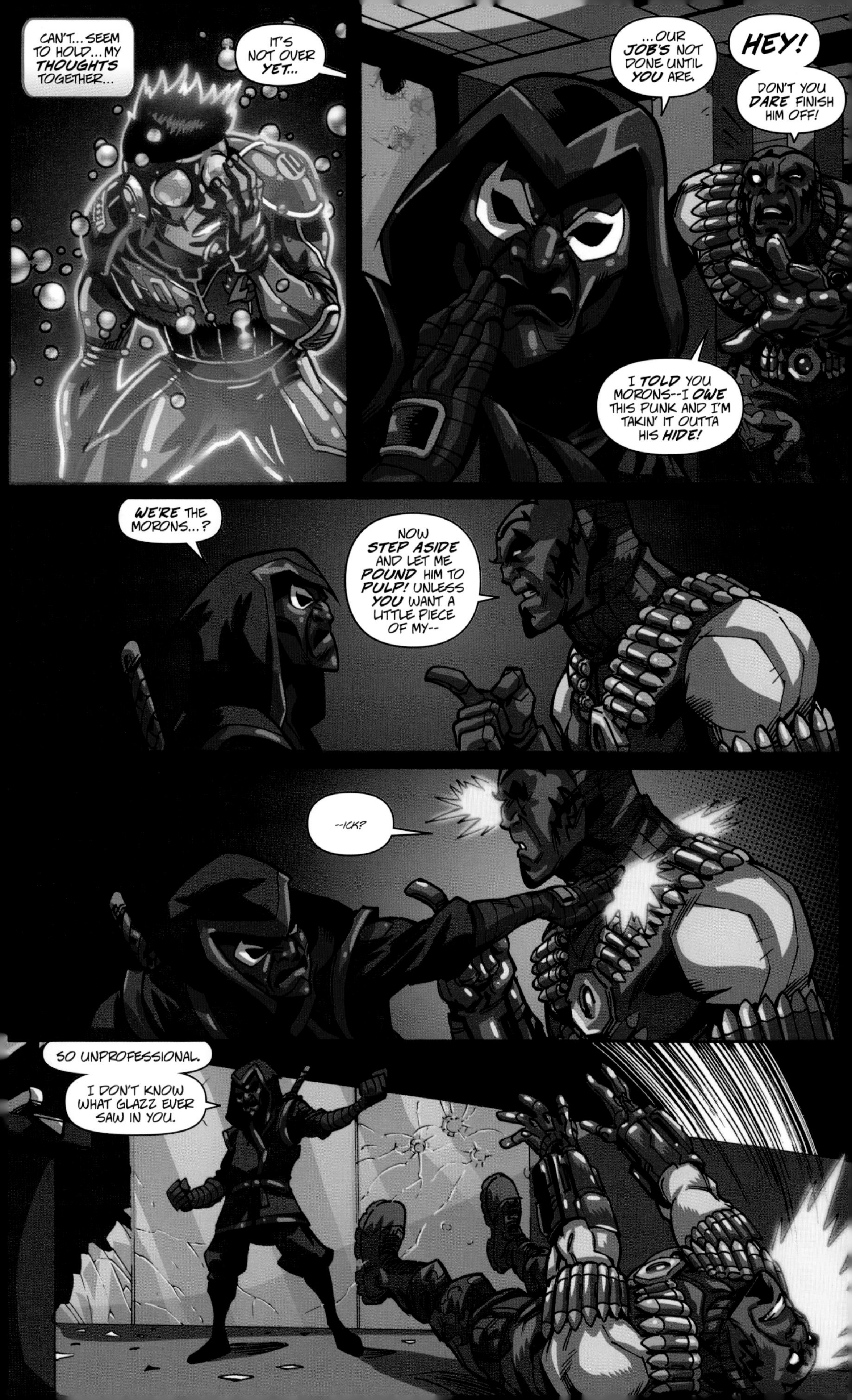
CAN'T... SEEM TO HOLD... MY THOUGHTS TOGETHER...
IT'S NOT OVER YET...
...OUR JOB'S NOT DONE UNTIL YOU ARE.
HEY!
DON'T YOU DARE FINISH HIM OFF!
I TOLD YOU MORONS--I OWE THIS PUNK AND I'M TAKIN' IT OUTTA HIS HIDE!
WE'RE THE MORONS...?
NOW STEP ASIDE AND LET ME POUND HIM TO PULP! UNLESS YOU WANT A LITTLE PIECE OF MY--
--ICK?
SO UNPROFESSIONAL.
I DON'T KNOW WHAT GLAZZ EVER SAW IN YOU.

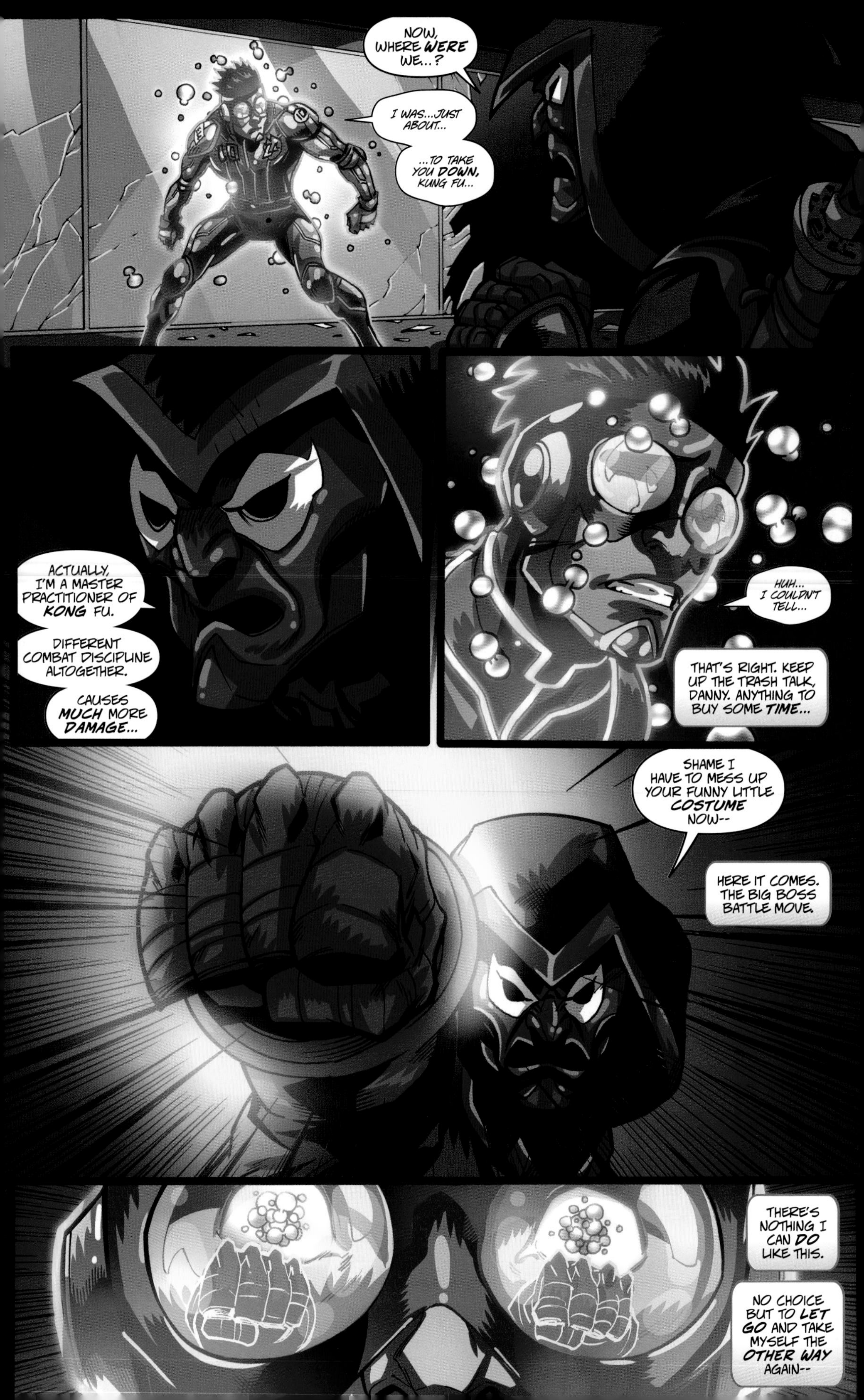
NOW, WHERE WERE WE...?
I WAS...JUST ABOUT...
...TO TAKE YOU DOWN, KUNG FU...
ACTUALLY, I'M A MASTER PRACTITIONER OF KONG FU.
DIFFERENT COMBAT DISCIPLINE ALTOGETHER.
CAUSES MUCH MORE DAMAGE...
HUH... I COULDN'T TELL...
THAT'S RIGHT. KEEP UP THE TRASH TALK, DANNY. ANYTHING TO BUY SOME TIME...
SHAME I HAVE TO MESS UP YOUR FUNNY LITTLE COSTUME NOW--
HERE IT COMES. THE BIG BOSS BATTLE MOVE.
THERE'S NOTHING I CAN DO LIKE THIS.
NO CHOICE BUT TO LET GO AND TAKE MYSELF THE OTHER WAY AGAIN--

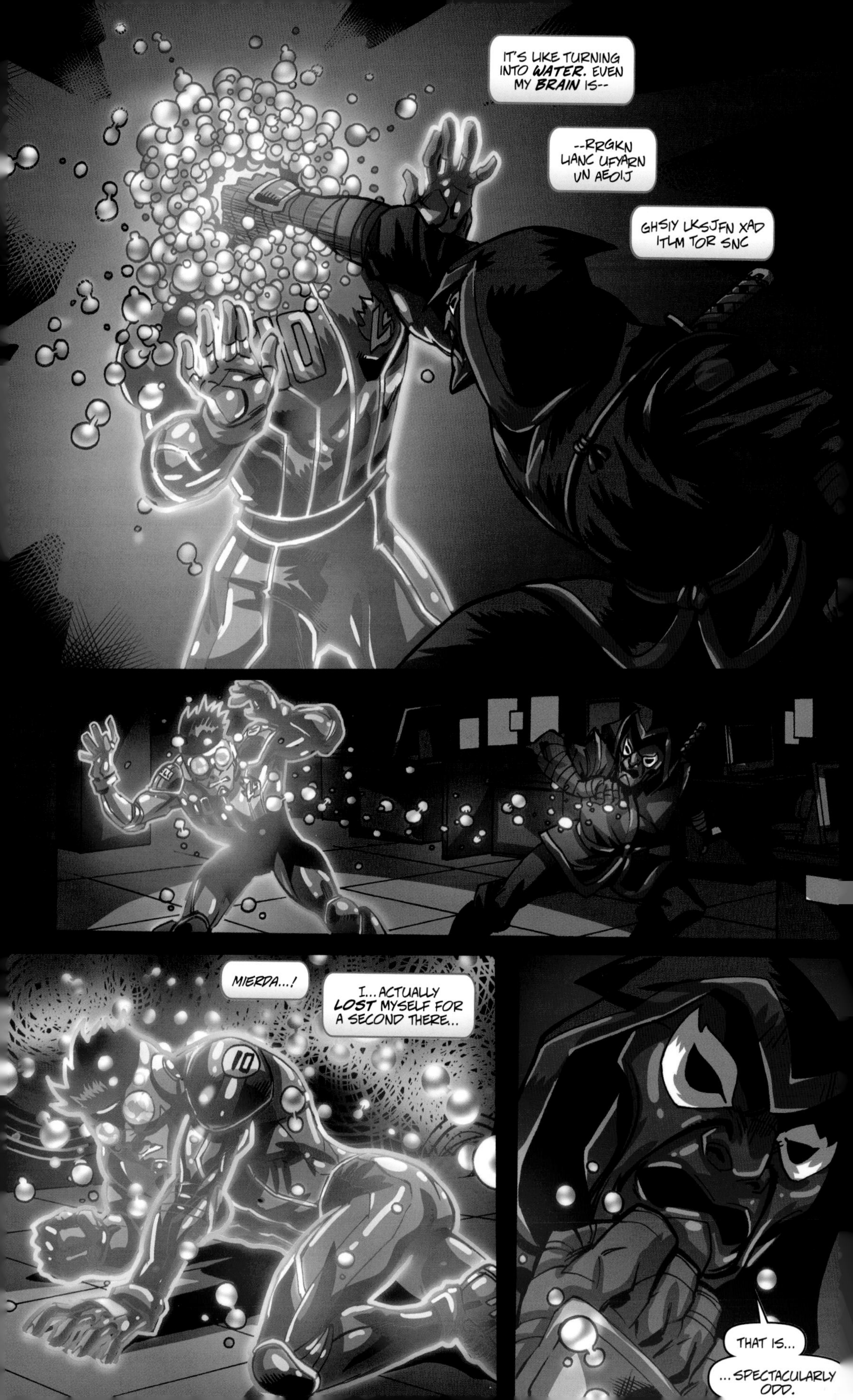
IT'S LIKE TURNING INTO WATER. EVEN MY BRAIN IS--
--RRGKN LIANC UFYARN UN AEOIJ
GHSIY LKSJFN XAD ITLM TOR SNC
MIERDA...!
I... ACTUALLY LOST MYSELF FOR A SECOND THERE...
THAT IS...
... SPECTACULARLY ODD.

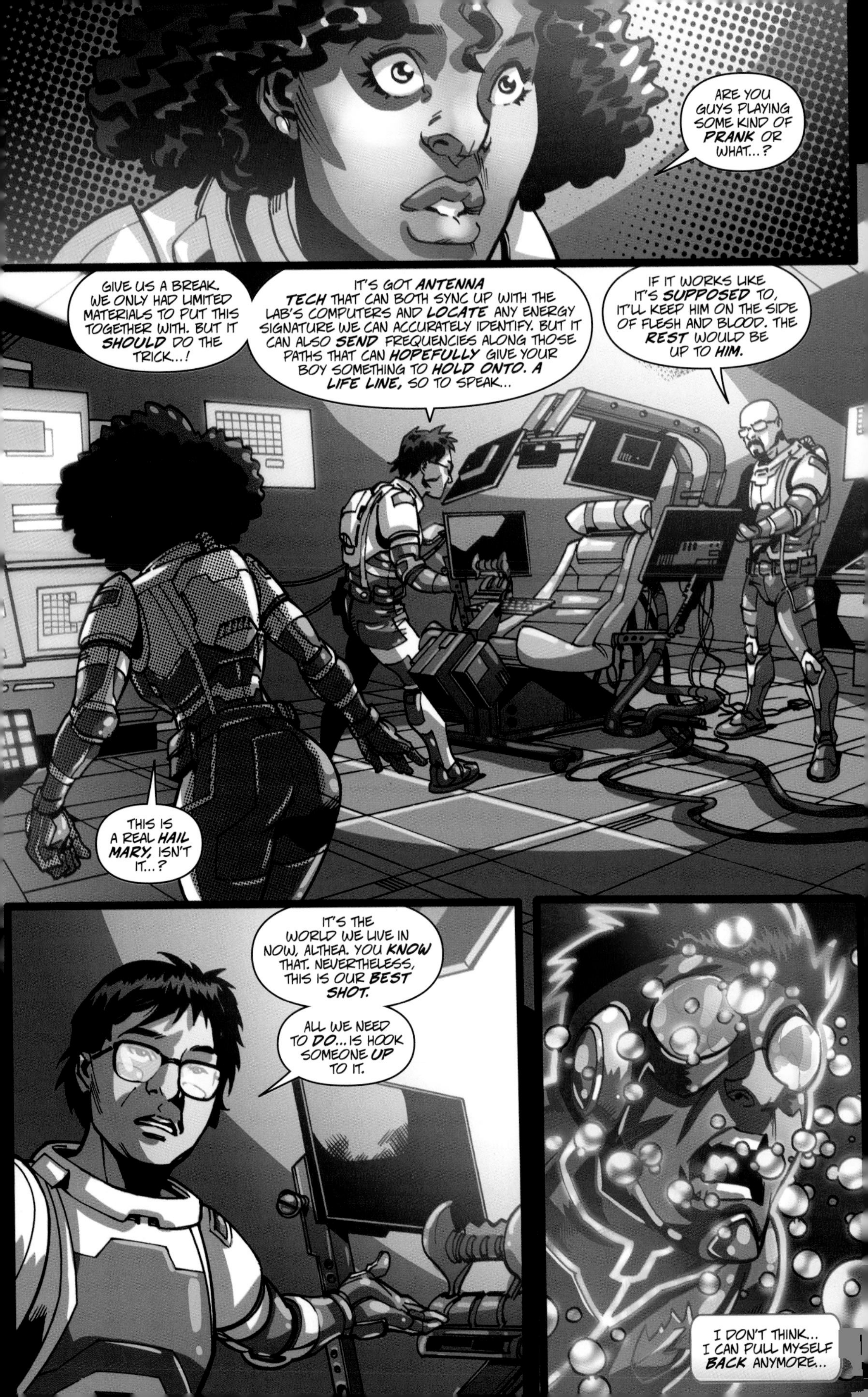
ARE YOU GUYS PLAYING SOME KIND OF PRANK OR WHAT...?
GIVE US A BREAK. WE ONLY HAD LIMITED MATERIALS TO PUT THIS TOGETHER WITH. BUT IT SHOULD DO THE TRICK...!
IT'S GOT ANTENNA TECH THAT CAN BOTH SYNC UP WITH THE LAB'S COMPUTERS AND LOCATE ANY ENERGY SIGNATURE WE CAN ACCURATELY IDENTIFY. BUT IT CAN ALSO SEND FREQUENCIES ALONG THOSE PATHS THAT CAN HOPEFULLY GIVE YOUR BOY SOMETHING TO HOLD ONTO. A LIFE LINE, SO TO SPEAK...
IF IT WORKS LIKE IT'S SUPPOSED TO, IT'LL KEEP HIM ON THE SIDE OF FLESH AND BLOOD. THE REST WOULD BE UP TO HIM.
THIS IS A REAL HAIL MARY, ISN'T IT...?
IT'S THE WORLD WE LIVE IN NOW, ALTHEA. YOU KNOW THAT. NEVERTHELESS, THIS IS OUR BEST SHOT.
ALL WE NEED TO DO... IS HOOK SOMEONE UP TO IT.
I DON'T THINK... I CAN PULL MYSELF BACK ANYMORE...

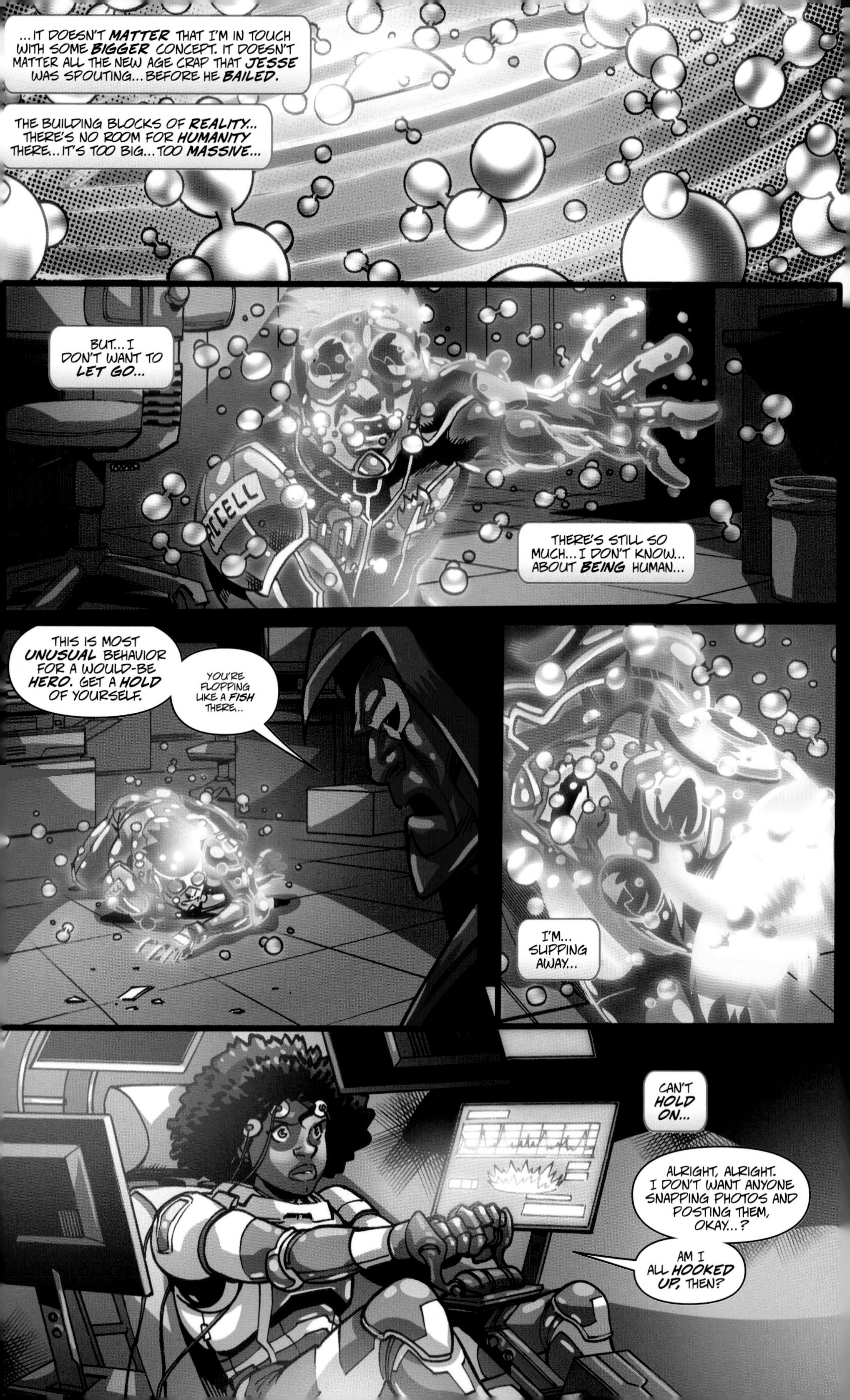
...IT DOESN'T MATTER THAT I'M IN TOUCH WITH SOME BIGGER CONCEPT. IT DOESN'T MATTER ALL THE NEW AGE CRAP THAT JESSE WAS SPOUTING... BEFORE HE BAILED.
THE BUILDING BLOCKS OF REALITY... THERE'S NO ROOM FOR HUMANITY THERE... IT'S TOO BIG... TOO MASSIVE...
BUT... I DON'T WANT TO LET GO...
THERE'S STILL SO MUCH... I DON'T KNOW... ABOUT BEING HUMAN...
ACCELL
THIS IS MOST UNUSUAL BEHAVIOR FOR A WOULD-BE HERO. GET A HOLD OF YOURSELF.
YOU'RE FLOPPING LIKE A FISH THERE...
I'M... SLIPPING AWAY...
CAN'T HOLD ON...
ALRIGHT, ALRIGHT. I DON'T WANT ANYONE SNAPPING PHOTOS AND POSTING THEM, OKAY...?
AM I ALL HOOKED UP, THEN?

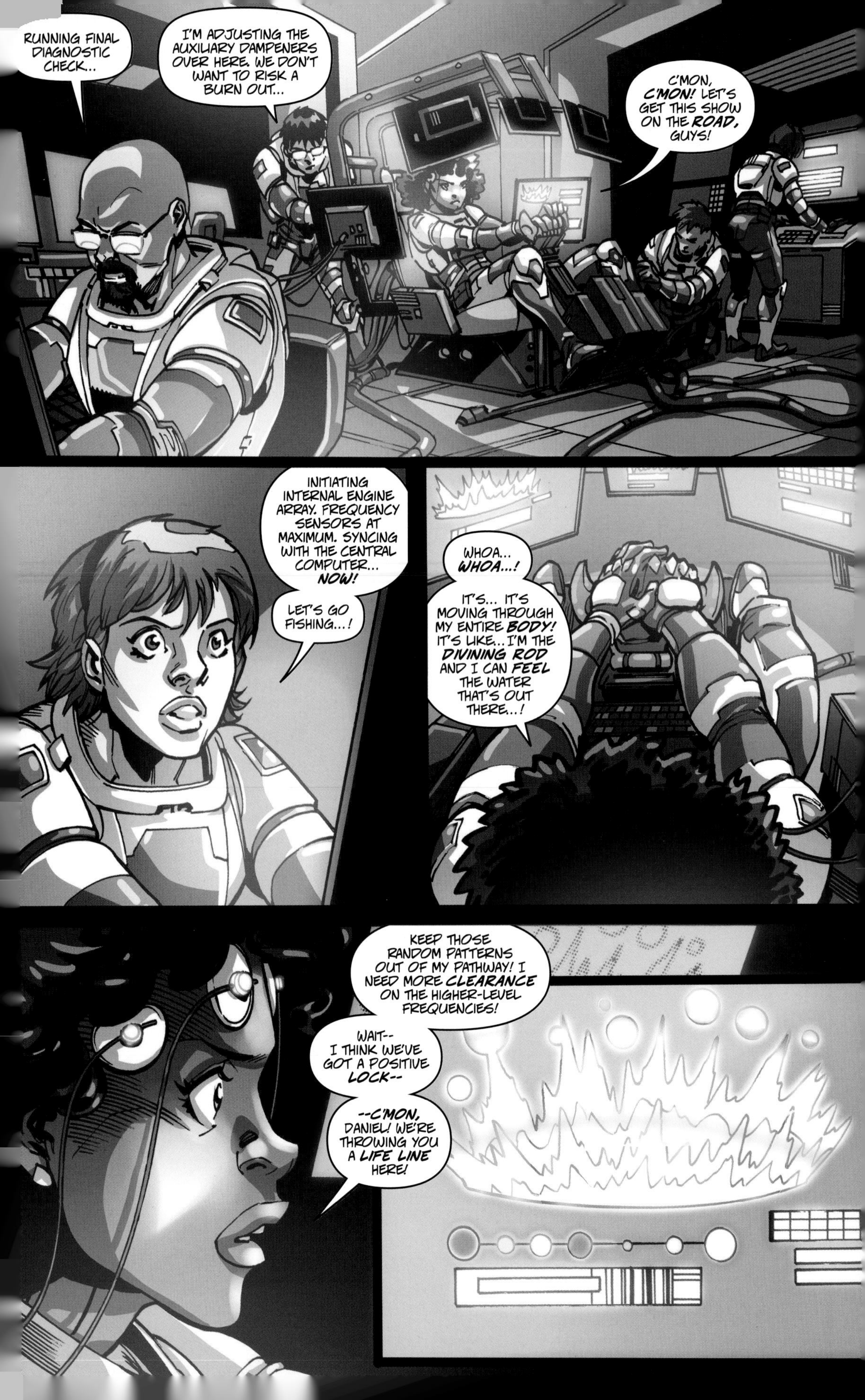
RUNNING FINAL DIAGNOSTIC CHECK...
I'M ADJUSTING THE AUXILIARY DAMPENERS OVER HERE. WE DON'T WANT TO RISK A BURN OUT...
C'MON, C'MON! LET'S GET THIS SHOW ON THE ROAD, GUYS!
INITIATING INTERNAL ENGINE ARRAY. FREQUENCY SENSORS AT MAXIMUM. SYNCING WITH THE CENTRAL COMPUTER... NOW!
LET'S GO FISHING...!
WHOA... WHOA...!
IT'S... IT'S MOVING THROUGH MY ENTIRE BODY! IT'S LIKE... I'M THE DIVINING ROD AND I CAN FEEL THE WATER THAT'S OUT THERE...!
KEEP THOSE RANDOM PATTERNS OUT OF MY PATHWAY! I NEED MORE CLEARANCE ON THE HIGHER-LEVEL FREQUENCIES!
WAIT-- I THINK WE'VE GOT A POSITIVE LOCK--
--C'MON, DANIEL! WE'RE THROWING YOU A LIFE LINE HERE!

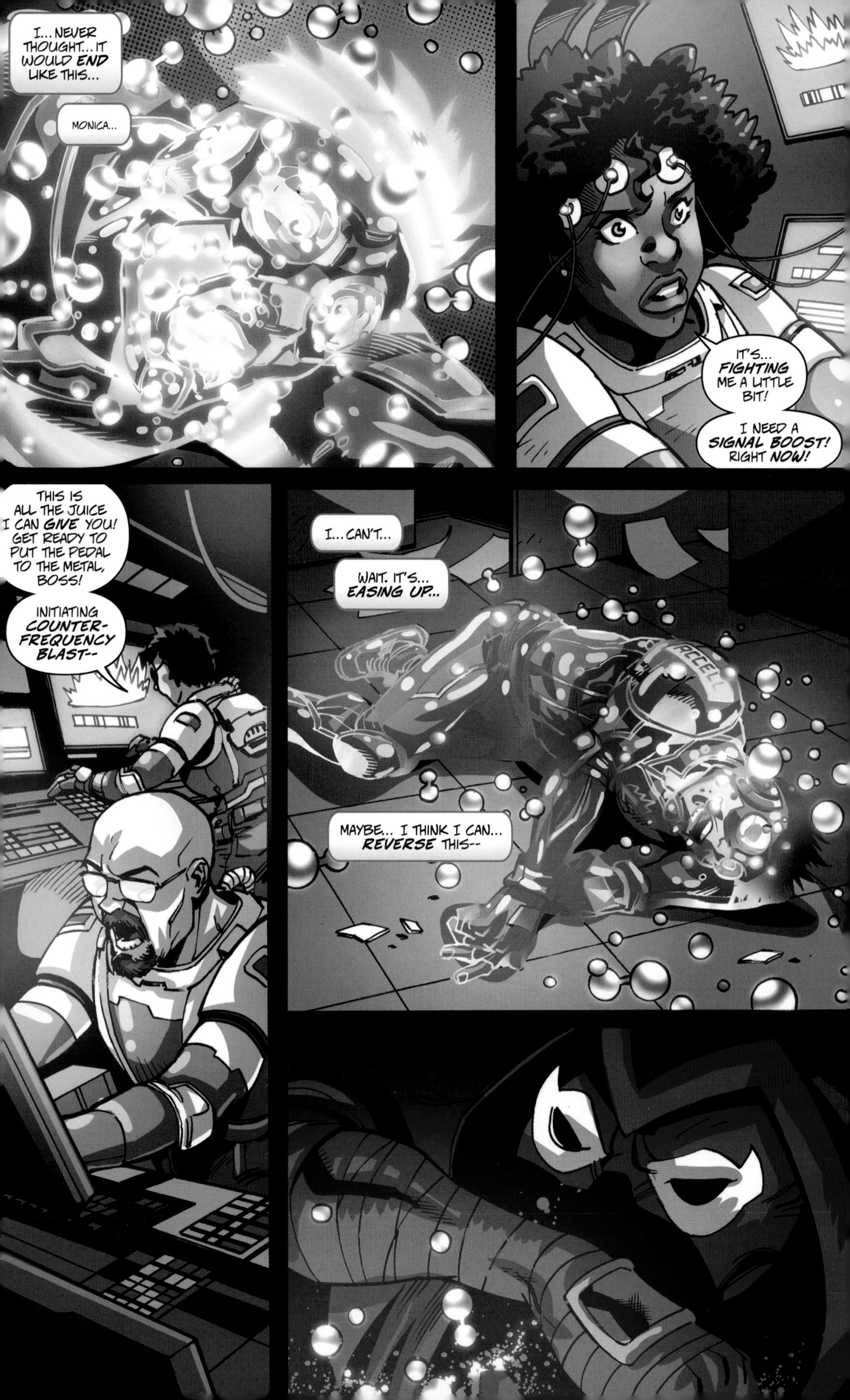
I... NEVER THOUGHT... IT WOULD **END** LIKE THIS...
MONICA...
IT'S... **FIGHTING** ME A LITTLE BIT!
I NEED A **SIGNAL BOOST!** RIGHT **NOW!**
THIS IS ALL THE JUICE I CAN **GIVE** YOU! GET READY TO PUT THE PEDAL TO THE METAL, BOSS!
INITIATING **COUNTER-FREQUENCY BLAST--**
I... CAN'T...
WAIT. IT'S... **EASING UP...**
MAYBE... I THINK I CAN... **REVERSE** THIS--

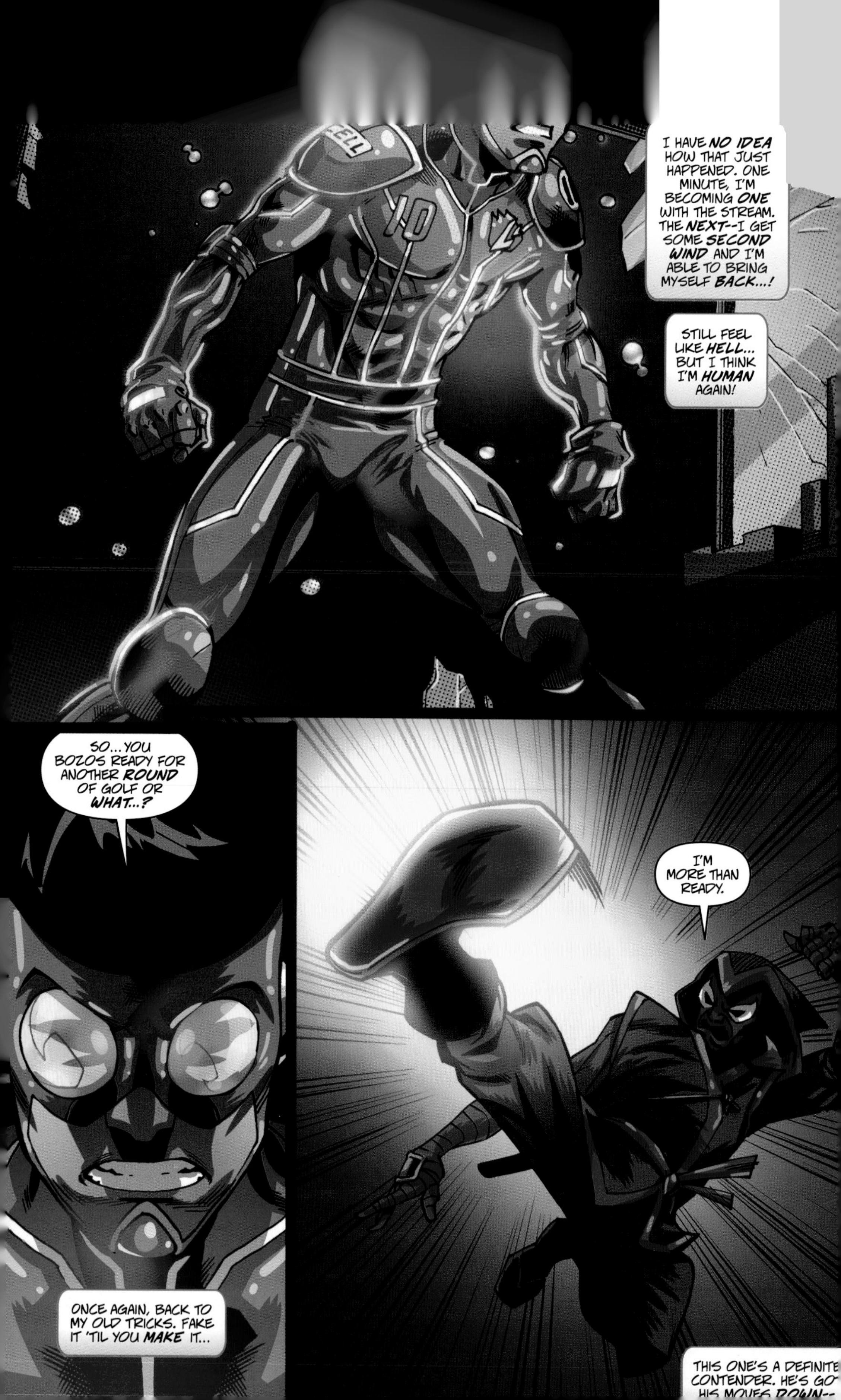
I HAVE NO IDEA HOW THAT JUST HAPPENED. ONE MINUTE, I'M BECOMING ONE WITH THE STREAM. THE NEXT--I GET SOME SECOND WIND AND I'M ABLE TO BRING MYSELF BACK...!
STILL FEEL LIKE HELL... BUT I THINK I'M HUMAN AGAIN!
SO... YOU BOZOS READY FOR ANOTHER ROUND OF GOLF OR WHAT...?
ONCE AGAIN, BACK TO MY OLD TRICKS. FAKE IT 'TIL YOU MAKE IT...
I'M MORE THAN READY.
THIS ONE'S A DEFINITE CONTENDER. HE'S GOT

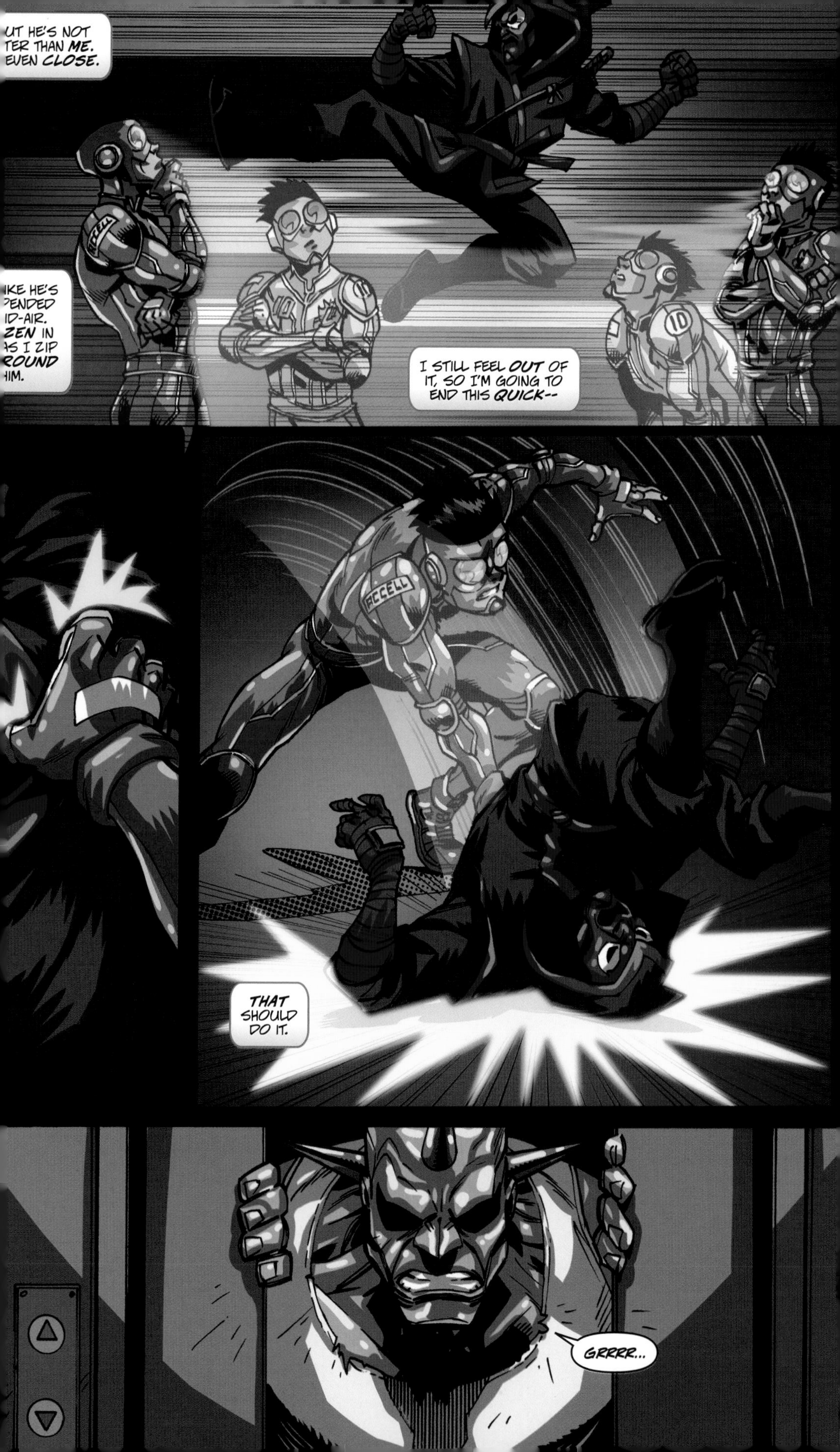
UT HE'S NOT
TER THAN ME.
EVEN CLOSE.
IKE HE'S
PENDED
ID-AIR.
ZEN IN
AS I ZIP
ROUND
HIM.
I STILL FEEL OUT OF IT, SO I'M GOING TO END THIS QUICK--
THAT SHOULD DO IT.
GRRRR...

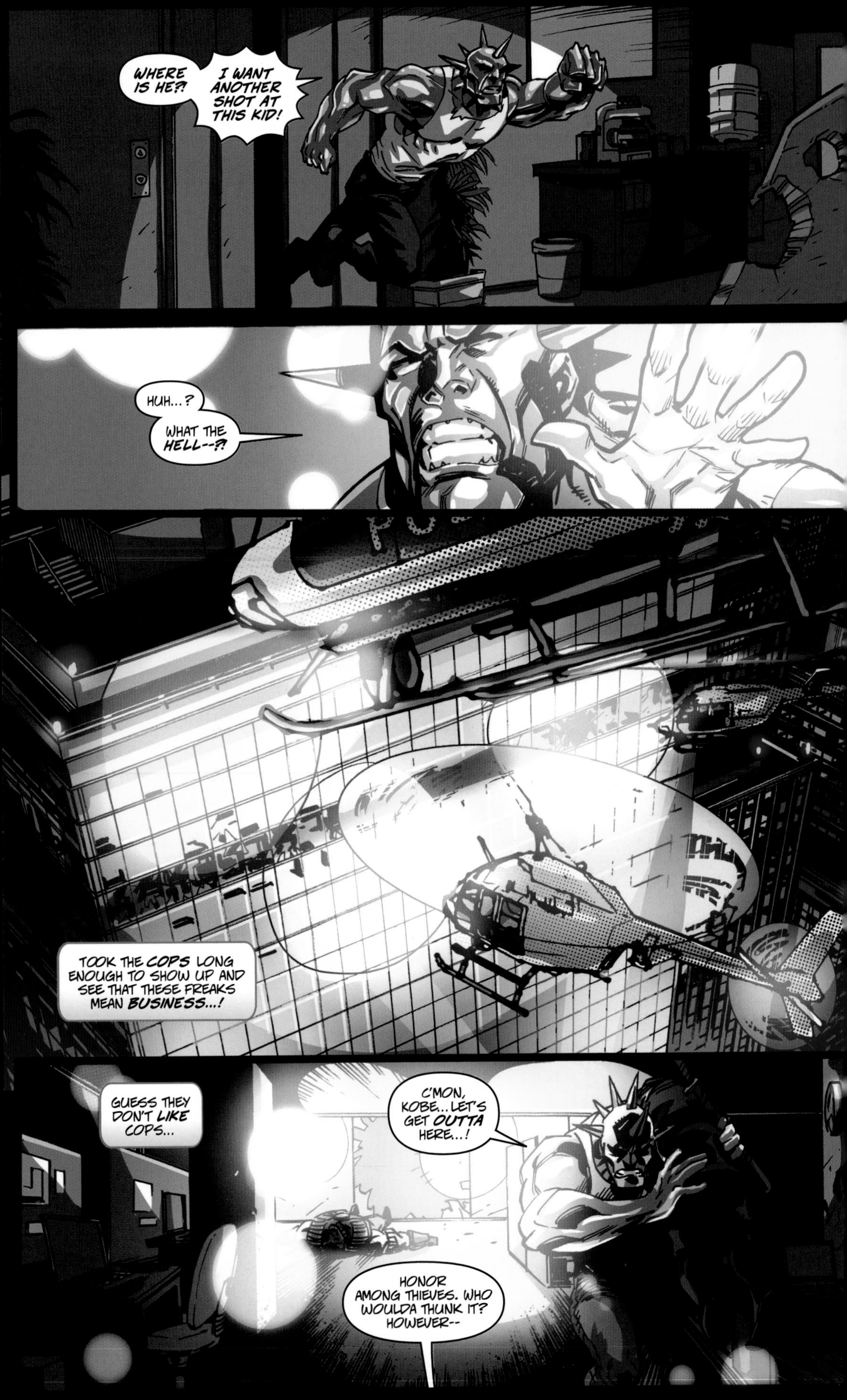
WHERE IS HE?!
I WANT ANOTHER SHOT AT THIS KID!
HUH...?
WHAT THE HELL--?!
TOOK THE COPS LONG ENOUGH TO SHOW UP AND SEE THAT THESE FREAKS MEAN BUSINESS...!
GUESS THEY DON'T LIKE COPS...
C'MON, KOBE... LET'S GET OUTTA HERE...!
HONOR AMONG THIEVES. WHO WOULDA THUNK IT? HOWEVER--

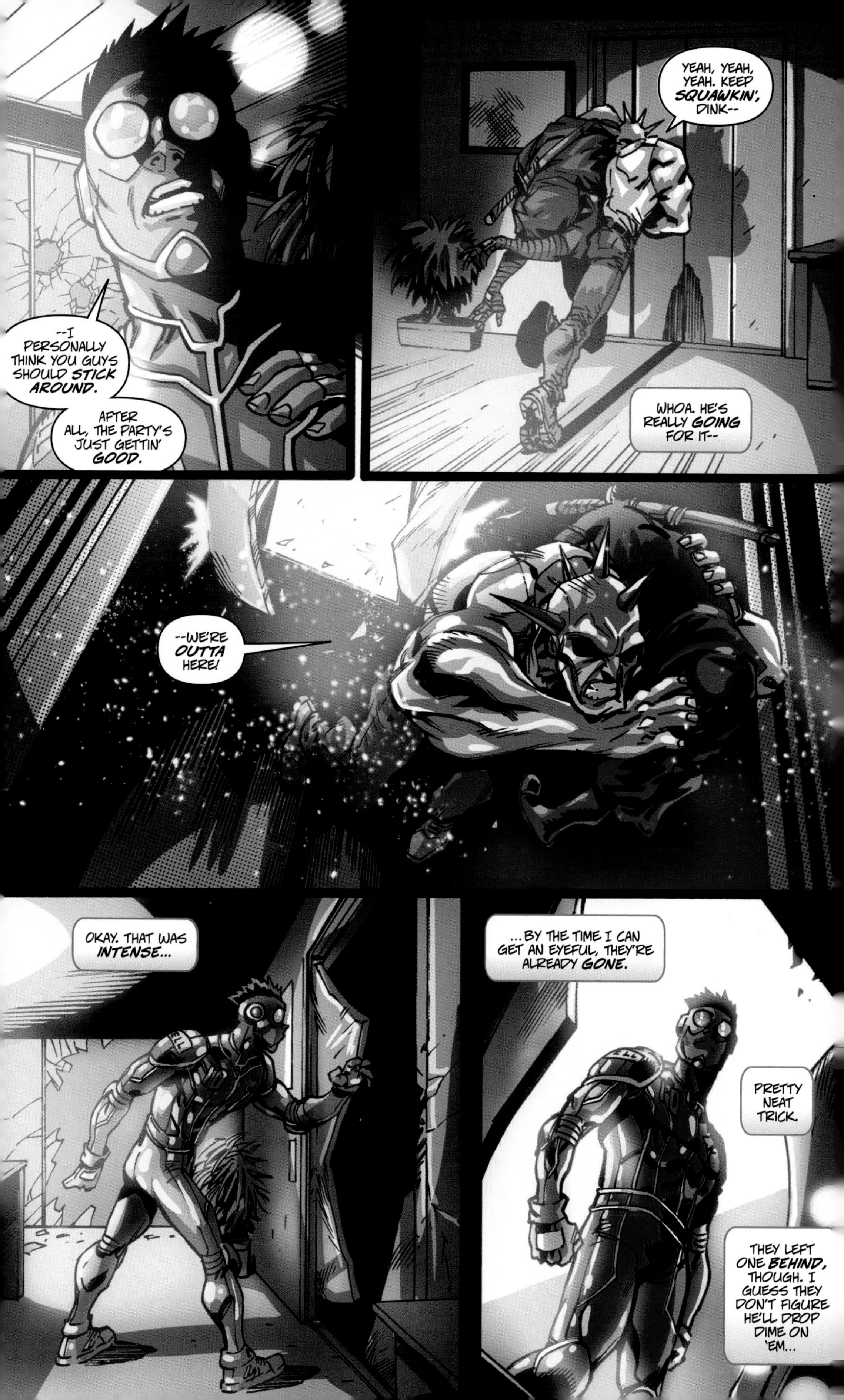
--I PERSONALLY THINK YOU GUYS SHOULD **STICK AROUND.**
AFTER ALL, THE PARTY'S JUST GETTIN' **GOOD.**
YEAH, YEAH, YEAH. KEEP **SQUAWKIN',** DINK--
WHOA. HE'S REALLY **GOING** FOR IT--
--WE'RE **OUTTA** HERE!
OKAY. THAT WAS **INTENSE...**
...BY THE TIME I CAN GET AN EYEFUL, THEY'RE ALREADY **GONE.**
PRETTY NEAT TRICK.
THEY LEFT ONE **BEHIND,** THOUGH. I GUESS THEY DON'T FIGURE HE'LL DROP DIME ON 'EM...

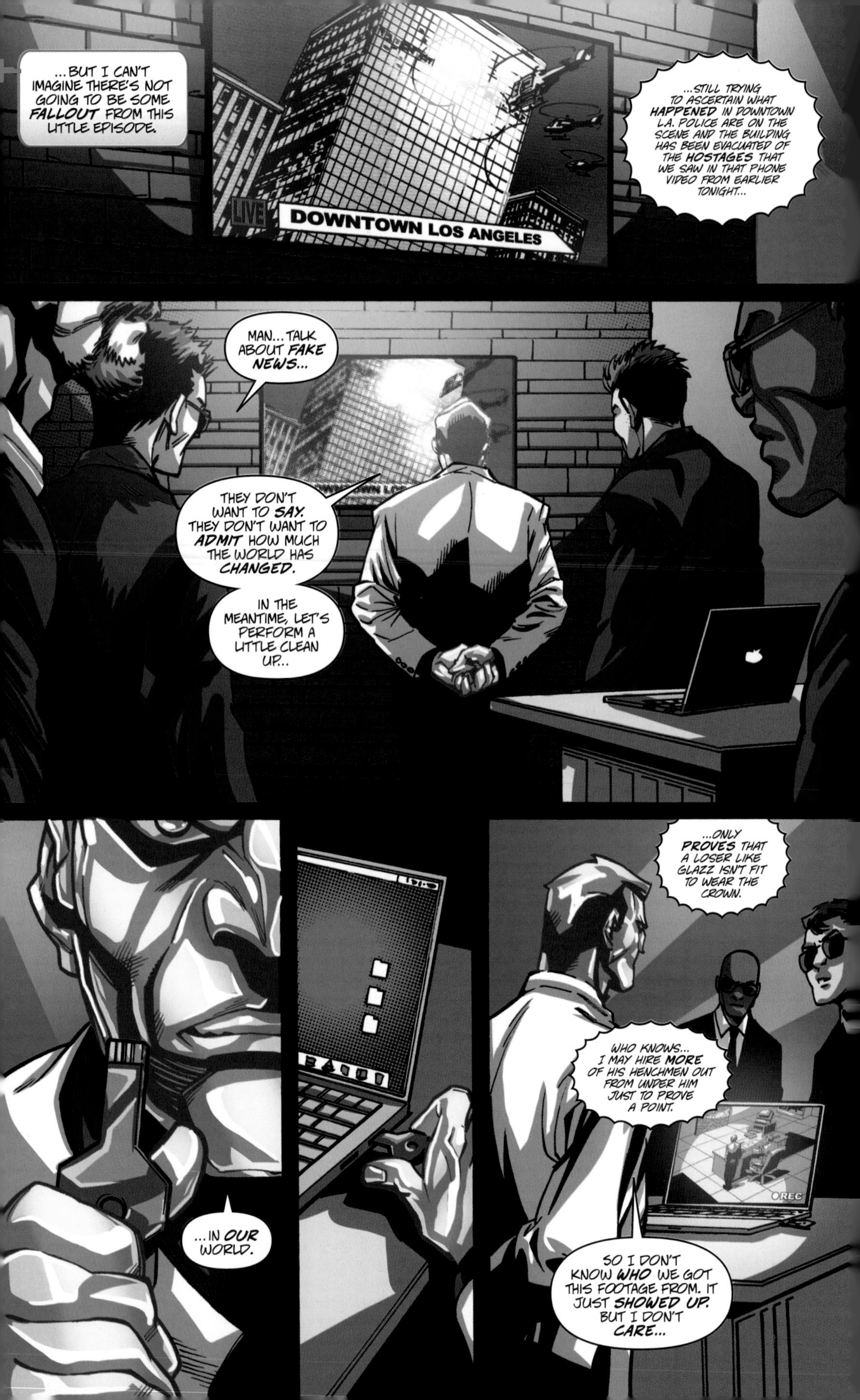
...BUT I CAN'T IMAGINE THERE'S NOT GOING TO BE SOME FALLOUT FROM THIS LITTLE EPISODE.
LIVE
DOWNTOWN LOS ANGELES
...STILL TRYING TO ASCERTAIN WHAT HAPPENED IN DOWNTOWN L.A. POLICE ARE ON THE SCENE AND THE BUILDING HAS BEEN EVACUATED OF THE HOSTAGES THAT WE SAW IN THAT PHONE VIDEO FROM EARLIER TONIGHT...
MAN...TALK ABOUT FAKE NEWS...
THEY DON'T WANT TO SAY. THEY DON'T WANT TO ADMIT HOW MUCH THE WORLD HAS CHANGED.
IN THE MEANTIME, LET'S PERFORM A LITTLE CLEAN UP...
...IN OUR WORLD.
...ONLY PROVES THAT A LOSER LIKE GLAZZ ISN'T FIT TO WEAR THE CROWN.
WHO KNOWS... I MAY HIRE MORE OF HIS HENCHMEN OUT FROM UNDER HIM JUST TO PROVE A POINT.
REC
SO I DON'T KNOW WHO WE GOT THIS FOOTAGE FROM. IT JUST SHOWED UP. BUT I DON'T CARE...

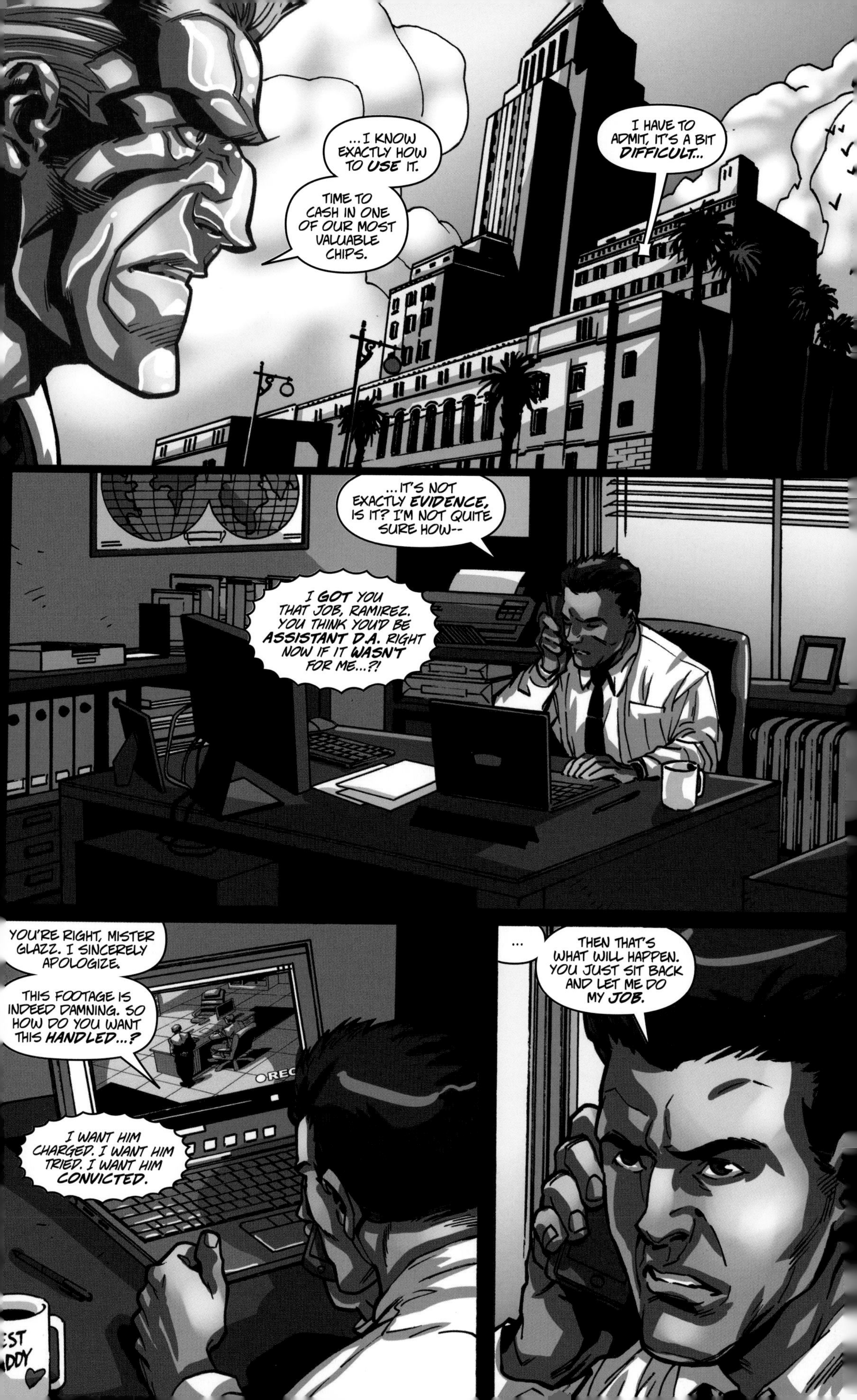
...I KNOW EXACTLY HOW TO USE IT.
TIME TO CASH IN ONE OF OUR MOST VALUABLE CHIPS.
I HAVE TO ADMIT, IT'S A BIT DIFFICULT...
...IT'S NOT EXACTLY EVIDENCE, IS IT? I'M NOT QUITE SURE HOW--
I GOT YOU THAT JOB, RAMIREZ. YOU THINK YOU'D BE ASSISTANT D.A. RIGHT NOW IF IT WASN'T FOR ME...?!
YOU'RE RIGHT, MISTER GLAZZ. I SINCERELY APOLOGIZE.
THIS FOOTAGE IS INDEED DAMNING. SO HOW DO YOU WANT THIS HANDLED...?
I WANT HIM CHARGED. I WANT HIM TRIED. I WANT HIM CONVICTED.
...
THEN THAT'S WHAT WILL HAPPEN. YOU JUST SIT BACK AND LET ME DO MY JOB.

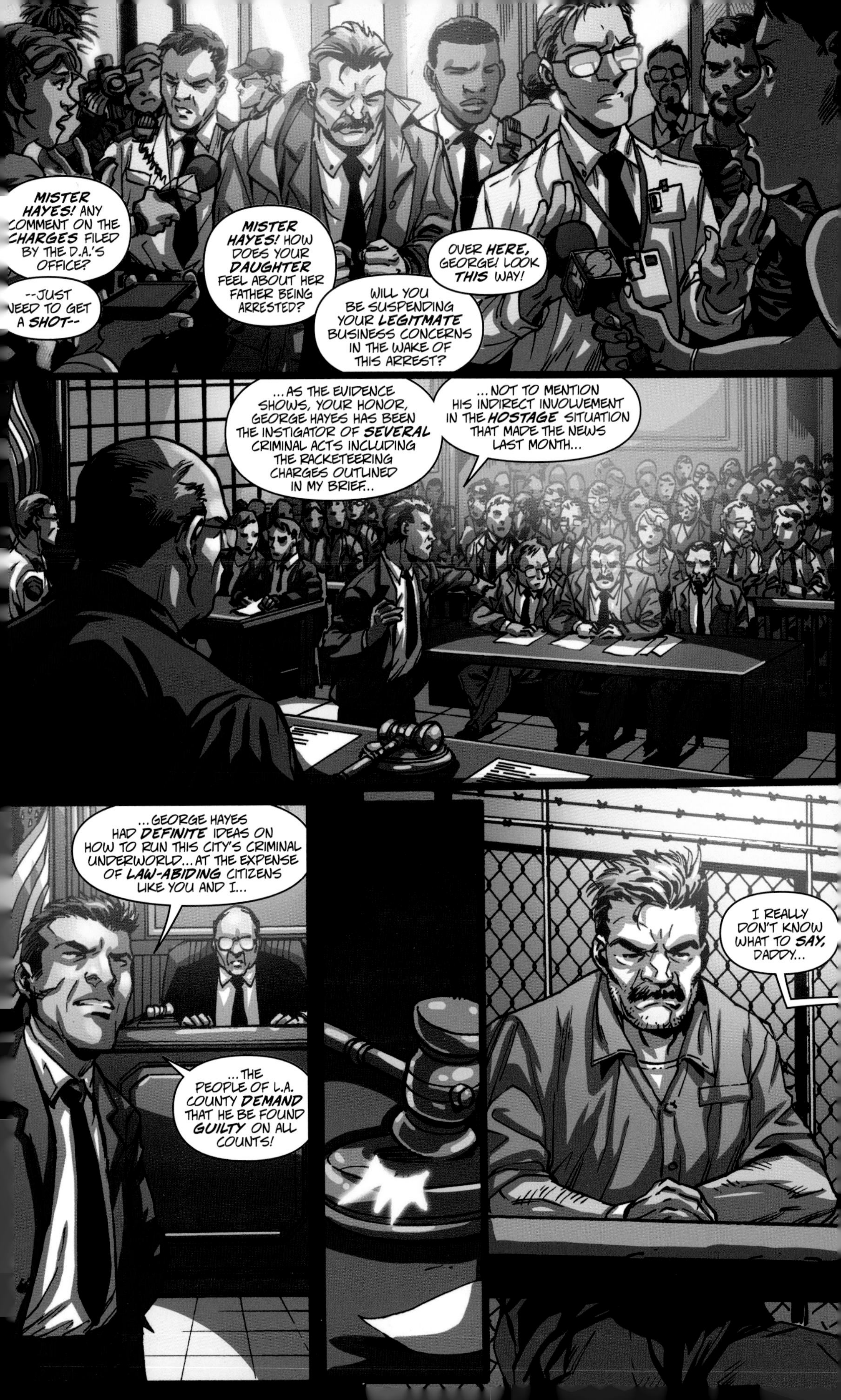
MISTER HAYES! ANY COMMENT ON THE CHARGES FILED BY THE D.A.'S OFFICE?
--JUST NEED TO GET A SHOT--
MISTER HAYES! HOW DOES YOUR DAUGHTER FEEL ABOUT HER FATHER BEING ARRESTED?
WILL YOU BE SUSPENDING YOUR LEGITMATE BUSINESS CONCERNS IN THE WAKE OF THIS ARREST?
OVER HERE, GEORGE! LOOK THIS WAY!
...AS THE EVIDENCE SHOWS, YOUR HONOR, GEORGE HAYES HAS BEEN THE INSTIGATOR OF SEVERAL CRIMINAL ACTS INCLUDING THE RACKETEERING CHARGES OUTLINED IN MY BRIEF...
...NOT TO MENTION HIS INDIRECT INVOLVEMENT IN THE HOSTAGE SITUATION THAT MADE THE NEWS LAST MONTH...
...GEORGE HAYES HAD DEFINITE IDEAS ON HOW TO RUN THIS CITY'S CRIMINAL UNDERWORLD...AT THE EXPENSE OF LAW-ABIDING CITIZENS LIKE YOU AND I...
...THE PEOPLE OF L.A. COUNTY DEMAND THAT HE BE FOUND GUILTY ON ALL COUNTS!
I REALLY DON'T KNOW WHAT TO SAY, DADDY...

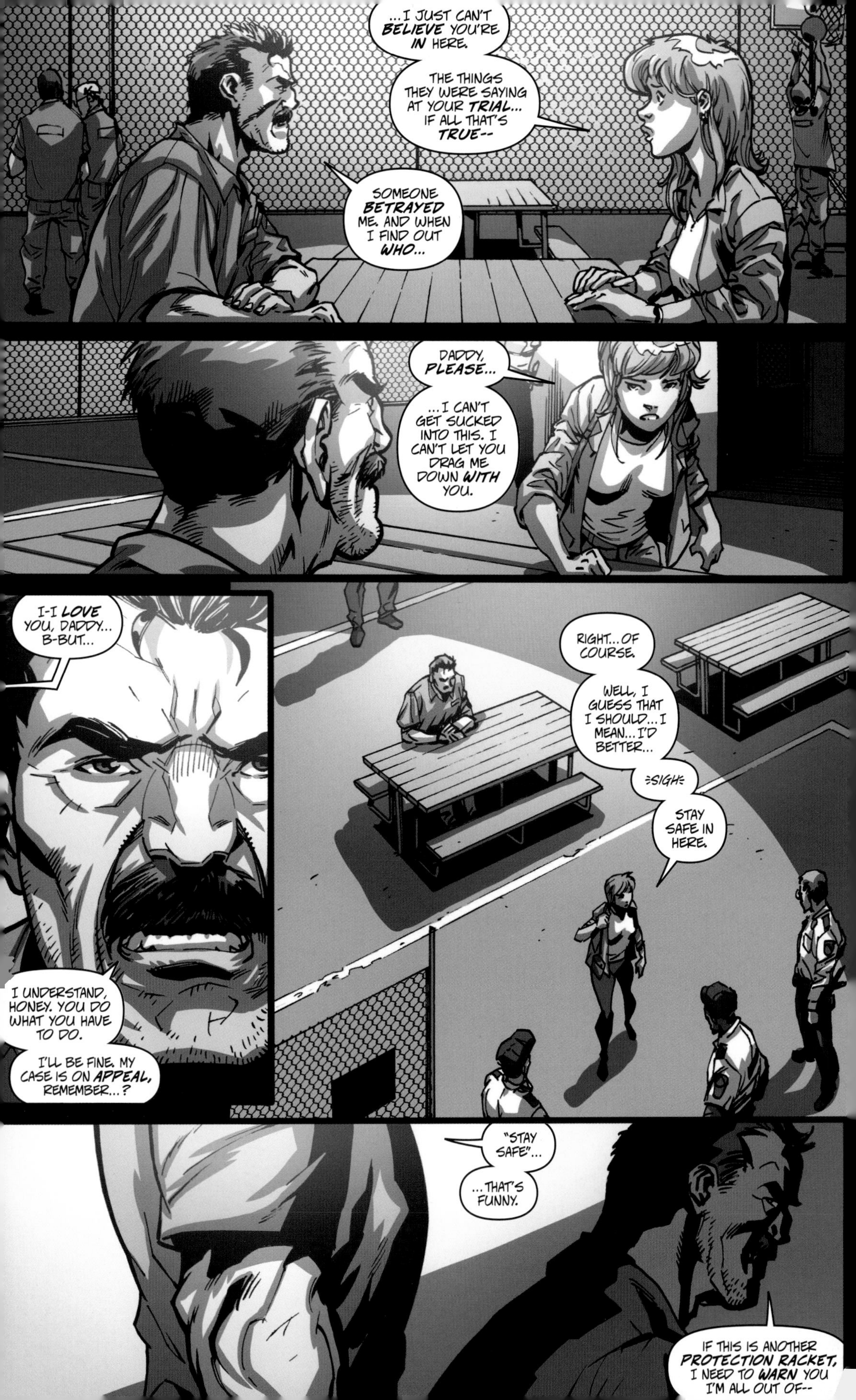
...I JUST CAN'T BELIEVE YOU'RE IN HERE.
THE THINGS THEY WERE SAYING AT YOUR TRIAL... IF ALL THAT'S TRUE--
SOMEONE BETRAYED ME. AND WHEN I FIND OUT WHO...
DADDY, PLEASE...
...I CAN'T GET SUCKED INTO THIS. I CAN'T LET YOU DRAG ME DOWN WITH YOU.
I-I LOVE YOU, DADDY... B-BUT...
I UNDERSTAND, HONEY. YOU DO WHAT YOU HAVE TO DO.
I'LL BE FINE. MY CASE IS ON APPEAL, REMEMBER...?
RIGHT... OF COURSE.
WELL, I GUESS THAT I SHOULD... I MEAN... I'D BETTER...
=SIGH=
STAY SAFE IN HERE.
"STAY SAFE"...
...THAT'S FUNNY.
IF THIS IS ANOTHER PROTECTION RACKET, I NEED TO WARN YOU I'M ALL OUT OF--

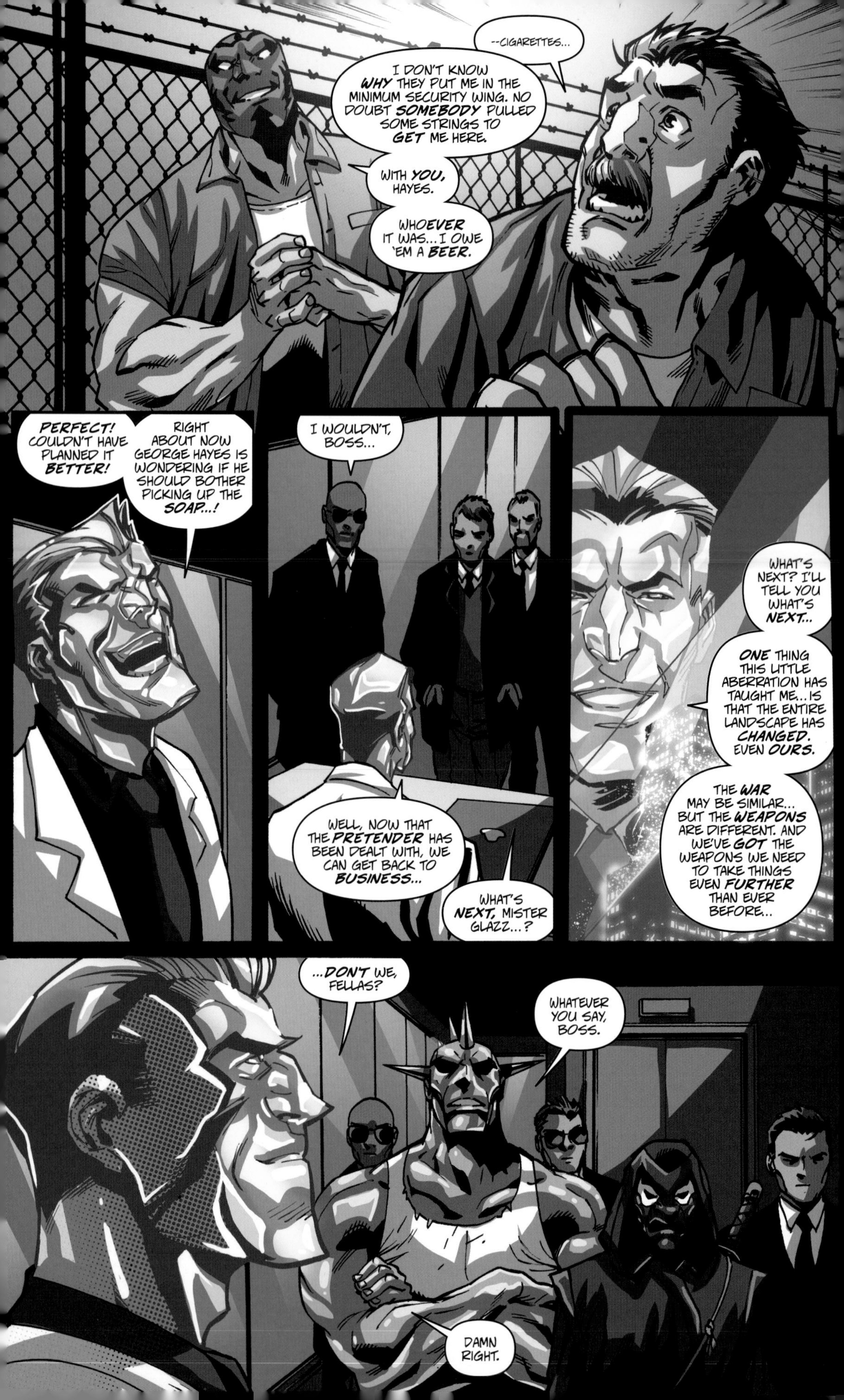
--CIGARETTES...
I DON'T KNOW **WHY** THEY PUT ME IN THE MINIMUM SECURITY WING. NO DOUBT **SOMEBODY** PULLED SOME STRINGS TO **GET** ME HERE.
WITH **YOU,** HAYES.
WHO**EVER** IT WAS... I OWE 'EM A **BEER.**
PERFECT! COULDN'T HAVE PLANNED IT **BETTER!**
RIGHT ABOUT NOW GEORGE HAYES IS WONDERING IF HE SHOULD BOTHER PICKING UP THE **SOAP...!**
I WOULDN'T, BOSS...
WELL, NOW THAT THE **PRETENDER** HAS BEEN DEALT WITH, WE CAN GET BACK TO **BUSINESS...**
WHAT'S **NEXT,** MISTER GLAZZ...?
WHAT'S NEXT? I'LL TELL YOU WHAT'S **NEXT...**
ONE THING THIS LITTLE ABERRATION HAS TAUGHT ME... IS THAT THE ENTIRE LANDSCAPE HAS **CHANGED.** EVEN **OURS.**
THE **WAR** MAY BE SIMILAR... BUT THE **WEAPONS** ARE DIFFERENT. AND WE'VE **GOT** THE WEAPONS WE NEED TO TAKE THINGS EVEN **FURTHER** THAN EVER BEFORE...
...**DON'T** WE, FELLAS?
WHATEVER YOU SAY, BOSS.
DAMN RIGHT.

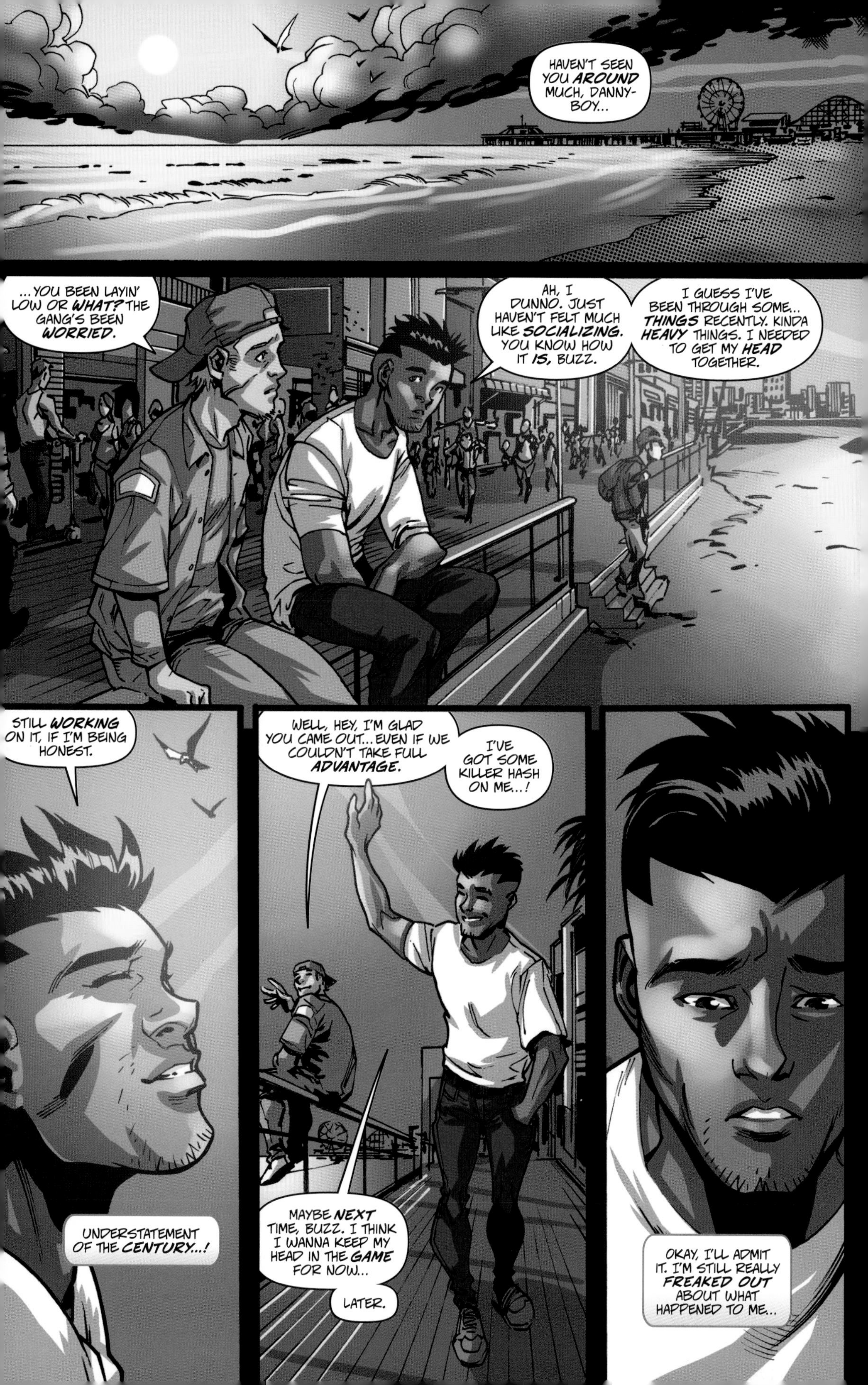
HAVEN'T SEEN YOU AROUND MUCH, DANNY-BOY...
...YOU BEEN LAYIN' LOW OR WHAT? THE GANG'S BEEN WORRIED.
AH, I DUNNO. JUST HAVEN'T FELT MUCH LIKE SOCIALIZING. YOU KNOW HOW IT IS, BUZZ.
I GUESS I'VE BEEN THROUGH SOME... THINGS RECENTLY. KINDA HEAVY THINGS. I NEEDED TO GET MY HEAD TOGETHER.
STILL WORKING ON IT, IF I'M BEING HONEST.
UNDERSTATEMENT OF THE CENTURY...!
WELL, HEY, I'M GLAD YOU CAME OUT... EVEN IF WE COULDN'T TAKE FULL ADVANTAGE.
I'VE GOT SOME KILLER HASH ON ME...!
MAYBE NEXT TIME, BUZZ. I THINK I WANNA KEEP MY HEAD IN THE GAME FOR NOW...
LATER.
OKAY, I'LL ADMIT IT. I'M STILL REALLY FREAKED OUT ABOUT WHAT HAPPENED TO ME...

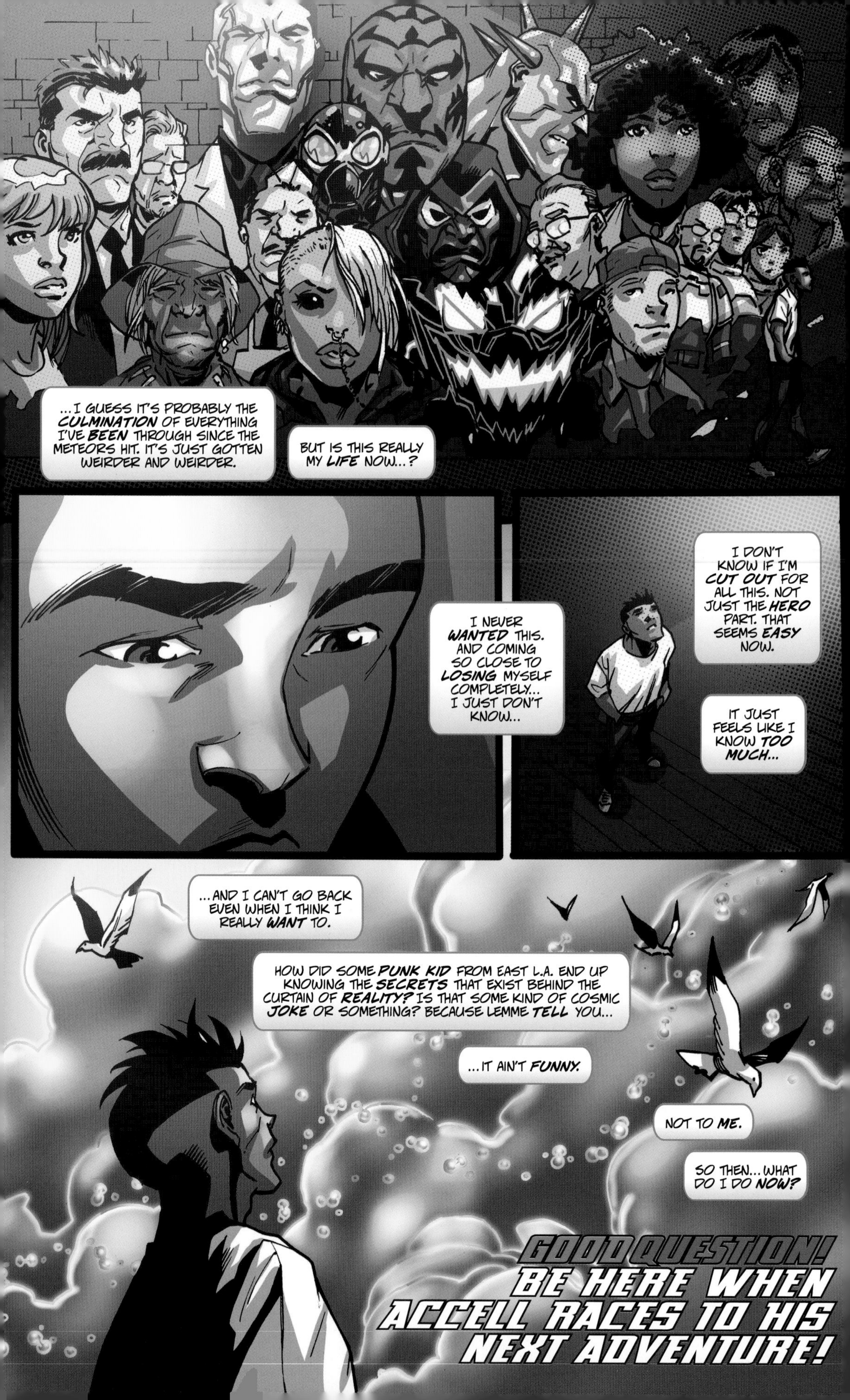
...I GUESS IT'S PROBABLY THE CULMINATION OF EVERYTHING I'VE BEEN THROUGH SINCE THE METEORS HIT. IT'S JUST GOTTEN WEIRDER AND WEIRDER.
BUT IS THIS REALLY MY LIFE NOW...?
I NEVER WANTED THIS. AND COMING SO CLOSE TO LOSING MYSELF COMPLETELY... I JUST DON'T KNOW...
I DON'T KNOW IF I'M CUT OUT FOR ALL THIS. NOT JUST THE HERO PART. THAT SEEMS EASY NOW.
IT JUST FEELS LIKE I KNOW TOO MUCH...
...AND I CAN'T GO BACK EVEN WHEN I THINK I REALLY WANT TO.
HOW DID SOME PUNK KID FROM EAST L.A. END UP KNOWING THE SECRETS THAT EXIST BEHIND THE CURTAIN OF REALITY? IS THAT SOME KIND OF COSMIC JOKE OR SOMETHING? BECAUSE LEMME TELL YOU...
...IT AIN'T FUNNY.
NOT TO ME.
SO THEN... WHAT DO I DO NOW?
GOOD QUESTION!
BE HERE WHEN ACCELL RACES TO HIS NEXT ADVENTURE!

COVERS SKETCHBOOK AND GALLERY

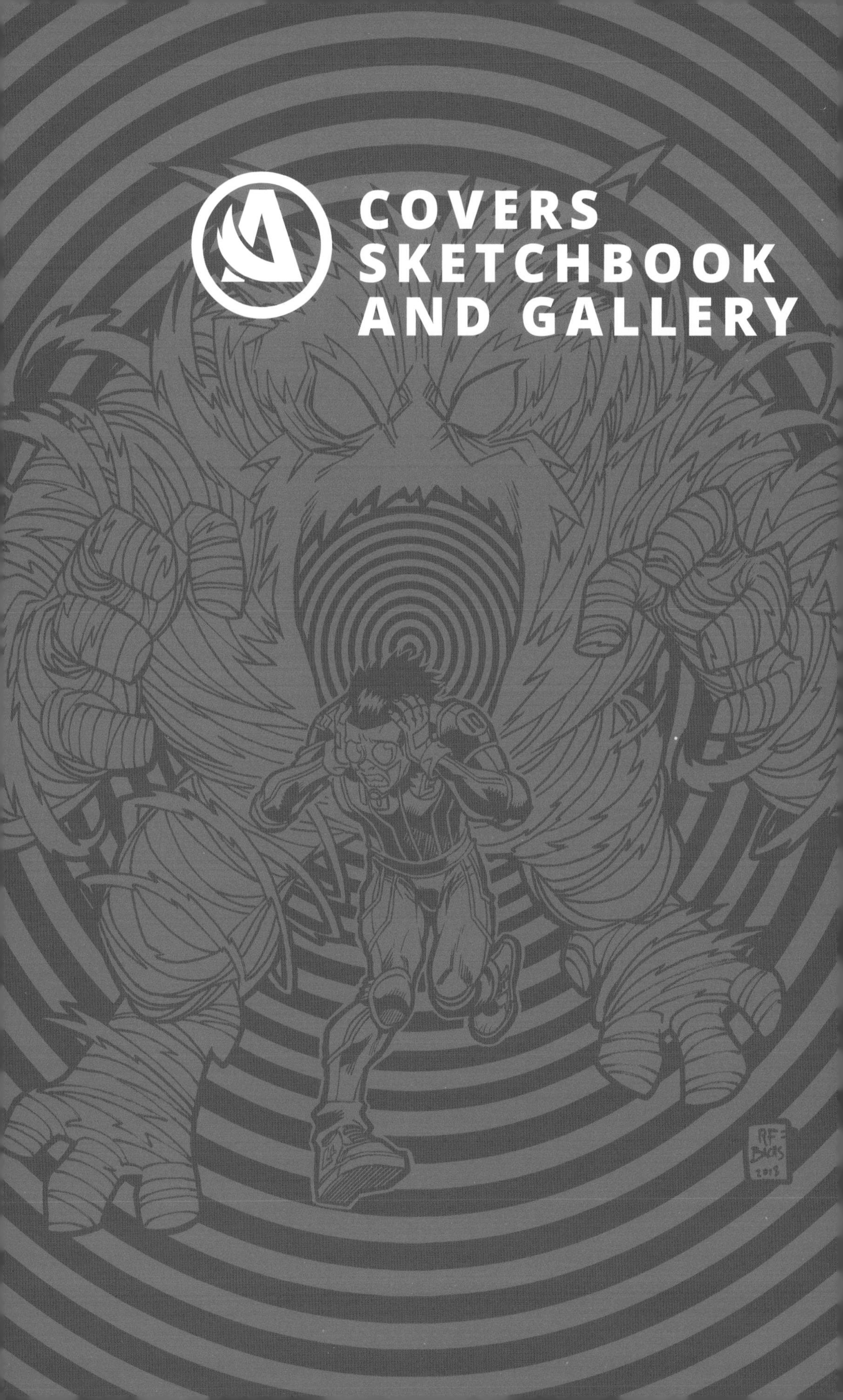

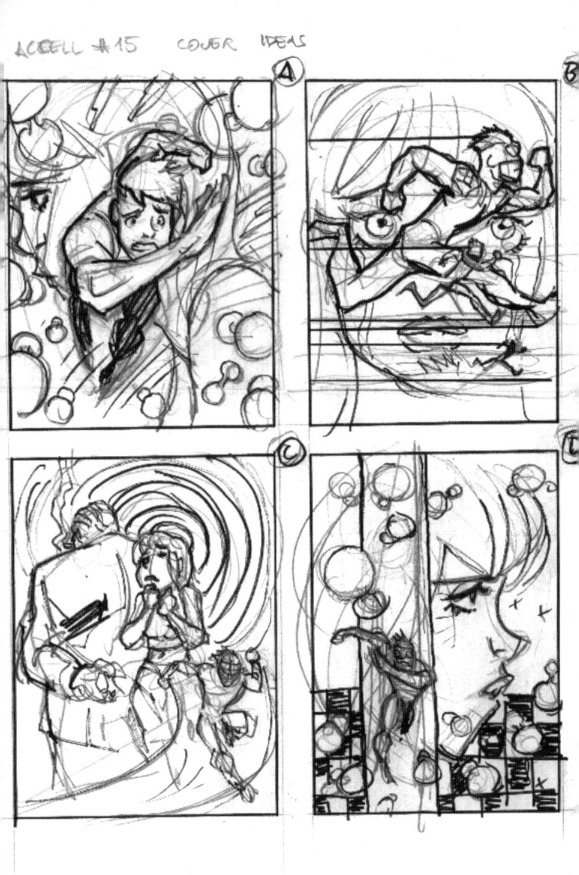

cover sketches by
RAMON BACHS

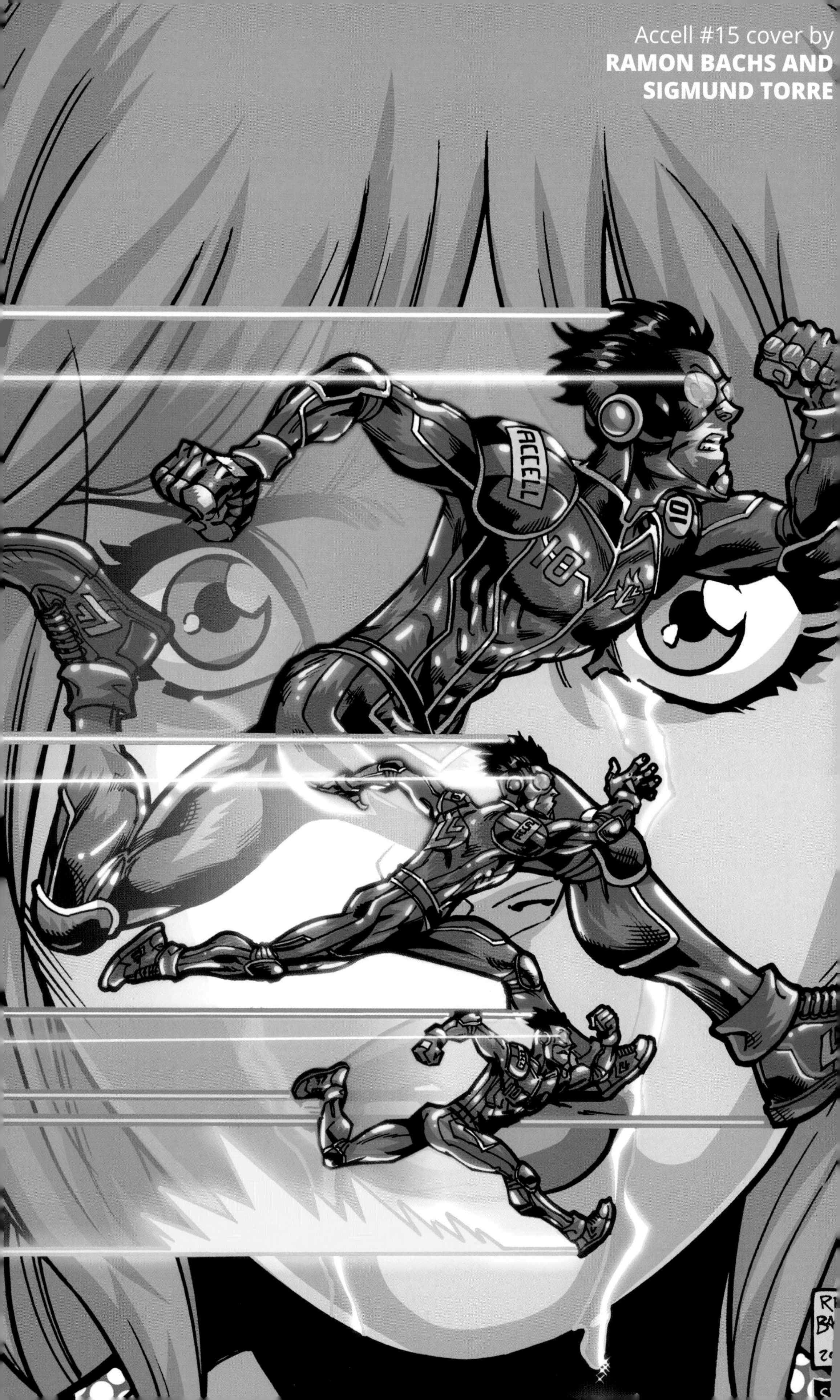

Accell #15 cover by
RAMON BACHS AND
SIGMUND TORRE

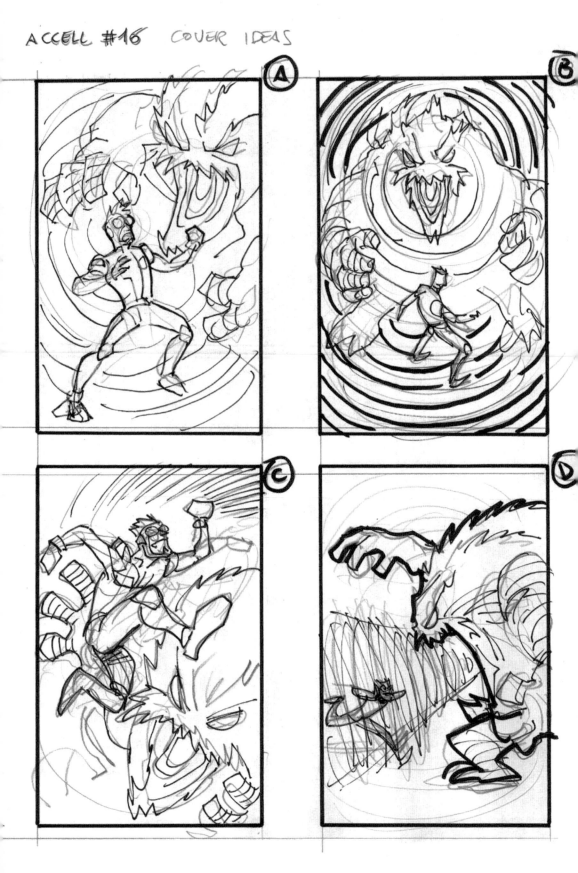

ACCELL #16   COVER IDEAS

cover sketches by
RAMON BACHS

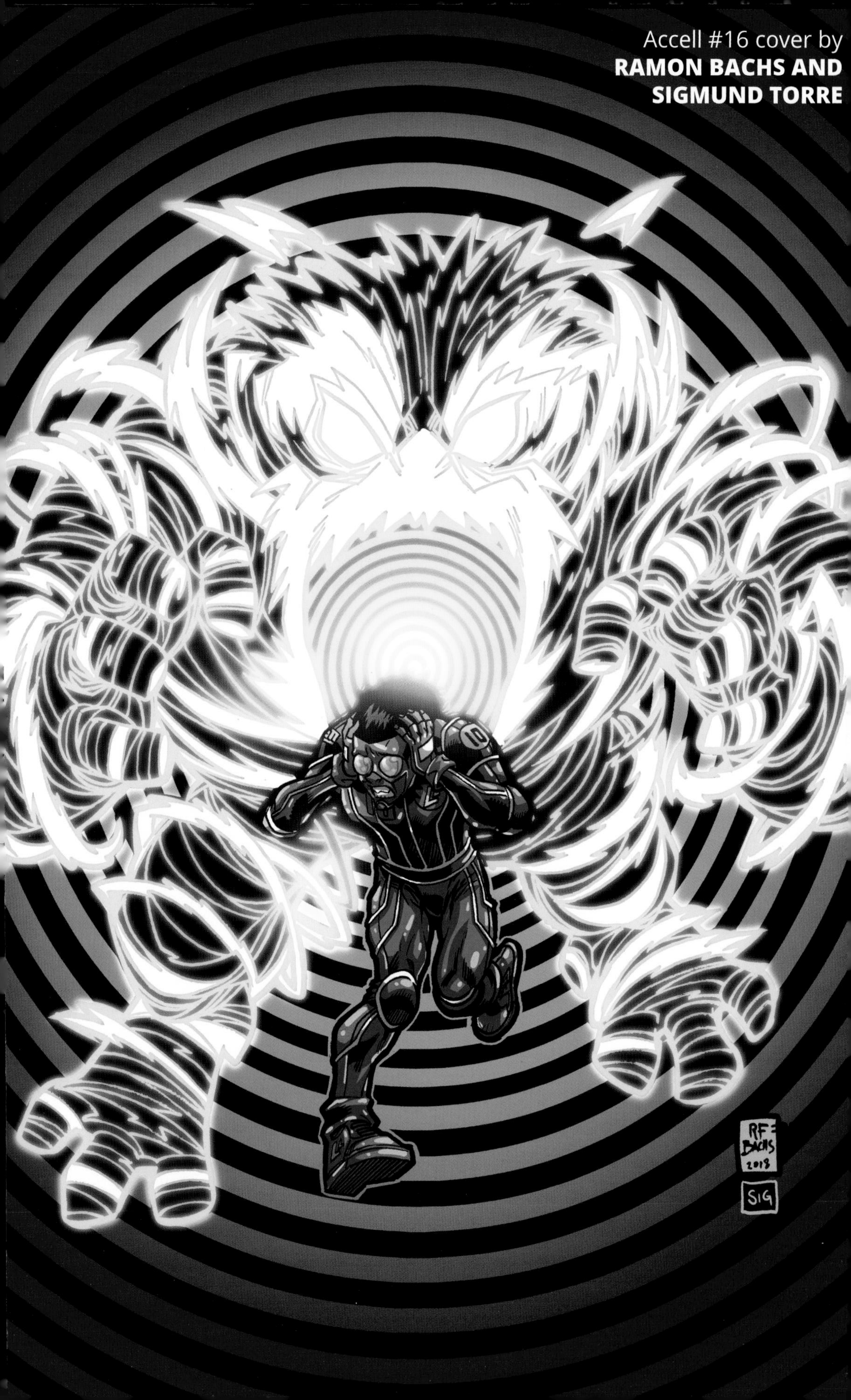
RF BACHS 2018
SIG

Accell #16 cover by
RAMON BACHS AND SIGMUND TORRE

ACCELL #17 COVER IDEAS

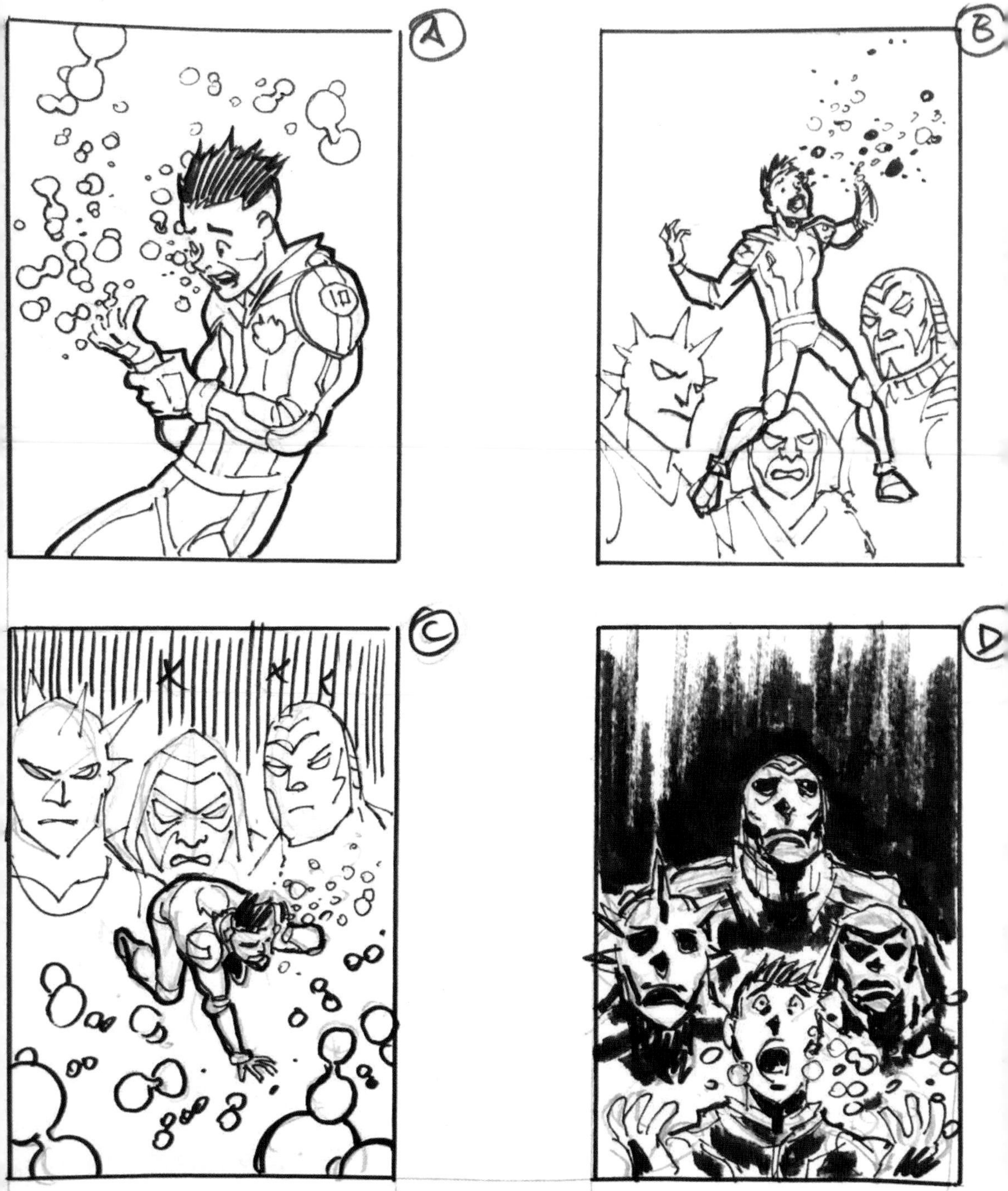
A
B
C
D

cover sketches by
RAMON BACHS

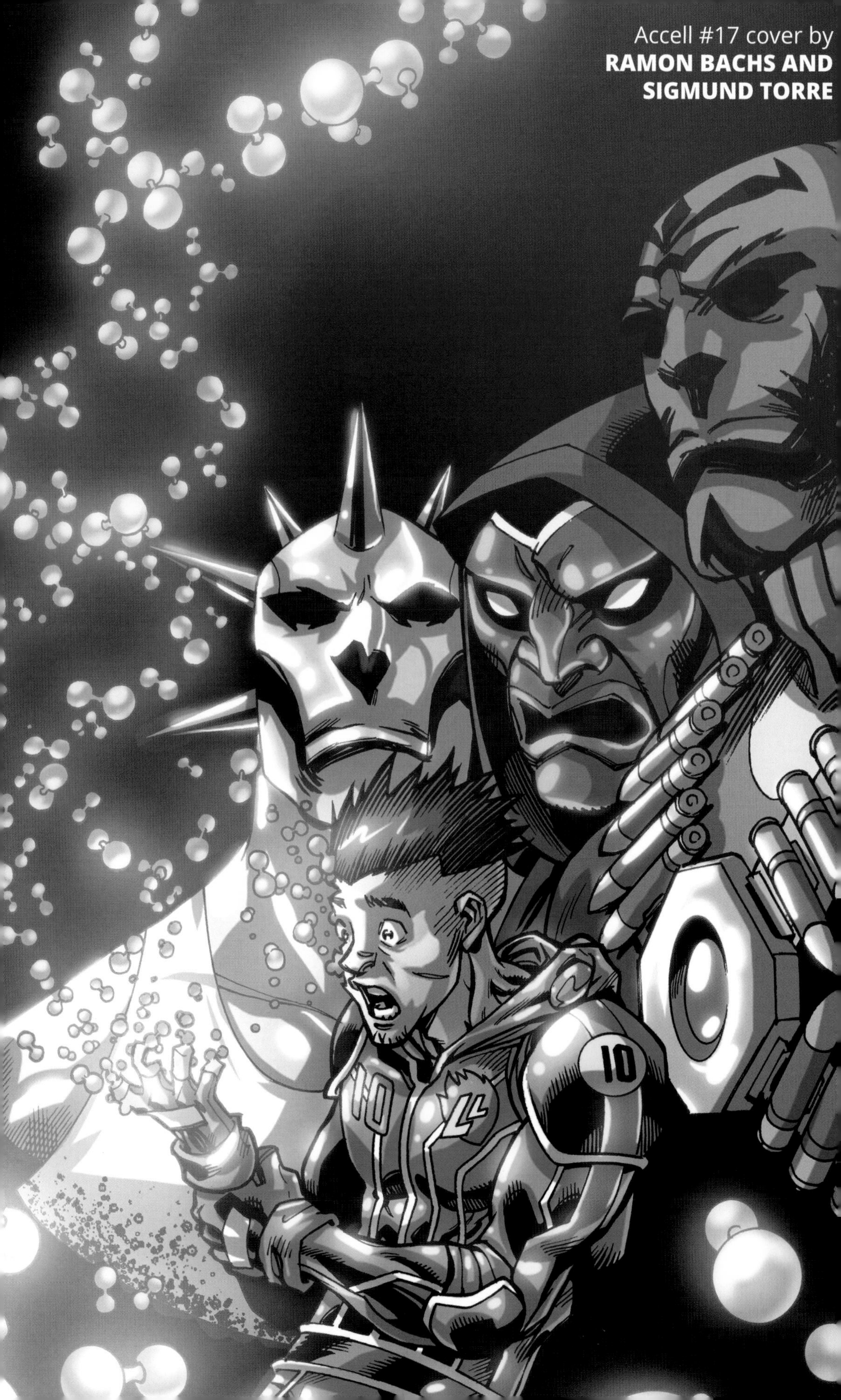
10
10

Accell #17 cover by
RAMON BACHS AND
SIGMUND TORRE

ACCELL #18 COVER IDEAS

A

B

C

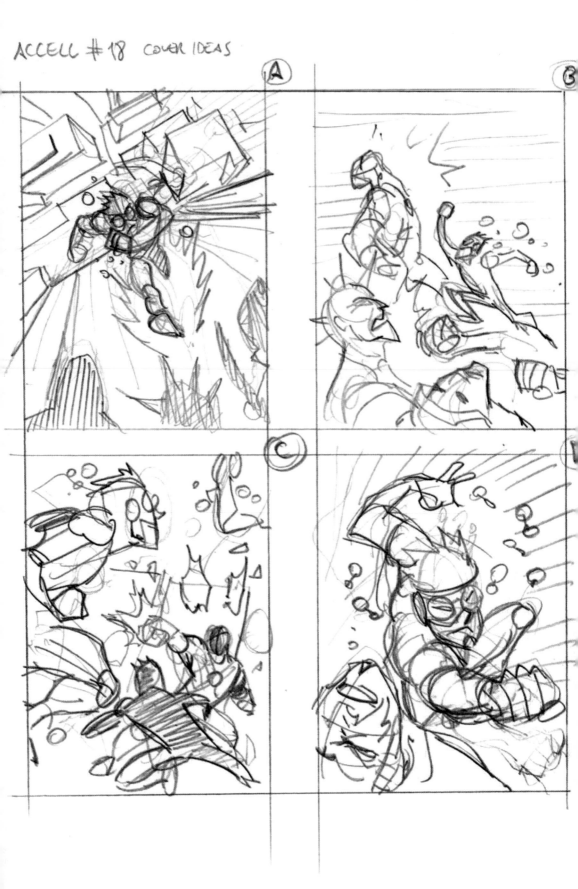

cover sketches by
RAMON BACHS

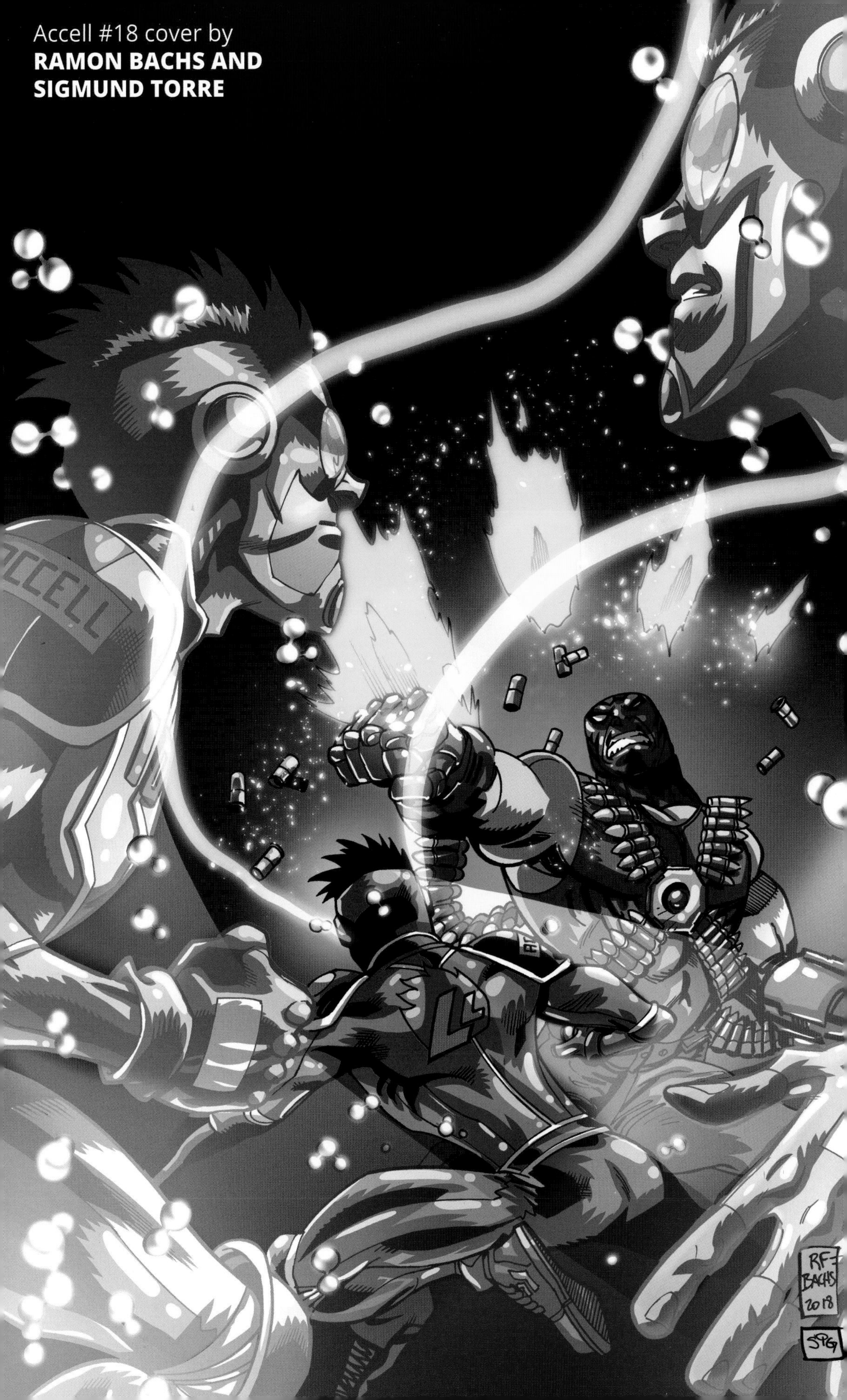
RF
BACHS
2018

Accell #18 cover by
RAMON BACHS AND SIGMUND TORRE

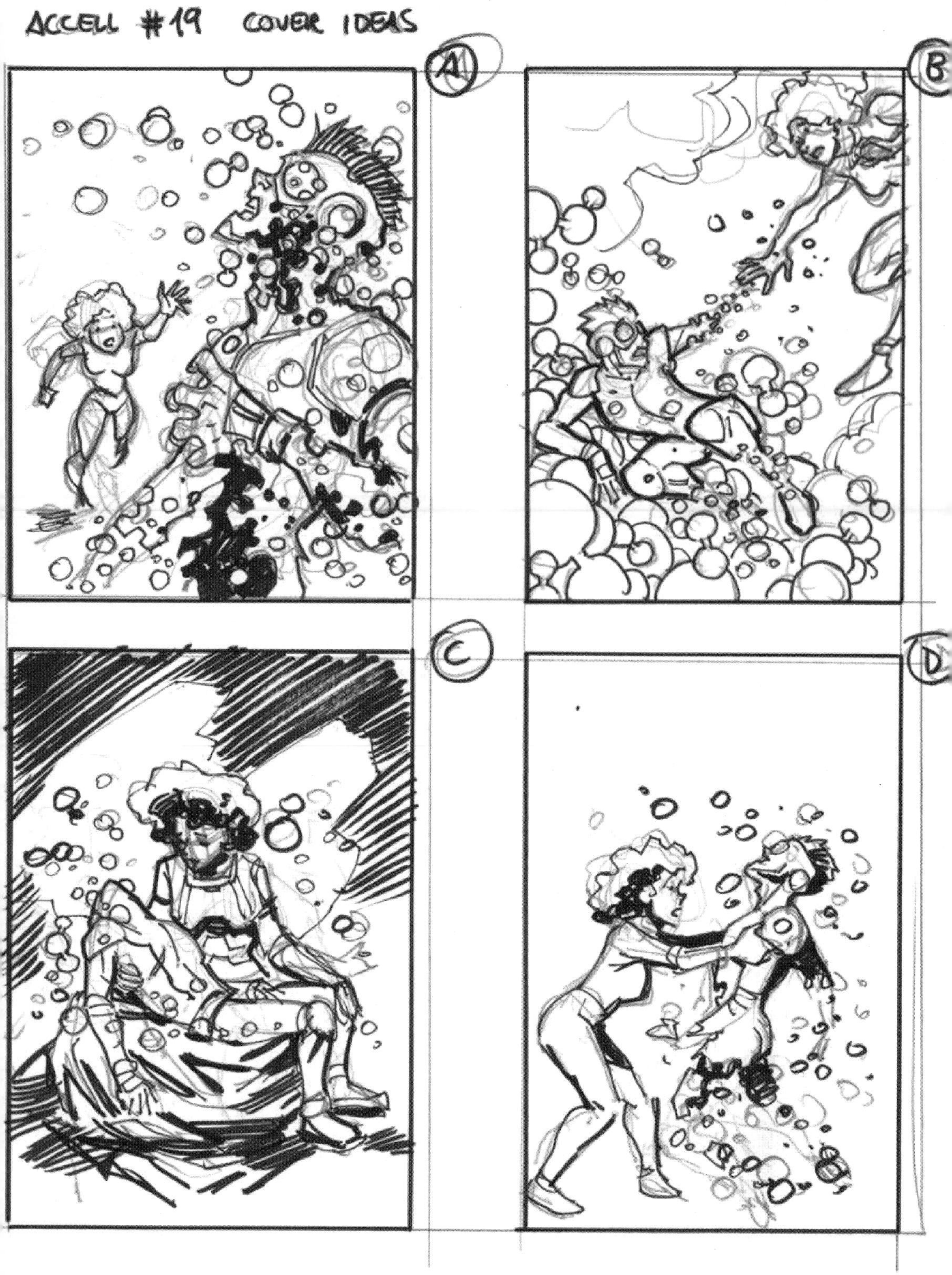
ACCELL #19 COVER IDEAS
A
B
C
D

cover sketches by
RAMON BACHS